# LORD of the AIR

## Tal Brooke

HARVEST HOUSE PUBL...
Eugene, Oregon 974...

**LORD OF THE AIR**

Copyright © 1990 by Tal Brooke
Published by Harvest House Publishers
Eugene, Oregon 97402

Library of Congress Cataloging-in-Publication Data

Brooke, Tal.
    Lord of the air: tales of a modern Antichrist / Tal Brooke.
    ISBN 0-89081-834-7
    1. Sathya Sai Baba, 1926-    .    2. Cults—India—Controversial liter-
ature.    3. Apologetics—20th century.    4. Brooke, Tal.    I. Title.
BL1175.S385B75 1990
294.5′092—dc20                                                    90-32273
                                                                          CIP

Deep in the heart of India, a man who claims to be God dazzles 20 million devotees with miracles and spiritual powers. In the midst of his glory, his most intimate Western disciple makes a shattering discovery.

Tal Brooke's eyewitness account takes you into the inner circle of the greatest "enlightened master" in the East. He goes beyond the supernatural displays of a man who claims to be God into a deeper world where a secret and terrible agenda is being fulfilled. The narrative suggests that, far from being God on earth, this "World Messiah" is in fact a modern antichrist, empowered by demonic forces bent on destroying the eternal hope of millions.

---

# *About the Author*

**Tal Brooke** spent two decades intently exploring the occult. His quest ultimately landed him in the heart of India where for two years he was the top Western disciple of India's miracle-working superguru, Sai Baba. A graduate of the University of Virginia, and Princeton, and a frequent speaker at Oxford and Cambridge universities, Tal has written six books, including his recent popular seller, *When the World Will Be As One*. Tal Brooke is President/Chairman of the Berkeley-based Spiritual Counterfeits Project (SPC) Inc., a nationally known research think tank and magazine.

# *Acknowledgments*

I want to thank my father (posthumously) as well as several others for their deep interest and help in the long stretch of writing this book, especially:

Professor Douglas Day, National Book Award winner and Chairman of the Department of English at the University of Virginia, who, as in my undergraduate era under him, became my mentor, encouraged me, believed in me, and took a special interest in this work over a period of four years.

John Casey—also a National Book Award winner and fellow faculty member with Doug Day—for friendship, encouragement, insight, and pensive workouts at Memorial Gym.

And Frank Ordaz for close friendship plus a second brilliant cover for me—one that surely equals his background scenes in *Indiana Jones*, *Return of the Jedi*, *Starman*, *E.T.* or any of the other award-winning motion pictures for which he painted breathtaking special effects.

# The Great Descent

One of India's five great spiritual Masters, the renowned sage Sri Aurobindo, looked deeply into the night sky on November 23, 1926. He saw a great descending power, a light speeding toward the earth and almost crashing down from the stellar regions.

In his touted enlightened state the great seer proclaimed it was more than a physical light, it was a spiritual light of great magnitude. Aurobindo saw it as "the ocean of Being" willing itself into birth, coming as an avatar. Aurobindo was the perfect herald for this cosmic event for he was universally accepted across India as having reached cosmic consciousness, One-with-God himself. It was a "realized God-man" declaring the appearance of the highest magnitude of divine embodiment—an avatar. Aurobindo, like Ramakrishna and Mahatma Gandhi, would be an enshrined saint great enough to appear on a memorial postage stamp. For Sri Aurobindo to see and proclaim the great descent of Vishnu was no small thing. If what he said was true, a soul on the order of magnitude of Rama or Krishna had just entered the earth.

At that very moment of proclamation, in the wilderness village of Puttaparthi, Sai Baba was born. Aurobindo named the locale in Southern India. That night local Hindus beheld supernatural signs that indicated that once again the great millennial drama was about to begin in village India. The eternal godhead was entering the earth to incarnate through the vehicle of Vishnu. Vishnu did this only at critical points of world history, to end one age and inaugurate another.

A sarod twanged and an 18-foot king cobra sat coiled next to the infant's bed. This was the sign of Shiva, Vishnu's counterpart. Astrologers began to appear in the region. Even the presences of the gods were felt as forms appeared and disappeared, lights went on and off. This was no ordinary child, it was like baby Krishna, possessed by a consciousness that was by no means human. The infant was given multiple consecrations to the gods, especially Shiva.

For a period of time the child refused food from his family as Brahmins do if it is not cooked by a Brahmin. He told them he was being fed by an "Old Man." They would see a form vanish into thin air as the child sprinted into view.

At eight Baba was manifesting signs. His schoolmates gathered around him. Out of an empty paper bag he pulled out varieties of sweets not available in the area. When asked about it he said that a certain "Grama Sakti" or powerful spirit being obeyed his will and gave him whatever he wanted. Then one ominous day a teacher encountered Baba's invisible agency. He had unfairly punished Baba by having him stand up on a table. When the class ended and it came time for the teacher to get up from his chair, he could not move. He was held down by some massive force. A psychic whammy. And when he did manage to get up, the chair stuck to him. He battled helplessly. The moment he released Baba from punishment, he was freed. Awe spread through the neighborhood. Meanwhile Baba's reputation for materializing items not found anywhere in the region increased. Baba was already semidivine.

Then the big transformation took place—the child hit the power line when he was 13. The cosmic personality took over with such force that his family did not recognize the former child, and it worried them. Events are garbled but the general version goes like this.

In March of 1940 at 7:00 in the evening, perhaps on a hillside, Baba suddenly screamed violently and collapsed. His body became stiff, his breathing faint, and he seemed unconscious. No one really knows what happened. He remained unconscious through the night.

People were worried. They first suspected that the local evil spirit in the cave known as Muthyalamma had taken possession of the boy.

Volunteers hurried to the cave and offered sacrifices to the demon spirit, laying flowers before its shrine while breaking a coconut. Immediately the unconscious boy lying at home muttered, "The coconut has broken into three pieces." Those who had gone to the cave confirmed what the boy had said while unconscious.

Baba revived after several days of unconsciousness. His family could not recognize the new resident living within the body, for there was a complete transformation of personality.

The boy spent most of his time in silence, not answering people. Sometimes he would burst into song, poetry, long Sanskrit verses, or religious teaching. Wisdom came from out of nowhere. His parents were terrified by what they saw. His body would become stiff intermittently, and he appeared to leave his body. Baba also began to share clairvoyant perceptions of surrounding events. A neighbor was brought in and humiliated by the omniscient boy who named his hidden evils.

The district medical officer from Ananthapur was dumbfounded. Astrologers said a ghost possessed the boy. Finally Baba's brother brought an exorcist to the house. The young Baba told him, "Come on, you have been worshiping me every day, and now that you have come here, your only business is to worship me and clear out."

The exorcist left in a hurry.

When the parents took the boy back to Puttaparthi, they watched his behavior with increasing fear. He would say to his sister, "Wave the sacred lamp, the gods are passing across the sky." Then his mood might shift violently.

Sometimes he evinced the strength of ten men, and at other times villagers reported that he was as weak as a lotus stalk. He argued with adults and exposed their inner secrets.

Then finally this transition period came to an end and a new power became fully operative in the boy.

In May 1940, three months after the boy fell unconscious, he called the members of his family together and made his formal announcement. But first he completely disarmed them. Out of thin air he presented them with sugar candy then flowers. As the neighbors rushed in, Baba then materialized rice balls and other objects for them. He also projected a kind of love. His brother arrived and was so distraught that he took a stick to beat whatever it was inside of Baba, declaring, "Are you a god, a demon-spirit, or a madman?"

Then the announcement came, "I am Sai Baba..." Then he told them, "Place in my hands those jasmine flowers."

They did. Baba threw them in the air and they hit the ground spelling out in Telugu the name, SAI BABA.

This was in the Penukunda district where the village of Puttaparthi ("the snake that lives in the anthill") lies. Travel was by bullock cart. The village lay timelessly in the wilderness of South India. But within 20 years this miracle worker would be known across all of India. By then millions of pilgrims would come just for a glimpse of him. Unabashedly Sai Baba would tell them, "I am God in the flesh. I am an avatar." As such, no spiritual figure in India would be his equal. Unlike realized gurus, he was never under a teacher or a spiritual path to attain enlightenment. Like an avatar he claimed to have always been in total oneness with the overmind. As a teenager Baba's encyclopedic knowledge of the sastras and Vedas and Upanishads was way beyond that of pundits and sastris who had spent years studying them in their original Sanskrit. Clearly, Baba's mission had begun.

# Chapter 1

# Landing
# in India

*A*fter flying across the Arabian Sea, the plane carrying me to Delhi drifted high above the northern plains of India. Contrasting with the living blue of the sea I now saw a land wrinkled with age and parched from the heat. I felt like an ant riding the shoulders of a giant. Below me, stretching from horizon to horizon, lay a dry, ancient face of sand staring back enigmatically—I believed that out of this waste of sand and clay had risen a race of men whose inner searchings had yielded ultimate truth. Without the advantage of laboratories and skyscrapers, India's wise men had returned from the veil of death with a system of thought that could stagger the green lands and empires of the West.

Suddenly I saw the outskirts of Delhi disappearing under the brilliant wing of the plane. What distinguished mud-huts from hotels, cars from pushcarts, I could not tell. Delhi resembled a dried-out wafer that had been channeled and gnawed down by wood mites. As we went down into the wafer by spirals, I got rare glimpses of color.

When the wheels hit the airstrip, the film-like quality of the flight ended. Now, as a soldier materialized suddenly into the heat of war, I realized that I had to route my own path as quickly as possible. I had no friends, no schedule, no routine, and little preparation. But the truth was my whole life was on the line, and little did I know that this was the beginning of an incredible journey.

As I emerged from the plane, a heat wave almost bowled me over. The air was unlike anything I had felt since my trips to Egypt as a child. It was as though nature had dammed it up on this side of the world, not allowing even a single draught to cross the land or sea. Unlike London's cool and familiar breeze moving among strolling people in parks, the air of India was like the dead-heated air inside a sun-baked sarcophagus. The effect of such intense heat was to give the atmosphere a feeling of close, lingering aberrancy; it was as if each door prized open to the mystic void had raised the temperature a few more infernal degrees. Soon I was out of Customs, joining a family of strangers in a taxi.

We flashed down mazes of little roads through occasional patches of countryside. We were going from Palam airport to old Delhi, bypassing as much of New Delhi as possible by sticking to the suburbs. Some of the areas must have been extremely old, perhaps even ancient villages that had been overtaken by the sprawling mass of New Delhi, and now incorporated into the diverse character of the city. Contrasted with these primitive huts and adobe houses were the new constructions going up right beside them. The net effect of grafting New Delhi upon ancient India was perhaps the most peculiar anomaly that I had ever seen, like the final campaign of an architectural madman.

In this hazy post-monsoon season of October, the afternoon sky took on a peculiar smoky glazing that seemed to burnish everything in sight. This gave things a certain otherworldly quality. Yet the vividness of the experience jarred me time and again.

For 40 minutes, the car raced through netherworlds. My reaction was to look for something familiar. I had heard about the sheer numbers of people in India, but now faced with it I was unprepared for what I saw. Like a slow-motion replay, streams and processions of people drifted up and down the road. Some were so dark that they were almost blue black, and all were emaciated and worn looking. Many almost naked, some practically choked by their tribal ornaments, and some painted and striped, they walked barefooted on the scorching road across occasional rivulets of semifluid tar. The feeling hit me time and again as I looked into their faces, that a great fear was in each of them. Not that it was always evident, but it sat beneath the surface waiting to emerge in moments of quiet.

In 15 minutes, we must have passed by ten thousand gaunt faces. Where did they go at night? Did they all stop in their tracks at sunset and, like june bugs, curl up in mud holes and heaps of refuse where the night world would scurry over them? And if they fell down in the noonday sun, did the human procession just stroll over them as they were glued to the road in puddles of tar?

Across the landscape were small fires, glowing coals, and things going up in smoke. Acrid mixtures filtered in through the window. Tar and oil-soaked rags burned while fires smoldered beneath metal drums. Blended with this came various smells of other burning things, among them, dried cow dung. And then there were odd human smells. As we passed open sewage canals, a putrid odor filled the air seeming to contaminate everything.

The new constructions sprouting along the road became commentaries on India's present state. That summer, when I was in Spain's Costa Brava, I thought that I had seen the worst civilization could offer in terms of skyscrapers. The plaster cracked before the buildings were done, water seeped through the walls, the exterior paint washed away in the rain, and in about three years, the "luxury flats" would be slum tenements. By three years' time, half the pipes would burst and clog with minerals, much of the plaster would crumble, and most of the electrical wiring would no longer work. By then, deep rivulets and cracks would run along the outside walls of these Spanish oceanside skyscrapers until they ran the length of the building and steel beams protruded. It would take little more than a firecracker placed strategically to get the entire wall to fall apart leaving the building open like a doll's house.

Yet compared to these new constructions going up along India's highways, the Spanish resorts were bastions of immortal rock. In contrast, they looked like Versailles, and had the indomitable strength of the Parthenon or the Great Pyramids. I wondered how the Indian buildings were even able to stand. Just then, a passenger in the backseat asked me if the buildings in America were really much better. I told him a little better.

The outer scaffoldings were logs tied together with rope, like crude tinker toys. Handmade cinder blocks were cemented in place with a mixture of mud and a trace of cement powder. The result was an array of buildings that leaned every way, resembling a work of modern cubism.

Another thing occurred to me—that many of the painted zombies along the road were the builders of these eyesores. The workmen stumbled around in the burning sun with cankers on their feet, carrying stones and cinder blocks. I wondered how much mileage each got per handful of rice. Their construction was like the desperate struggle of a wounded soldier realigning the sandbags of his bombed-out trench. How could there be artistry or beauty here? By what rationale was Delhi modernizing? Was it not in pursuit of some illusion by which India could walk into the drawing rooms of the

Western nations, and have problems in common with them, problems in mega-technology? Yet the fuel for this illusion of modernity was India's dying men constructing symbols of affluence on a stark desert.

The car swung out of the suburbs toward the heart of old Delhi, the twin of New Delhi.

The late afternoon air of old Delhi smelled like sugar syrup, rose perfume, and cow dung. We entered the heart of it, moving down past the Red Fort and the Bazar. We whirled past beggars, cripples, street-sellers, abandoned children among the masses of people. The road itself was a sensory overload consisting of scrambling people, herds of bicycles, cows, cars, motor scooters, taxis, and auto-rickshaws. The family of strangers disembarked and I moved on.

The driver bobbed and weaved at such a high speed and so haphazardly that on about 20 occasions I was positive that we had maimed someone. Finally I yelled at him loud enough to make him jump. He flapped his hands and sped on babbling for a while about "if a man has an accident, it is his *karma* (see Glossary) only." Soon we entered New Delhi.

Yet even with a new westernized veneer, New Delhi still contained a basic seediness of character. New as much of it was, nothing seemed to keep the process of disintegration in check. Behind even the most freshly whitewashed hotels and buildings loomed this feeling of decay. There was a quality about Delhi that no amount of westernization could hide, and yet I could not quite put my finger on it. Perhaps it was more than simply a common attitude of the Indians or their way of life. Perhaps I was sensing a wholly different reality hanging in the air—a philosophic entity that colored and infused everything in its realm.

In the haze of Connaught Circle, through crowds and pavement-sellers, I managed to get my bags from the cab and up the steps of Hotel Continental, a dilapidated old British hotel. I was moving in no matter what. I had been awake for days and it was now late afternoon.

The heat of the seedy little room made sleep impossible. All I could do, as noises and smells filtered through the walls, was roll back and forth in bed. The voice of Bill Buckley, who did "the Naz" rolled through my mind saying, "... And if you go off to some place ... and you get there and can't get back, then there you jolly well are, aren't you!"

The room was so humid that it was like floating on a cork in a thermos bottle of hot bouillon. A Lifesaver would have melted on a table in about three minutes. Not only that, but what must have once been a good bed now sank right down to the floor like a hammock and if you tried to lie on your side or your stomach, it was like a sustained yogic posture on a bed of nails because the springs came through the mattress like burrs, and made such a loud noise that they sounded like the day shift at an iron foundry.

I watched the large blades of the ceiling fan spin around, and soon noticed the road map of cracks networked across the whole ceiling and down the walls. I also noticed fleeting movements at the periphery of my vision. When I moved my eyes to catch the fluttering, it stopped. Suddenly from nowhere, I saw the source of the movement. Fluttering then freezing, I saw a large lizard. It ran along the ceiling with as much ease as most creatures move along the ground. I pictured it losing its grip at night right above my head, falling on my face, or worse, in my open mouth, where it might flutter for a while and leave an amputated tail to dance on my epiglottis. It was the hideous thought of an exhausted mind.

Dismissing this last horror, I decided to pursue the movements of the lizard across the ceiling. Perhaps it had meaning to its existence, perhaps it had none. It just went on without the thought of not going on.

The movements of the creature across the ceiling and walls became a battlefield of forces on a miniature scale. It was no longer so much a lizard as it was a symbol of a conscious force putting its life on the line for fulfillment, whether this be a small fly or the logistics of getting from the cellar to the third floor via an intersurface. I lay there in a growing abstraction in which the noises and smells of New Delhi seemed to vanish, and the scene above my head became a haze of crazy patterns. It began to dawn upon me that these hazy enigmatic patterns were a representation of myself, working through different paths and obstacles toward some sort of incredible goal. Somewhere on the map, be it far or near my destiny, was my present location, where I now lay alone, staring up at the ceiling of an old British hotel in New Delhi. I began to trace the forces and events that brought me to India.

# Chapter 2

# A Crack Through Time

As I lay eyeing the ceiling, I was riddled with self-doubt. The culture shock I was experiencing made me feel empty. I began to question things that I was so certain of when I boarded the plane in London. Now I was looking for almost any excuse to fly back.

Enervated by heat and fatigue, I mulled over my life as it seemed to unravel in the cracks above me, its quest now represented by the lizard on the ceiling that darted, then froze. In essence, I had come to India with the impassioned intent of reaching the highest goal that the mystics, yogis, and spiritual masters down the ages have spoken of, namely cosmic consciousness, enlightenment, or nirvana, all terms of oneness and identity with the godhead—that bliss state of "the Supreme Self." The teaching of Eastern mysticism, especially Vedanta, which has become the foundation of New Age thought, was that "the true self within all of us is none other than the eternal consciousness of the godhead, the ocean of being." This was a promise that paled anything that this world seemed to offer, and I had tasted it, experienced it! Now I felt a desperate need to recall my moment of mystical awakening, for this overwhelming experience had driven me all the way to India with an uncompromising single-mindedness.

## The "Tree Experience"

Suddenly the lizard lunged into a hole, and my mind's eye came out on the other side in the spring of 1966. A friend and I were on our motorcycles. We crossed Memorial Bridge into Virginia, then plunged down abandoned highways, through forgotten towns and villages into a part of Virginia I had never seen. The grocery stores and houses we passed seemed out of the nineteenth century. Even the roadside leaves sat as though they had not been moved in 50 years.

The rains that had covered the Atlantic seaboard left the air crisp and clean. In the late afternoon, mists sprang from the ground lacing the forests and roads with mystery.

In the twilight, we passed down an archway of eight-foot hedges. After a maze of rivers, paths, and hills, we entered an abandoned farm. We parked in a distant field and laid our sleeping bags against a giant old oak tree that stood alone and rose into the sky, its branches like tremendous ganglia. The fog cleared almost immediately as the stars popped into view, through the branches of the black tree above us. Neither the sun nor the moon was present, only the stars which stretched across the cool sky like burning jewels.

My purpose was to take the largest dose of LSD 25 either of us had ever heard of anyone taking, 3000 micrograms (or ten times the standard dosage). I was sold on the psychochemical approach by Alan Watts' book, *The Joyous Cosmology*, that I first read in 1963. Here was the testimony of a contemporary mystic. He did not pray in the desert, he did not fast in the wilderness, he did not stick to rigid covenants, nor was he required to spend months in isolation. Rather his meeting with God was as subdued as a New England tea, in part because he took LSD on a farm in the country, and spent the time surveying deeply significant things in this newly altered state of consciousness. Watts was propelled perhaps by his academic learning in Oriental metaphysics, for he, like Alpert and Leary, was a Harvard professor. Watts the explorer could record his observations to a world in waiting. In flowers and leaves lay subtle *mandalas*, behind winds blowing through fields was a joyous cosmic dance. And behind all things, asserted Watts in a characteristic statement for mystics, was an absolute consciousness; that it is all-permeating, and that it expresses itself through diversity, and yet is not that diversity.

At a fraction past midnight, I swallowed the capsule. It was to be a lone voyage. My friend was not in the mood for anything but sleep. I was ready to stay awake all night I was so charged. I accepted the fact that I was, in effect, sitting on top of an atom bomb. And that I would either come out on the level of Guatama Buddha or the coyote in the "Roadrunner" cartoon.

An hour later, what looked dead was conscious, as all of creation crackled in dialogue with itself. Meanwhile my thoughts and perceptions began to fuse. Stars joined together like drops of mercury across the night sky forming multicolored webs—breathing and arching across the heavens, across galaxies and onto the very ground where I perched. Grains of sand, pebbles, and trees, ebbed and flowed with this impersonal consciousness.

If my own consciousness was layered and branched in a million places like a banyan tree, it was now as though the rest of my being had squeezed what was most essentially me into the top stem of the uppermost branch. Down to the deepest root, there were a thousand astral levels at war within me, as my uppermost self was fighting to stay aloft through the aid of a million subordinate parts that were straining and tugging. Even below these, there were endless rumbles and shifts, like a subterranean city, while every archetype that I had ever encountered was presently being held at bay.

Soon I was above even the dazzling beings and demigods that were so special before. The celestial cities and realms were like the lower strata of a pyramid whose fascination I had sacrificed—things great enough to inspire the master poets and painters, I later reflected—in order to approach the level of the truly abstract, pure thought, pure knowing, and pure being. If I did reach the purest state, I could diffuse like a drop of bright mercurochrome throughout the ocean of thought.

Every second that passed, one of my million parts was answering something comparable to the riddle of the sphinx to propel me on to the level of superconsciousness. A new truth came. That I, like every man, was a hierarchy of men, a living society, a kingdom and a nation, and before I became enlightened I would have to bear the weight of all truths, to encompass the total history of my nation within a fraction of time. After a thousand other thoughts, I passed on to the next level of realization.

I shrank and became so small that "humbling" doesn't describe it—I became insignificant. Far less than a blade of grass that has just been given the brief consciousness to realize what it is. It might hear the voice that shakes the mountains of the worlds, "You thought you were a god and you stir only to find that you are a blade of grass lying helpless on the forest floor—even the ants walk over you. How tiny you are. Your delusions end. Can you bear this? and yet live?"

Then the sheer jet-like force of what was happening to my mind became too great. I became a twig riding a tidal wave. I clutched the field as though clutching the rigging of a hurricane-swept deck. It seemed that something other than the drug had taken over, something supernatural perhaps.

As a force drove my mind at a speed greater than thought, I could feel something far older than I navigating my course. I passed 10,000 crossroads per second, and took the proper turn on each one of them. I feared that if I tried to grind down the gears at this point, I might wake up on the outer edges of the galaxy not much higher up on the phylogenic scale than a cucumber. And after all the billions of years it took me to work my way up to becoming a human being, I didn't want to blow it now, and enter a form of loneliness that was unthinkable.

My speed increased even more, as I became a diamond wedge cutting the finest possible arcs, from one juncture to another. Then it occurred to me that on some level I was helping to open the doorways for the wedge. That I was being asked questions in which a correct turn could only be made by means of a totally spontaneous truthful answer. Anything else would veer me off course. Like the Day of Judgment, a lie would be impossible damnation, because there was not an atom of time to deliberate. And anything but the truth, it seemed, would have fragmented me all over the cosmos.

Immediately before I lost all grasp of language and thought, I saw a doorway into a new universe. It was a pinpoint of light. To fight the acceleration required to approach it was to fight the mass of the entire universe. I could not tell whether the distance within the pinpoint of light was as minuscule as the angstrom units between atoms, or almost infinitely huge, as the distance from one side of the universe to the other.

At the barrier of the pinpoint of light, I enter the eternal present. All 13 billion brain cells within me seem to turn inside out, as though reforming into a complex and higher structure that was latent. Each cell recites one of my former names, and as a nation, I hear the 13 billion names of my subjects who are me. Once in the pinpoint, all ties with the world vanish. I enter "the unborn."

A caterpillar cannot experience the butterfly transition and remain a caterpillar; one structure cannot be smuggled across into the other. That is impossible. That also went for me. Thus at most, my experience could be paralleled from one universe to another, but nothing could cross the barrier.

I have never been able to summon what happened for that stretch of time after going through. Months later I assumed that I had entered into the "... void, also known as the clear light or the Ocean of Brahman." That I had been allowed to experience the highest mystical state, what the Hindus call *Nirvikalpa samadhi*. Years later, Baba would call it a "taste."

Before dawn I was coming down fast, yet still within a hallucinatory sea. My main object was to remind myself of the great truth I had encountered and not lose hold of its intensity. I knew of the distractive irrelevance of the post-LSD comedown, and how it could quickly muddy up anything no matter how overpowering and brilliant it was. Therefore I preferred to go sharply from one continent to the other, and be in the world crisp and awake with a clear memory, not battling bullfrogs and hearing monsters scream in the swamps.

As the dawn broke, I chewed a Thorazine tablet, the popular LSD antidote. But that didn't stave off the invasion of absurdity; indeed, I could hear what I termed "the cosmic super chuckle" well on the way.

While spitting out stems and weeds to kill the taste of the tablet, mocking sounds filled the air. The trees started to scream with laughter; they shuddered, flapped, and wailed with scorn.

In the harsh glare of dawn, I could hear squawks,

screams, and whistles amid a constant babble of innu-
endos and trivial conversation. It sounded like resurrection day for the social snobs of the world, and to coin a
Twain phrase, the air was "all full'a tears and flapdoo-
dle." It sounded as though all the former members of the
Boston social register were in opposition to the royal
lords and ladies of England. Perhaps, I thought, I am
tuning in to a sector of hell where this really exists.
Where every self-important fool has to battle it out with
armies of other "creme de la creme" for an eternity.
They'll have incredible charts and tables referencing
genealogies and purity of family blood, cross-referenced
and carbon-dated for authenticity. And there will be
libraries of photostated family emblems, shields, rib-
bons, and coats of arms, and all hell will break loose over
these things.

Then I saw the source of the sound. The trees, on that
early spring morning in the mountains and pastures of
rural Virginia, were weighed down with birds that hung
like clusters of grapes, of every size, shape, and color.
Quadrants within a given tree would be in opposition to
other quadrants in the same tree or in other trees. Then
it turned on me.

I caught them out of the corner of my eye. The heckling
began, in hoarse impersonations. "Kothmick Conchussness...honk honk, peck peck...Kothmick Conchussness...honk peck...KOTHMICK CONCHUSSNESS???"
And scornful laughter rippled from tree to tree..."Don'd
bee Prupostrus..."

Finally I saw about five giant crows hogging an entire
section of a tree, cramping the other birds. They were
smoking cigars, wearing top hats, and dressed in different formal dinner jackets. Amazed at this find, I looked
around and noticed that, sure enough, all the other
birds were rather fashionably attired, some in recent
Paris fashion, others more sedate. The babbling got
louder.

Within ten minutes I had blown a circuit, and was climbing the tree like a demon, stoning and shaking other trees, and finally chucking huge sticks and logs at all the trees. My friend awoke by the time I had emptied every tree in the neighborhood, and told me later that rather than resembling a "Maha-God-possessed-what-ever-it-is," I looked like a werewolf, covered with twigs, drooling, and almost purple with rage. Hours later I would try to tell my friend about cosmic consciousness over peppered eggs and hot coffee, in some roadside cafe in the hills of backwoods redneck Virginia. Then some hillbilly music blared out of the jukebox. So I had to start screaming at my friend on the other side of the booth. "Right now while I'm eating these eggs, there is an underlying consciousness at work inside them that makes their existence possible. I know, I've been there and that was only five hours back."

Suddenly the whole place started filling with red-necks, and it got noisier and more absurd, and we must have looked weirder and weirder, screaming about God being in the eggs ... and the table salt. And the jukebox sound became more outrageous with Nashville holler-ing.

If only hours back, I reflected remorsefully, some neu-rological cybernetic had shifted my cortical relays and boosted my IQ to half a million to give me a mystical experience, I must be somewhere near the bottom of the rainbarrel right now. So the answer was to exit before the pinball machines exploded, and before a whole crew of really sophisticated demons, dressed like true blue hominy-grits-eating cowhands, appeared on the scene to yodel, howl, stare, finger triggers, and tear the place apart.

In the shimmering air of American highways, en route to Washington, D.C., we motorcycled back into civilization passing glinting chrome and neon signs in the suburbs. The midday sun was baking me like a reptile, and I felt dull again, and a stranger to all the truths that I knew so deeply only a few hours earlier. So too, as I remembered this experience in Delhi, I felt equally as distant from the incredible "truths" that had driven and inspired me for years now.

# Chapter 3

# *Immersion Into the Subcontinent*

With memories of cowboy cafes, country stores, glinting chrome, and hot exhaust of rural Virginia still hanging in the air of my mind, my doubts about India still remained. In part because I knew that I had blundered in my imaginings. My preconceptions from all the guidebooks were almost irrelevant to the India I was now in. And I wondered if my spiritual preconceptions were not equally divorced from reality. I still had to assure myself that everything fit together.

After my "trip" in the late spring of 1966, when I returned to the University of Virginia, things started opening up. Truth became like a medieval lover in the window of a palace, sweet but remote. And the ecstasy of life was the pursuit of those rare glances as I, like an enraptured lover, would try to discern her form as she changed to more elusive guises. Truth became not only the rock-hard surface of the Bible, with the dazzling power of the parables of Christ, it was also the sublime and the beatific, and came as a cosmic lover. Like the woodwinds of Krishna in Brindavan, it danced across planes of existence, bringing all things to their source. Yet like the Universal Form that Krishna showed Arjuna on the battlefield of Kurushetra, it was also awesome and imponderable. I became a natural syncretist, insisting that all paths lead to the same God.

I was having the most positive and confident period of my life. It was a manic rush, a never-ending up of confidence and energy. I expected a revelation around every corner, I read *Sri Ramakrishna, The Great Master*, by Swami Sradananda. Immersing myself in the mystical book, I decided to overlook any disagreements it might have with the Bible. When I was spiritually more mature, then I could synthesize all "apparent" differences and spot the unity between the two traditions. Of this, my intuition was certain.

Other enlightening books soon joined it on the shelf. The common denominator of all of them was that with amazing optimism, they portrayed a universe free of any ultimate evil or absolute peril. And the seeker was prodded to march ahead fearlessly into the center of a cosmic playground.

Contrasting with the simplicity of the Bible, the path of the mystic was, in the higher esoteric systems, labyrinthine and fraught with introspective paradoxes. Yet to the seekers, such challenges magnified their own sense of achievement, exalting their efforts like a climber on the crest of a mountain peak.

My bookshelves mounted with books from India's most respected orders including the Sivananda, Aurobindo, Ramana Maharshi, Maharishi Mahesh Yogi, and Yogananda ashrams. Each school claimed to have the most evolved means of yogic salvation and enlightenment for the *Kali Yuga* (the present age by Puranic doctrine), be it *Naad* yoga, *Mantra* yoga, *Hatha* yoga (mechanically attuning the nervous system to transmit the high voltage of enlightenment), *Vichara Atma* (pure philosophical self-inquiry into the nature of self), or any of 30 assorted systems of *Kriya*, *Raja*, or *Kundalini* yoga. LSD led to Indian mysticism, which in turn brought me to India. Yet my perplexity in the Delhi hotel room was unabated. My faith was under assault.

I reminded myself that another key Eastern axiom was, "Don't let outward appearances sway you from the truth within." I knew I was still overreacting from the trauma of culture shock. Yet what could I trust?

Now I even let myself ponder something that I would have considered to be blasphemy during the last three manic years following that powerful mystical experience. I wondered if the entire mystical system was not a subtle deception in itself. The yogic antidote to doubt is, "Do not think. Do not conceptualize. Trust and relinquish your self totally to the process." The final barrier to my trusting would be the abolition of that last inkling of a suspicion that such an admonition was not the cosmic mind after all, but Satan in the garden all over again.

The answer to my stalemate was to get out of bed and take a walk in downtown New Delhi. Ten minutes later, I emerged into the night air of New Delhi amid a smog of curry and spices from the jumble of sidewalk cafes and stands. Beggars and peanut-sellers still lined the pavements. Apparently my probings had not changed the nature of Delhi.

As I moved ahead, it was as though I had become radium coated in a Geiger-counter society. Peace of mind on an Indian street was impossible. It was like being under the spotlights of World War II Munich at curfew, where every movement is indelibly recorded by a thousand searching eyes.

I looked and saw that diagonally across from my hotel was something that was either an amusement park or a bazaar.

It had more colored lights than Rockefeller Center. The high wall around it was a painted muslin with a barrage of disproportionate ten-foot demigods, like a madman's Disneyland. Over these chain-linked creatures blared big metalic loudspeakers. They looked like British military surplus goods from World War II, dented and banged as though forever being packed off on trains with the fair. It was a far cry from my impression of an India bathed in a rich harmony of sitars at every street corner.

As I left the fair I saw the 15-foot monkey god *Hanuman* fluoresce above the fair, winking and scowling, perpetually ready to hammer a huge mace down on the people with its giant muscular arms. I stood for a long time scanning the lights of Delhi. The sounds were beginning to quiet down as most of the stores closed, and much of the crowd thinned out. Under the dark arcades of the circle were the glowing coals of peanut-sellers, as well as a number of human forms stretched along the pavements. In the central grass area I looked over the fence in front of me. Beyond the glow of hashish pipes and *beedies*, I discerned that the small group of people, though dressed as Indian peasants, were gigantic in size. Then as I took a closer look at the lightness of their features, I visualized who they were, the original trippers from Big Sur, Laguna Beach, and Marin County, leaving their crash pads and geodesic communes for an Indian pilgrimage.

Now in a seedy downtown night in Delhi, sprawled out in a public park in clouds of hashish smoke, they gave off distinctly "wasteland vibes." It was as though what they had found was such a terrifying "bummer," their only recourse was to shut it out and pretend that, whatever it was, they never saw it.

Nevertheless, they kept their cool as they passed hashish chillums, knowing "it's all a dream" because life was a child's paradise of candy-cane gardens and lollipop boulevards. Observing them over the fence, I experienced cultural embarrassment for my own people.

I was also afraid that they were an omen of what was to come as I went on the road in India.

Then I saw what was no more than a 90-pound frame. Teetering against the night lights of the cinema-house like a skeleton, I saw that it was a girl. Then bending over a sprawled body I saw her proceed to lift it. It didn't appear as though she had the strength to lift a small bundle of newspapers. She tugged and leaned all her weight back and jerked again and again, straining and stumbling. Finally the body managed to turn half sideways, while bracing an arm on the ground to begin a gradual process of lifting up. She stood rigid as a lamppost, as the arms of the body worked its torso up her like shinnying a tree. Finally it stood and swayed against her, a head taller than she was, and I saw that it was a man. While balancing him, she reached down and picked up two giant black pretzels. Then as he got into the two body braces while she continued holding him, it resembled an insect dance. Apparently he was paralyzed from the waist down, and judging from the carved wooden pretzels, it had happened in India. Was it one of India's countless legendary diseases? A hideous fall from some precipice, all in the search for truth. Now the impersonality of the godhead felt frightening. There was no protecting hand underwriting your life.

They entered the street light as the stoned-out chortles of their California buddies intimidated the night air. He looked like a decadent "Jesus" with stringy blond hair, goatee, hollow eyes, and a single large brass earring. Barefooted and dirty, he wore a shredded white cloth wrapped robe-like around him, revealing two bird-like shoulder blades. Around his neck were Hindu prayer beads, and tightly pressed between his fingers was a tiny smoking beedie that glowed against one of the braces. The girl was equally wasted, a little scared, a little defiant, holding her own, and proud of it. I would learn that there were many like them in India, like a plague.

They had become obscene. It was as bad as watching a man who has to carry his stomach and intestines in a clear plastic bag that flaps over his belt buckle. Yet I wondered if the humbling fact of becoming an abomination had lessened their arrogance. Or did the pride of defiance grow like cancer?

Trying to numb the raw edges of the experience, I watched the two "freaks" make their way slowly across a downtown street. At a distance they pumped up and down like two rusty automobile cylinders, as his lower half dragged and swept above the hot pavement like a giant paint brush till they vanished into the shadows. That ended my night in horror. That first night in India in the hotel room was a kind of hell.

By the end of three weeks, either things had changed or I had adjusted. Whatever the case, I was ready for full immersion into the vast body of India, like sliding into a scalding bath by inches and degrees. I had moved to a youth hostel in the diplomatic enclave. The only terrible inner diary I had kept were the tales of Westerners who had come through, all of them following various wild dreams. On one unforgettable night I slithered home on the Delhi pavement at midnight with a temperature of 104 and blood coming out of my bowels. I was up all night dripping blood and liquid. My guts felt like steel wool was being dragged through my colon on a fish hook. It was the famed "Delhi belly" and it felt like Cholera, far worse than anything I had experienced in the Middle East growing up. Yet I continued to jump over obstacles in my path like a mad hurdler. I was determined to see this thing through to the end.

## Himalayan Journey

My first jaunt, at the end of the three weeks, was to the Himalayan hill station of Rishikesh, one of the most sacred places in India, famous for its hermitages, ash-rams, and yogis. My companion was a Californian whom I had met at the hostel. He was all I could find for the trip. He had a Sanskrit name, a ponytail, spoke English like an Indian, carried a flute, dressed like a monk, and continually reminisced about Lord Krishna.

We blasted to the huge, crusty, clamoring railway station in old Delhi at 1:00 A.M. by motorcycle-rickshaw. We raced through back alleys and slums, bouncing along cobblestone roads as our luggage bounced around in the open booth. At the railway station, we waded over bodies half asleep, pushed through crowds with our lug-gage over our heads.

It was hard to believe. At 2:00 A.M., the platforms were loaded to the brim. Like all huge British-built prewar terminals, the old Delhi station had over 18 platforms, two-thirds of which had long steam locomo-tives hissing and blasting. And the empty platforms were no less packed with people, luggage, freight, and farm animals. Our platform was halfway across the station, a good quarter-mile walk, where the narrow-gauge trains pointed to the mountain regions of Punjab, Simla, Kashmir, and Uttar Pradesh.

When we finally boarded the right train, I realized why people reserve berths three weeks in advance when riding third class. I had a narrow wooden board to lie on, perched above the seats, where the skeleton of a midget might just barely have room to turn over. And at peak hours, lying on one of these resembled being tucked on a ledge overhanging hell. Thirty people right below me played cards all night long amid the clucking of chickens. And anytime we pulled into one of 25 stations, tea-sellers would pop their heads in the window to scream "Chai." By early morning we had gone less than a hun-dred miles in eight hours, and that was as far as the train would go.

---

We immediately hustled a taxi with a number of middle class Indians and roared off. After an hour's driving, I asked the driver when we would get to Rishikesh. As dust spilled in the window from some cow-packed fruit bazaar, the driver said, "This is it." I almost went into shock as the other passengers filtered out in front of a tea stall with a blaring radio. Controlling my temper, I told the driver that he would have to do better than this, and drive on till it even vaguely resembled what I had expected. He didn't understand me, but kept on, seeming to know where to go. To ward off depression, I entered into the spontaneous mode of narrator.

"So this is the timeless abode of the great yogis and meditators," I announced. "And the perennial source of Vedantic inspiration." I had pictured caves, waterfalls, and forests tucked in the evergreen foothills of the Himalayas where men of vast wisdom sat in ethereal silence. I did not expect this. I had been led to believe that this was a spiritual magnetic pole on the earth.

But the town of Rishikesh had no such magic, and that hurt. "The woodpecker," a name befitting my companion, and I were the only ones left in the taxi and were beginning to wonder if there was any place worth getting out for. When we got to the famous Sivananda "Divine Life Ashrama," we got out above a chain of crusty nondescript buildings overlooking the Ganges. I was hoping that this was really a nightmare and that I would wake up any minute now. There was no escaping the dirt of India. In time, I would learn to blot it out. But there always remained the bizarre fascination of the unexpected.

Our goal was the ashram of the famous Maharishi Mahesh Yogi on the other bank which indeed did look more like the picture book Himalayan foothills as green mountain vistas rose above the clear Ganges.

---

After we passed through lines of beggars to get to the dock, we crossed the Ganges on a motorized barge. Along the opposite bank, we passed scores of multi-colored temples until we reached a gravel path that went up a mountain to the barbed-wire gate of the Maharish Mahesh Yogi Ashram. This was our point of separation. They let me in, but they would not have a thing to do with "the woodpecker," who was becoming increasingly hysterical.

He ranted and threatened to write to the President of the United States, the United Nations, Indira Gandhi, as well as Interpol. Then he spent hours sitting outside the gate, to protest their persecutions and hypocrisies against him, to embarrass them before the world, and to hasten cosmic judgment upon them.

Once on the ashram itself, I was reminded of the more plush areas of New Delhi transposed to the mountains. By any Indian standards it was high class, and by Rishikesh standards it was like an elite country club overlooking an abyss of confusion. Herein lay a fragment of a chance that my Eastern dream would leave the rubble that it had fallen into, and find some kind of resurrected hope.

As I sat patiently in the reception office near the gate, I looked at all the pictures and billboards of Maharish Mahesh Yogi, on television, in San Francisco, boarding planes, and sitting in transcendental serenity.

Maharishi's house sat on a far corner of the ashram, perched on an overlook where far below glinted the Ganges and vistas of Rishikesh. It reminded me of some Hugh Heffner layout for bachelor yogis. Maharishi entered from behind the curtain, as the room went quiet in response to his patient hand gesture and smile, which immediately established the gulf between the enlightened man and the average person.

By the end of the meeting I was depressed. Maharishi had not given off a really noticeable aura of spiritual incandescence. Nevertheless he agreed to initiate me without charge, something he rarely did. Some of his Western troupe were very impressed by this.

The night before I was to be initiated, a week later, Rishikesh was ablaze with one of its major yearly festivals. All night long, loudspeakers screamed away, parades combed the streets, and firecrackers exploded amid religious rallies and local plays. By 11:00, I gave up trying to sleep. I wandered from festivities to street corner debates between yogis from different holy orders. One of them, who looked like Michael Jackson complete with wraparound shades and fire-engine red tunic, latched on to me till 2:00 A.M., giving me his life story with the inside word on various local gurus.

By the time I reached Neelam restaurant, mentioned in Fodor's Guide as marginally acceptable and yet eight levels above any other stall in town, it looked like Jazz Festival Week at The Heavy Metal Kid Cafe, East Village.

After maybe three and a half hours of sleep, I was up with the land at 5:30 jarred out of sleep as usual by the tubercular hackings and coughs of the janitor of the badly deteriorated Rishikesh guest house. In the raw morning air, I dashed across the crusty cement courtyard to take douses by squatting under a freezing faucet in a dark slime-coated metal shed.

By 8:00, I was making the two-mile walk to the river barge in front of the Sivananda ashram.

The only other unsettling thing after that was the odd silence of the religious arcades on the opposite bank. The temples interconnected with weird gates, entrances, and hallways painted in ghastly bright pastels that highlighted their otherworldly shapes. The most un-hinging section of all was a temple with a courtyard of huge cement lotuses and figures that portrayed scenes out of the Hindu epics. Above the main pathway at the entrance, elevated glass cases protruded from the walls containing life-sized manikins of the main Hindu gods, clothed, four-armed, blue black with enigmatic death-mask expressions that either stared far off or right down at you through either two or four perfect glass eyes.

On every trek to the ashram they confronted me from their elevated dusty cases, and I inevitably wondered what state of mind a man would have to be in to see them as divine. Certainly the smell of cotton candy combined with the sickly bubblings of a Wurlitzer organ would end my ambivalence. But for now, there was always the possibility that I was hung up by "cultural variables." Their system would say that for every man there is a unique way of approaching the absolute. Yet why did these temples generate a feeling not of exuberance or sanctity, but rather of voidness, desolation, and death? And if this feeling was a sample of what the rishis called nirvana, and should nirvana be an absolute increase of this force, then perhaps it was the most terrible cosmic insanity conceivable. This was a haunting thought to have on my way to a mantric initiation in Maharishi's own house.

Half an hour later, with flowing beard, serene blue eyes, and wearing a cleanly pressed white silk kurta, Dick Britton-Foster, Maharishi's closest disciple, who looked like the Schweppes man, met me in the garden of Maharishi's house signaling with silent gestures. Pausing for a moment, Dick looked down the overlook to the clutter on the other side of the sparkling Ganges where the tent ashram of the yogi from Calcutta could very clearly be seen. We heard a faint din of honkings, gongs, cymbals, drums, and chants. Then with a look of almost transcendental disdain Dick said, "I really wish those idiots would learn to shut up."

As we continued toward the house, I envisioned a hundred transcendental yogis of the Maharishi camp attaining at least a "causal plane" consciousness, siphoning off some of the creative energy of the universe, and then erecting an impermeable barrier around the tent ashram. Then I pictured "the Calcutta Guru," calmly wandering outside, with hands on hips scanning the local geography, and then with a calm blowing of the nose and perhaps the utterance of a *mantra* or two, obliterating the entire mountain from the face of the earth.

The "cave" beneath Maharishi's house was dark except for a little flickering candle. Built entirely of natural stones, the inside wall had an altar containing flowers, and incense, and other initiatory items, including fruits, flowers, and white handkerchiefs that we were told to bring.

In the dim blackness, I knelt with my eyes shut and hands on knees.

After a long silence, Dick recited a Sanskrit prayer in a subdued voice that resounded about the cave. Then he began a series of chants, following this with the slow repetition of a single word, the mantra "Iyengar," a seed name or primal syllable for a being whose likeness was in some South Indian temple.

By the end of several more weeks, I had meditated steadfastly every day at the prescribed hours from early dawn till late at night, often, picturesquely enough, on the banks of the Ganges. My mantra had lodged itself into such a fixed tape-loop, that it would reappear of its own accord at all times of day and night. Maharishi had enthusiastically queried if I was getting good results, and not wanting to seem ungracious, I replied that I was.

But the intuition that brought me to India knew that Maharish was not my reason for coming. A greater spiritual dynamo would appear on the horizon. And more than one Rishikesh old timer referred to Maharish as an "export item." These were low yield spiritual fireworks.

Yet I shuddered at the prospect of having to comb India alone in search of this unknown light on the horizon.

# Chapter 4

# *The Ocean of Light in Sandals*

$M$y sojourn had gone from bad to worse and this was to be my final try, a last ditch effort. I was about to see the most powerful spiritual figure in India, a modern-day miracle worker with a following in the millions. *Newsweek* magazine had just called "Baba" India's Christ, citing that he had been observed by a large crowd on the Indian desert as he turned water into gasoline when his car had run out of fuel. Some of his miracles had almost become legendary in India.

But recent events for me had been especially bad. Traveling all over India for months on trains had been debilitating. I had been alone much of the time and had to face all kinds of incredible obstacles. Things that took courage and energy. Not only that, the decade of the sixties had just ended two weeks back as winter closed out 1969. I was now on the outskirts of the city of Ananthapur in the heart of South India and stood in the large compound of a private residence. It was the evening of January 15, 1970, and no more than 40 or 50 close Indian followers were present as three limousines entered the driveway.

Seated in the backseat of the main car was a figure donned in a brilliant red gown, whose hair raised up like a giant cumulus cloud of wiry black strands. It was Bhagvan Sri Sathya Sai Baba, whose name meant "God."

Baba claimed to be God incarnate coming as the world savior, and was well known throughout the continent as being able to back up this claim by a profusion of miracles. His miracles, as far as I knew, distinguished him from the one or two other miracle workers throughout the world because they were unceasing, and had been known to occur on rather large scales.

Sai Baba emerged from the car, and I felt an instant shock wave of force I would be hard put to describe. Quite unlike any feeling I had ever experienced before, my near bankrupt emotional state dispersed like a faint mist floating through the blazing white corona of a helium arc welder. The privileged within the courtyard stood in awed silence with hands held in prayer to Baba. Others fell on their faces before him, some trying to touch his feet.

### Trials en Route

During the time I was waiting for Baba's car to arrive, I accepted the fact, after four months of traveling around India, that I had been defeated and that my search had reached its end. I almost hoped it would be a failure, so that I could leave the exhausted continent and think things out all over again in some land of the living, be it Virginia or California. If Baba was as disappointing as the other gurus, that would be the final straw, and I would leave satisfied that I had persisted in my search beyond reasonable expectation. The one thing that kept me in India this long was my dogged refusal to accept the invalidation of my beliefs, no matter how much evidence to the contrary kept rolling in. Yet I wanted to be dead certain these prized beliefs were wrong before letting them go.

If I scrapped the mystical view of reality and was thrown back to the starting position again, the ordeal that I feared most was the knowledge that my greatest cornerstones, intuition and experience, had betrayed me and could no longer be a standard. Then I would be in the limbo of wondering what reference point to trust if I could not even trust my highest mystical intuitions and promptings. There had always been less spectacular contrary intuitions. But these were the old run-of-the-mill puritanical rights and wrongs that kept firing tracer signals regardless of circumstance, like some vestigial intellect stuck like a doorbell on "duality."

One source of inertia that had been constant was a steady dull despair that I probably could have tolerated indefinitely. But the despair was brought to a head after a series of lesser stages going from Calcutta to Goa to Bombay.

When the boat pulled into Goa, ten or so days before I went to Bombay, I was convinced I had found the ruby of India, especially after sailing 300 coastal miles of Maharashtra and much of the old Portuguese-Indian state Goa. Riding on the deck in the breezy sunshine and the temperate night, the boat rocked gently on the jade green of the Arabian Sea, passing beaches dotted with lush palms, black fishermen, and brilliant white sand reminding me of a south sea "Typee."

But once I disembarked in Panjim, the capital, the pristine natural goddess began to show signs of acne. For one thing, the beach was the main hangout for hippies besides Kathmandu, Varanasi, and Kulu Valley, and inundated with people who "burned" each other on one hand, and then complained about the depersonalized societies from which they came without seeing any contradiction.

My stay in the fallen paradise ended with a frenetic rock festival, instigated by the local guru, an ex-Harlem jazz artist named Eight Fingered Eddie. It was on Christmas eve, when the mean temperature of the night air and the sea was around 80 degrees. The 500 participants looked like what Woodstock would have become, had it lasted for three years instead of three days. And from late afternoon onward, processions of tribes strolled up the beach from every far corner along a two-mile stretch, emerging out of their thatched hut communes, rented cabins, tents, or campers, and gathering at a center point on the beach where the time would be spent gathering twigs and sticks for a giant bonfire. By dusk, several sand dunes were littered with semiclothed people whose bodies had been painted, striped, polka-dotted, nose-ringed, long-haired or head shaven, and any combination in between.

By midnight I headed back for my cot on the beach. By then things were really "groovin" in a constant roar of Nepalese gongs, ceremonial Tibetan thigh-bone horns, guitars, violins, sitars, and top volume acid rock. As columns of red smoke billowed up into the moonlit sky from the glowing bonfire and hundreds of hashish pipes, it resembled Mount Vesuvius erupting on the foul city of Pompeii. There had been distant screams in the night air. In this paradise, the rule of anarchy had taken effect.

The next day on the boat back to Bombay, I got to hear the rest from two travelers who decided that Goa was not the answer. During the party, one group of soul brothers ransacked almost all the cabins along the beach, grabbing anything from cassette machines to passports, including the host's cabin where the music was provided. There, they made off with the entire stereo system, when everybody thought that the record was just being changed.

Meanwhile, three of the less popular Frenchmen sold scopolomine instead of LSD to several girls, then raped them, stealing their passports, and almost killing one of the girls in the ocean. By early morning the girl was found naked on the beach, unable to speak, and by late morning it had turned into a manhunt as half the beach was out for blood.

Also found that morning in a cabin at a far end of the beach were nine or ten people either dead or completely insane. The place looked as if a hurricane had hit it, according to every report, and the blackened room was outlaid with black sulphur candles, pentagrams, strange curios, stashes of the powerhouse psychedelic STP, and several dusty volumes on sorcery and the occult. Local rumors agreed in their explanations on the major points. One, the group in the cabin had been constantly "tripping" for over three days without sleep. And two, they had been trying to summon up and control some sizable demonic force.

Briefly in Bombay, after Goa, I stood in the huge Bombay Victoria train terminal ready to give intuition one last chance at guidance. I spun away from the ticket window for the northeastern regions of Bengal, and went over to the Madras booth. I knew without a doubt that my last resort was the miracle worker, Sai Baba. Plans to see Krishnamurthi, the Aurobindo Ashram, and the Ramakrishna Math in Calcutta were dropped.

I had one last afternoon and evening in Bombay, Saturday night, and I decided to spend the evening changing money. I had met an Indian at the tourist office early in the afternoon, and he told me that his brother needed dollars desperately to go to an American university and would pay a very good price in rupees for them, since there was no official means of obtaining dollars in India.

That Saturday night at around 9:00, we met in the rear gardens of the Taj Mahal Hotel. My feelings were divided. Strictly speaking, I sensed that I was breaking the law. But by a more liberal interpretation, I would be helping an Indian by virtue of a direct swap of "property." And which, according to *Time* and *Newsweek's* table of international monetary standards, was the true value of the rupee.

On the way to the hotel, I did an instant replay in my mind of every solemn warning I had been given about moneychangers, from Calcutta back-alley counterfeiters, to Delhi con men who double count, palm notes, and call false police raids midway through the deal to scatter in five different directions with your money.

As these fears mounted, I was awakened to the reality of evil as being not just an abstraction to be easily transcended, but a power as concrete and lethal as a manta ray. Then I began to feel like a goat going for slaughter.

In the rear garden of the hotel, the "student" in the purple shirt squirmed in his chair as he talked to me across a small English tea-table. He stressed that the sum of rupees at stake was an amount he could not carry around, and that I would have to wait while he went to get the money from an intermediary in room 306. His voice wavered, as a trace of fear shot across his face which he subdued while mentioning that a delay could arise while his friend examined the notes for authenticity with a magnifying glass. This was the minute to pull out, screamed the witness in me. It smelled of a con game a mile off. But by now I was too hooked on making the whole thing work out.

Just before he got up from the table with the envelope of notes, I stood up, reached over, and pulled it out of his hand. "How do I know I can trust you?" I asked threateningly.

He tried to remain composed but underneath was a starved street mongrel scowling at a washed, collared, pedigreed German Shepherd, but nonetheless, a German Shepherd. At first looking insulted, as though I had forgotten his brother's need and had approached him instead of vice versa, his expression changed to a testy bravado look of, "What's-a-big-rich-American-like-you-sweating-over-a-couple-of-bucks—you-big-pampered-fool—what-do-you-know-about-real-back-street-tough-ness?" As he talked, he almost forgot the transaction, occasionally looking slightly testy, "I wish that you had told me before that you were not really serious. This has taken a lot of trouble, and this friend is waiting up there now. This is risky for me and due to the risks, this is the way I have always done it. Besides, your traveler's checks can be replaced." It wasn't his words that got me, it was what was coming through.

As I stretched my arm back across the table to give him the envelope, I felt a blip pulse out of my eyes. In an almost psychedelic abreaction of hell-consciousness, my stare proceeded to "out-demon a demon," saying, "Now you've thought all along that I was basically a big ami-able naive hot dog who would probably whine in dread if you pulled out your rusty pen knife...so take a long look into these pupils, while I open them up for you to see a few things. Don't let the force scare you, after all those slums you've been through. Just take a closer look and don't let me see you chicken out and break the gaze. Now what's this stuff about you being a jerk? No. It's no joke, there's something, a thing, back there called the Tennessee Mountain Spirit, and it's going to jump into your mind for a second...and...if...you don't...show...the...right kinds...of...terror...it'll...have...to...tear...out...your...large...intestine...pull...it...up...through...your...nose...sinuses...and...out...through...the...top...of...your...skull...and...then...over...your...head...like...a...cellophane...bag....And...if...you...whimper...once...it's...going...to...clean...off...the...membrane...with...tur-pentine...and...a...wire...brush.

Burn Out of Silent Abyss Demon Consciousness.... A "Well... bet you never thought this could come through a stare, eh?" I felt like killing him and he knew it.

As he left the table, there was really terror in his eyes, and I was no longer quite the same person. I waited and waited.

Half an hour later, I was burning up with a kind of rage I had not felt in years. It was an agonizing predicament. I was tied down and unable to confront the enemy. Not only had I been conned, but I was a laughing stock to any accomplices stationed around to keep an eye on me. "In fact... 'the dying machinery of my brain concluded as the last traces of lucidity vanished, leaving a psychic Doberman Pinscher.' Every jaded witness in this garden knows just what happened." A doorway of paranoia opened up in the polluted consciousness of my mind.

I suddenly pictured accomplices snickering under their breaths, while I continually fidgeted, trying to hold back the rage and anxiety so as to look perfectly normal, if for no other reason than to deprive them of the pleasure of seeing me sweat it out. Yet the more I tried to hold my cool by looking reflectively up at the sky, the more my face twitched and the closer to violence I was, and I was sure that this probably looked hilarious. And if one of them laughed, I'd rip his arm off and make him chew on it for a while in front of all the others, and then go on a few little friendly visits from table to table, staring silently at some of them, and giving others a neighborly smile, while laying a meat ax on the table with a modest collection of internal organs and severed limbs.

I sat in the shadows, eyes enlarged with rage, staring up at the Bombay night that seemed to shimmer and ripple with a jet-black liquid energy. I was entering an alien dimension of mind-evil and it was hideous.

Cold sweat poured down my face. Added to my rage was an element of fear, that I had been seduced into opening the wrong spiritual door, and there was no way of telling what I had let in, or how long it would take me to stabilize and get back out.

Within minutes I was on the streets, pacing the area of the Salvation Army and the Gate of India. Soon I resorted to asking people after giving them a description. I rode a taxi to the area of the American Express, even though it was late at night and almost everything in the city was closed.The obsessional rage continued all night long.

On the train to Madras from Bombay, it began to dawn on me that I had either gone insane or suffered some kind of antimystical state. My nerve endings had been unshucked and torn down to bare wires. I needed some kind of sign to show that the Cosmic Gatekeeper was still guiding my life. And then it happened, right there in front of the Madras train station as soon as I arrived—an event that utterly defied concidence, one in trillions.

A Mercedes Benz stopped in front of the Madras Railway station as soon as I emerged. I was invited inside. This had never happened to me once since coming to India. I was curious, so I cautiously sat in the front seat. The ignition key chain had a picture of Sai Baba. The man driving happened to be the only human being in Madras who knew exactly where Sai Baba was. As I gazed at the Baba picture he announced: "I am president of the Madras Sai Baba Seva Dal." I was in Madras no more than ten minutes and this is who I am guided to. He graciously gave me specific directions to Baba concluding, "No, he is not at his main ashram, but is traveling to Bukapatnam then Ananthapur. Here is how you go. . . . *Bhagavan* is bringing you into his august presence, be assured." Of millions of residents in Madras, what was the probability of this one man being there in that ten-minute span? I suddenly felt as though I was back on track again continuing the trip with greatly renewed hope.

## The Encounter with Sai Baba

The Bombay episode added to the Madras encounter echoed on the periphery of my mind as I stood in the Ananthapur compound waiting for Sai Baba's arrival. I wondered how deeply Sai Baba would detect it and my consequent despair and sense of having blown it.

I refocused on the central limousine that had just entered through the gate. The door of Baba's limousine closed behind him. Then my mood suddenly repolarized by Baba's force, as I felt the contradiction of emotions one feels when he comes head-on to a presence that is superhumanly great; on the one hand I felt insignificant. On the other hand I wondered what it was that might be important enough about me for a face-to-face meeting with a God-man. If Baba could peer through people like so many tumblers of water, then he was the litmus test of their true worth, which made a direct confrontation with him something of a gamble.

As devotees flowed in a circular pattern around Baba, I saw that I was not the only one who felt his dynamo effect. Undoubtedly Baba was the most magnetic human form I had ever seen. Unlike every other Indian holy man I had visited, Baba did not project a thanatopic serenity or an austere severity. Baba was incredibly youthful, fresh like a spring flower and with the vibrant energy of a bee.

Then I felt a second jolt of power as I saw Baba talking to an Indian near the car whose arms remained held up in a prayerful gesture. The Indian had made some kind of request which Baba had already known about, telling the devotee the problem before he could even get the words out, in a quick musical raspy voice. As the devotee's mouth dropped in awe, something else happened.

I had been studying the physical structure of Baba, who, six inches shorter than the man he was standing before, or for that matter any Indian there, resembled a dwarf-sized giant. His huge head of wiry black hair flowed above a neck so thick and muscular that it looked as though it was transplanted off of Bronco Nagurski of the Chicago Bears. Underneath this floating head was a diminutive, well-muscled little body narrowing down to two tiny feet, cloaked from neck to foot in a brilliant red robe, which made Baba's head appear to hover over an eternally frozen fiery jet of red flame. Suddenly the flame flickered as Baba pulled his sleeve up. In an abracadabra motion of spinning his arm in circles with the open palm down, I did a double take, noticing suddenly that the hand was no longer empty. My God, he had worked a miracle! From nowhere he had a hand full of gray powder that he was pouring into the devotee's hand, instructing him to eat it. While the shaking devotee jabbered a thank-you, Baba spun around flashing me a large sparkling smile. Before I could even react, he was busy talking to another man, explaining the man's personal family problems before the devotee even had a chance to tell them to Baba.

There was an immediately obvious nonhuman quality about Sai Baba, but I wasn't sure I could define it. All that I could conclude was that "nonhuman" suggested "super-" rather than "sub-" humanness, and only a full master could transcend the human condition. As Baba proceeded from person to person, he seemed to act in absolute spontaneity, suggesting the busy impersonality of a bee vibrating pollen out of a flower. And this rebounding from person to person made me ponder a key idea of Vedanta—Baba's access to people's thoughts in spontaneous short order could only be explained by the concept of "thoughtless-all-knowing." That only an enlightened person without the limiting ego could harbor the infinite impersonal mind of god, as the mystics explain it. And this implied to me that Baba was like a walking doorway into the absolute. When he talked or acted, it was merely the meeting point of the impersonal godhead tuning down to the comprehensible personal aspect of deity.

Baba suddenly spun away from the people he was talking to, presumably a family with a common need, and came straight over to me, while I reminded myself not to blow it by losing my poise.

Baba's English was practically baby talk, while his black eyes told an entirely different story, radiating vibrant awareness. He didn't seem to assess me, but already seemed to know me. "Hello, Rowdeeee," he chimed with taunting playfulness. Then looking concerned he asked, "What's wrong, some sickness in the stomach?" Then almost without thinking I patted my stomach, looked up from the ground and said, "Yeah, Baba," more astonished at my informality than anything else, "a little stomach trouble." Which was true of course, since I had been having stomach trouble on and off since entering the country, switching from one brand of bacillary dysentery to another with probably some amoebas to boot.

Turning my head sideways a little, I looked down from his hand to his eyes several times and gestured with a look, "What's that stuff Baba; do you have any for me?" The answer was a quick audible "Oh yes... called *vibhuti*, divine ash." Again, Baba's hand began rotating in wide circles for at least the fourth time in five minutes. In an instant he had a handful of gray powder sitting in his hand, which he immediately poured into mine saying, "Eat, eat, it is good for the health."

Feeling almost like a different person than when I walked through the gate, I stood there licking off the palm of my hand as a slight tremor ran up and down my arm. Baba was still smiling as I cleaned the last traces of ash from my palm. Then as suddenly as he had come over to me, Baba left, quickly entering the house on the compound owned by the principal of the local engineering college. Meanwhile I stood there absolutely stupefied, thinking to myself, "No big thing mind you—just about half an ounce of stuff miraculously summoned into existence from the causal nexus by a single act of will. Just elaborate lattice structures of crystallized carbon, whose sum total energy quotient would melt a subcontinent if unleashed properly." I had just seen a miracle then eaten it!

It was getting dark outside, and the few of us permitted in the compound were immediately invited inside the house for what they called a small *bhajan.*

As I entered, there were about 40 people seated along the living-room floor, men on one side, women on the other. The room was fragrant with incense and fresh flowers, and on all the walls hung assorted pictures of Hindu deities, and in key places, large mounted photographs of Sai Baba. Facing the audience in the front was a large flower-garlanded chair.

I sat right on the aisle near the wall. Music lit the room about the time I heard Baba's raspy voice from behind the kitchen curtains, as the host and hostess skittered in and joined us. Baba sat down, keeping time with his hands, and the singing became louder as faces lit up all over the room.

Baba nodded his head from side to side with the music while tapping his foot on the stool. Then I noticed that he was rolling up betel leaves and popping them into his mouth, which in a matter of moments turned a bright cherry red, lips and all. And like a broken record, couldn't escape the semblance—god or no god—Sai Baba resembled a big happy golliwog. If he gave someone a special look one second, the next moment he would appear bored with the whole room. Repeatedly he looked at me as he swayed his head and chewed away, as if to say, "I know who you are."

Suddenly Baba was on his feet. As Baba sprang out of his chair, the Indians stood up and chanted a Sanskrit praise to Baba and then stood in silence. A few people came up to Baba, knelt down, and touched his feet.

The words of an aristocratic Indian girl I knew in Delhi rang in my ears: "You foreigners will accept anyone as a guru—people like Maharishi are export items as common as tea, but we Indians will have nothing to do with them. There is only one I have heard of whom the Indians trust, he is Sai Baba—he doesn't go politicking like the others, they come to him, from all over India. His miracles have been discussed by almost all my countrymen, and after 15 or 20 years, they have been accepted without question. There have been far too many instances of his miraculous abilities for people to doubt any longer. People may doubt whether he is equal to Lord Krishna or Jesus as he claims, but they have ceased doubting his miracles."

I walked up to Baba, who immediately switched all his attention on me, and did what the Indians call *Pada Namaskar*. I kneeled down and touched my head to Baba's feet, and remained there as he patted my back saying, "Very happy, very happy—*santoshanam*." With both hands he finally grabbed my shoulders and slowly raised me up, smiling affectionately. The host waved those of us up front to resume our places.

As Baba walked down the aisle by the crowd of beseeching and prayerful devotees, he ignored everybody but me, after abstractly smiling at the entire group. He stopped right in front of me and whispered in his raspy voice, "Tomorrow, sir, tomorrow." When Baba had left the room, almost half the room encircled me asking what he had told me. Sensing this was a supreme gift of confidence from Baba, I held my silence and left. As I passed the host on the veranda, he called me aside and said that Baba had told him to make sure to tell me that he wanted to have a private audience with me on the following day. Seeing my joy, the host remarked, "There are very few whom Baba notices this readily. You have no idea how lucky you are."

I was driven back to Ananthapur that night by one of the wealthy local businessmen, owner of the largest automobile parts store in the city, who had been a Baba devotee for 20 years. He told me what I was starving to hear, details about Baba, his childhood, his miracles, his behavior patterns, his claims, and every bit of it was astounding. "You are indeed fortunate that Bhagavan has plans for you—just accept these things by faith. They are no mere coincidences, but the will of God."

As I entered my hotel amid a whine of beggars on the porch, the owner pointed to a greasy section of the wall where there was a permanent menu painted. It was the only nonvegetarian menu in town, revealing another fact about South India, vegetarianism.

Soon a boy in rags plopped down a small glass of water that he had been carrying with his thumb halfway down the center. The contents splashed across most of the slab. As he ran off to get a rag, I noticed that the glass was not transparent but rather translucent with what looked like a yellow glaze of coatings of accumulated grease. As usual in predicaments like this, I yelled for a Coke, which international standards should ensure against amoebic dysentery and jaundice. Sure enough, he came trotting back holding the bottle not in the middle but right on the mouth, and I swore that if I found his thumb jammed in the mouth, I'd break it on the table, using the bottle as a hammer. He had the good sense not to cork the bottle with his thumb.

Suddenly in midtrack I realized that I was already quickly falling from the grace that I had just received from Baba, and that India's squalor was like a raw nerve. It was also an unpleasant echo of what had happened in Bombay. I also realized that those escalating rage levels had really taken effect in my life after I first tried psychedelics, starting with mescaline and ending with LSD 25. One could call it a new freedom of expression.

# Chapter 5

# *An Embrace with Eternity*

$A$t 6:00 in the morning, I rolled out of bed to begin washing up. Before I could even finish my coffee on the veranda, I could hear a motorcycle sputtering outside. It was the nephew of the wealthy Baba devotee who drove me home the night before.

We buzzed off on a medium-sized Indian motorcycle shooting through crowds before I could even get a grip.

As we reached the edge of town, the strange barren Andhra Pradesh countryside looked almost beautiful in the yellow morning light. I noticed in the distance several conical mountains that jutted out from the flat ground in almost perfect symmetry. Anomalies of topography, they resembled immense termite mounds that instead of shaping along the contours of the ground, looked as though they had been plopped down as land grafts from some prehistoric volcano world. Already the sun was beginning to bake the air, even at 6:30 A.M. at a time of year when most countries were knee-deep in snow. And before too long it would be soaring up into the nineties in this arid region of South India.

We pulled into the driveway of the compound in an almost irreverent cloud of noise, between a long line of devotees who instantly saluted us. I felt like a caricature of Arjuna on the horse, as I looked up at Baba's window. His silhouette was shaking a chiding finger in my direction. Then I heard Baba's low laugh addressing attendants in the room, from where I thought I heard, "riding on a motorcycle." With the rest of the crowd, I stood quietly listening for the faintest stirrings in the house while eyeing the windows for movement, hearing nothing more than the occasional buzzings of Baba's voice.

At the end of over an hour, suddenly Baba emerged from the house. The crowd jumped to attention, making way for Baba as he headed toward a car. He briefly glanced in my direction but gave no acknowledgment.

Then I noticed people waving to get my attention. The merchant who had driven me home the night before ran over to me sputtering, "Baba says you are to come with him, I am to drive you." Baba had not misled me and a new hope appeared. Out of all the hundreds there, Baba had singled me out to come with him.

We made haste out of the driveway behind Baba's car, while the merchant informed me that Baba was inspecting the site of a massive new college to be built in his name. It would be the largest girls' college in the state and would have an allotment of as much as "40 lakhs of rupees" or several million dollars. He told me that there were already 96 schools of one sort or another named after Sai Baba. This one, in two years, would look like something built for a Felini movie and would be the location where I would have an absolutely unpredictable experience.

Once we were on the barren plain for 40 minutes or so, the jaunt almost seemed irrelevant. Baba would strike out in different directions, and a small party of architects and engineers would go running after him with palms constantly cemented together and blueprints rolled up under their arms. And every time one of them tried to unroll a blueprint to show Baba, it resembled an elaborate ritual of eating an ice-cream cone without using any hands. Meanwhile Baba seemed to pose, wink at some people, smile at others, and essentially make light of the whole thing.

The upper echelon devotees continued to be as stiff as penguins. With morbid solemnness they walked about as though carrying the crown jewels. Motioning, waving, and trotting back and forth, they inscribed huge arcs along the ground with their feet to delineate vital parts of the future structure. I was sure that if Baba had proposed bulldozing one of the local volcano-mountains and paving a palacial driveway with hedges and date-palms straight up it at a 70-degree angle, they would not have flinched but would have dutifully called Bombay to get it underway, and ship up the machinery.

Baba suddenly headed over to his car, got in and was driven off.

When our car pulled into the compound, almost immediately the surging crowd was calling for me in a low voice. "Go, go...in the house...Bhagavan has called you." I followed several people single file up the stairs. Among them was a white man in his early thirties who looked like a cross between an Old Testament prophet and the perfect Occidental mystic yogi.

Baba stood in the open doorway smiling as we walked in. The fragrant room was so opulently decorated that it bordered on garishness, but then it was to be expected as a certain cultural variable. Our audience with Baba was given a feeling of exclusiveness from the rest of the world as the curtains were drawn.

Remaining in the room near the window were a handful of the engineers, architects, and I assumed financiers of the building site that we had just surveyed. I was bothered by their presence. Somehow their awkward insensitivity led me to suspect that they lacked the capacity to appreciate who Baba was, grunting and flustering over engineering symbols, stress points, relative strengths of materials, and what not. How could they be oblivious to what I perceived as paramount issues of Baba's true significance? Yet they still bickered on, apparently satisfied with a worm's-eye view of one, who if he revealed even a facet of who he was, would release a dazzling brilliance that would leave them quaking in terror. Krishna said to Arjuna, "If you saw me as I truly Am, you would not live." Baba made the identical claim. He dismissed them in a note of chiding as they tiptoed out.

When the door closed, there was a brief silence. As though trying to catch an elusive plant filament in a stream, I realized that no matter how hard I tried, I could not keep in my mind who Baba was. There was a familiarity and yet an unfathomableness that would not mix. I felt similar to an amnesiac hearing the voice of his father and searching through the family photo album, constantly feeling a strong visceral tug, but never quite pulling the memory to the surface. And this was denuding.

With quick bristling movements, Baba's gown swept by me as he mounted the stage on tiny child-sized feet. He sat on the floor of the platform, supporting himself by an extended arm, with feet curled up beneath him. It called to mind the emperor in *The King and I* whose head was always slightly above every other head in Siam.

Everybody was slightly nervous except the Western mystic who was beginning to resemble a lion, exuding a fiery boldness out of his eyes. And when I met his eyes, they didn't flicker, they just burned on like two steel beams as two of the most powerful eyes I had ever seen in my entire life. Perhaps he had gone through a thousand "dark nights of the soul," and knew something about the avatar-man that no one else did, and maybe he had gone through so much that he could take in a lot more than other people. I didn't know, but this is what he seemed to project with an unflappable self-confidence as he sat in a half-lotus with widening nostrils. My eyes would run into his huge lion's mane beard and flowing head of hair and I'd begin to think, "He's no hippie. That's the real McCoy that the sheep have been imitating solid as the wall of China, and he knows that he knows."

I looked back at Baba on the platform. Unlike the lion who looked like he had fallen through the center of hell and come back heavier than mercury, Baba was an immortal flower. Stronger than anyone on the continent, he didn't need to come on strong, yet could probably melt the center of the moon with one single titanic thought. Clearly a force was enhancing my imagination—call it an extra door opening up.

Baba spoke, "God is Love. God is everywhere," cutting to the core of everything in utter simplicity. It almost mimicked Christ's parables.

"God is like the sun and man is like a flower. The sun shines on the flower and the flower grows up toward the sun, becoming beautiful and giving off sweet nectar. The nectar is prema—love ["lowve"]. Love is one, love is God. To love is to know God." Baba nodded while his eyes affirmed beneath their sparkle, "I know of what I am speaking. I am not just spouting off silly words to titillate you."

With some sadness Baba went on, "But if the clouds of ignorance, ego ["yeeego"], jealousy, and hate come in the way, then the light of the sun is off the flower. There is no *prema*, no nectar and the flower is wasted. The sunlight of God's love is always shining. It is only the clouds of man's thoughts that get in the way."

Baba's parables were almost like modern day billboard slogans. Maybe, I thought, the only thing that can cut through our twisted complexity so that we can be brought to the heart of the issue.

From Baba's viewpoint, enlightenment seemed almost pedestrian: so easy, so inevitable that the idea of undergoing the required *tapas*—discipline—was almost superfluous.

Looking over the entire group, Baba waved his hands to ask, in a standard Indian gesture, "What do you want?" He looked at the Pakistani family and asked in a light chiding tone, "What is it, family arguments?" Then he shook his finger at each one of them playfully indicating he knew their deepest secrets and was by no means fooled by their best behavior. He saw them when they were being nasty, but he was not fazed because Baba had the strength to cope with every single sordid secret on the earth, and could see down to the divinity behind the rotten little areas of human nature.

Baba diagnosed their problem: "Anger, ego, jealousy, hate, greed, desires. Too much desires and no understanding, just confusion." They bowed their heads in shame. Baba's tone became kind again, and they perked up instantly.

Baba looked at the father who was flushed with emotion and said, "Love is very important." But Baba's tone also said with a note of warning, "The discipline to love that you are afraid of is nothing compared to the impersonal and harsh justice that can befall a negligent man." As Baba became stern again, the father was brought practically to sobs, as the other members of his family began to gleam in triumph. The kids sat up, the mother looked proud, arching her back like a painting of Sita.

"Anger," Baba declared, "is weakness, big sign of weakness, not strength." The man's face puffed in shame to hide the source of his weakness, rage. "A strong man has self-control, gentleness, not rage." The wife and kids reflected the quiet satisfaction of those who have been suppressed now standing by as the bully, their suppressor, gets cornered by someone who is ten times as big, becomes, like them, cowering and humiliated. And the rage in him knew that if it escaped, it would be obliterated in cosmic fire. The Pakistani pleaded with Baba, holding out his hands to indicate helplessness, and Baba soothed him like a mother and showed him a standard to follow, love.

As they huddled together, children's heads on their mother's noble and long-suffering lap, they refused to accept the stench of their own sin, playing to the hilt, righteous victimization.

In their greatest moment of weakness, Baba forgave the entire family, endearing himself to them forever. With abundant kindness, he smiled at the kiddies, told the parents to cheer up, and said that he would soon see them privately to give them "special help."

Suddenly a ubiquitous force seemed to fill the air as Baba began rotating his open hand, palm down, clutching something, then opening the hand again. Baba revealed four metal plates with a photographic likeness of himself in color on each one of them. The plates were at least three-quarters the size of Baba's palm, maybe two inches and a half oval. Both Baba's hands were in crystal-clear visibility, the whole time. If this wasn't enough, right after Baba handed the four plates to the Pakistani family, he began rotating his hand again. The same shock wave undulated through the air, only this time Baba's palm was full of gray powder. "Vibhuti," Baba cheerfully announced, "divine ash."

Baba turned to me then. "You have a nice place to stay in Ananthapur?"

"Sure, Baba," I replied with total abandon, hoping not to lapse into incoherence. "Hotel on main road, best one in town, Baba. Good facilities—not important though, Baba, anywhere will do."

"Yes, I know Rowdie. What is the name of the hotel?"

"Oh, you know that, Baba, Vidya Bhavan, or something like that."

"I know, I know," Baba laughed. "Food is good?"

"Yeah, Baba, the food is okay, not bad at all."

"No Rowdie, the food is not good. Too hot, too dirty, too much spice, not pure food, not *satwic*."

Baba gave me a look of mock chiding. "Driving on a motorcycle, very noisy, very rowdy." He motioned at the group, "I see him this morning, driving through the gate, sunglasses on, looking like a gangster." We all laughed, except the Lion-man.

Baba looked at him and nodded, to inform us who this creature was. "Mr. Freedom," Baba announced as I heard a low groan. "Freedom means *moksha*, no more birth, no more death, only union with God." Mr. Freedom rolled his eyes like a suffering lion, and groaned loudly. It was a deep male voice that resonated in bass tones like the bellows of a huge organ in an old European cathedral, suggesting to me that there was a supernatural potency added to his natural voice.

Baba responded reassuringly, "Be patient, freedom coming, freedom coming." He looked at Baba with a gaze that didn't soften in the least—the two implacable eyes fixed on Baba and became the eyes of a samurai swordsman pinioned between a blazing forest on one side and an approaching armada on the other—never showing fear, but remaining aggressive, even in the face of certain annihilation. Such was the difference in magnitude between him and Baba. But Baba seemed pleased with this sort of audacity and exclaimed under his breath, "What a man!" He smiled gently and let the suffering lion roar. Something I was sure was an out-of-bounds relationship with Baba for the Indian devotees. And I was sure that if any of the former penguins tried to pull it off, Baba would verbally slap them down, and they would decompose on the spot like gelatin aspic spooned out on some burning equatorial concrete.

Then Baba addressed the whole group to say that enlightenment is no easy matter or random gift that one happens to stumble upon. It is difficult. But without grace, Baba assured, it would be impossible to attain.

Baba arose from the platform and went over to the door, bidding the Pakistanis to follow him into the room across the hall, at the top of the stairs.

After ten minutes, the door opened and a troop of bleary-eyed, hyperemotional Pakistanis filtered out in a haze of powder-filled air. Their foreheads were smeared with a bright red powder (*kum-kum*) that Baba had materialized for them. Someone ignorant, for a second, might have gathered that a grenade went off in the room. They carried a handkerchief loaded with vibhuti plus a large gleaming silver container. They announced to the entire room that Baba had materialized the silver vessel for them as well as the sackful of vibhuti, staggering me with the fact that something weighing several pounds and as big as a grapefruit cannot be palmed.

Baba's eyes and mine locked as he stood in the doorway of the private interview room. "Cyam on, Rowdie." Legs wobbling, I went through the door of the little side room as Baba's hand slapped me on the back.

My viscera seemed to know that the stakes were incredibly high.

As though hearing the voice of an archangel, the thought entered me as a siren from heaven: that by a single act of free will, from some vast summit of choice, a man can either be glorified beyond measure or impaled for eternity. I should take heed.

The God-man, *Sathya* (truth) Baba, whose robe today was the color of blood, closed the door behind me. I knew that even if there was a remote possibility that this Being was not who he said he was, the only way I could win in the end was to be absolutely honest about myself. Nor could I get hung up over the fact that millions across India were teeming for even one word or a smile from this person which would be enough to send them back to their villages rich in blessings for the rest of their lives.

The room was small. It had a little window on the far end, a chair or two, a dresser, and a bunk bed. Baba stood in front of me, a full head shorter, and spoke in the sympathetic tones of a mother who is tending a son convalescing from a catastrophic accident, still wincing from the pain. This simple gentleness of Baba disarmed me, soothed my fear of being vulnerable, and bathed the thousand seeming inner centuries of desolate cold.

Certainly the tenderest part of me I had fortressed like the Wall of China around the Temple of Solomon, and almost no one was allowed into the temple of my heart. My own emotional past had been a wasteland of the spirit where I was very selective about those I could love. I was usually content, aloof, and independent. Those times I had opened up to love with intensity, I always burned out like a meteor over some Cinderella flower of a girl, knowing that it would never last forever, that something brutal and harsh in the world would stifle the love, like frost killing a honeysuckle. Spiritual love I knew was the next step beyond the infidelity of romantic love.

Describing my runnings to and fro Baba said, "Confusion, much confusion. Not happy, not happy. Often traveling from America, Europe, India, Bombay, but only finding trouble. I know, sir, you are looking for the truth but finding only confusion, no peace." I nodded as though to a doctor cleaning out a wound with salve and dabbing other wounds.

"Not happy in America, too much materialism, and no love. Always looking for love, the pure love of God, but only finding a small sample."

"Yes Baba, just a sample."

Then came a dose of tonic. "Dedication to the truth, sir. Coming to India alone—very brave—taking many chances: bad food, pains, always alone, thieves..." And Baba's eyes gleamed but I wasn't going to say anything about the Bombay rip-off yet.

"Yes, Rowdie, money stolen in big city, causing great spiritual fear and confusion." Baba was humming like a top.

"Yes Baba."

"I know your whole past. Very unhappy childhood. Bad adjustment to the world. Hating school, not happy with family, looking for love, but never finding. Not satisfied with selfish love, looking for divine love." With a note of reassurance, "That is the way to God, never give up, search with a pure heart, and you will reach the goal in the end." Feeling awkward looking down at Baba, who stood about six inches away, I sat down on the edge of the bed and looked up.

"Some worldly desires, many impure thoughts." I agreed to that wondering what the spiritual X-ray would dig up next. "You must control the mind, the mind is like a drunken monkey. More desires, never ending from birth to birth can only be conquered by faith in God. Life for most men is only eating and sleeping, food coming in and going out like a tube."

"You still have some doubts, some questions?" Baba asked.

"Yes Baba, but they are difficult to translate. Very complex metaphysics, Baba. Subtle things." And I wondered if I shouldn't scrap all that extra luggage and be like a child.

"Yes, I know, I am in your heart."

A *sloka* from the Bhagavad Gita suddenly pricked my mind. "The guru appears when the disciple is ready." Maybe my whole future weighed on my response to Baba right now. The thought weighed on me that I now had to give myself to Baba and this was that critical moment. I may never get a private interview again.

"Baba, I want to be under your guidance. What do you want me to do?" It was like letting steam out of a cooker.

Baba dazzled. "I want only love. That is my life, that is my mission, to love my devotees. Krishna once said to

Arjuna, 'I am your servant, I am the servant of my devotees' love.' This is true."

Rubbing my belly, Baba suddenly noticed, "You are still having stomach trouble." The room filled with a crackling force. Baba stepped back, sleeve up and hand twirling with palm down. I warned myself to accept whatever it would be with the humble grace of an orphan—but I was still swept off my feet.

Baba's hand in a fraction of a second exploded from an outstretched empty palm to a massive half-open fist clutching an egg-sized object.

In one second of the world's history, I had stood witnessing the kind of gargantuan miracle that would have caused pandemonium in the major scientific institutions of the Western Hemisphere. But none of these considerations mattered to Baba, who held the object like any other object. It was a large structure of pure transparent crystal which looked like quartz at first, but was in fact a large chunk of rock sugar. Trying to ward off the beginnings of a gem collector's greed, I wanted to study it forever and build a glass case around it as a monument of the miraculous.

But the incarnation of "Truth" would have no such thing. He motioned and I tilted back my head and opened my mouth like a baby robin as Baba jammed the entire thing in my mouth. Then Baba wrapped his arms around me and held me in a tight hug, as his hair bristled in my face. While returning the embrace, I didn't want to seem ungracious of this sacrifice of mind-blowing affection, so I tried to gather what wits I had left and use them to dispose of the miraculous chunk as unoffendingly as possible, muffling the slurs and crunching sounds. There was a brief moment of infant-on-the-bottle helplessness, as I stood there gagging and watery-eyed, but I was determined to get all the gravel of sugar crystals down my throat so that I could more heartfully return the embrace and really be the prodigal son returning to God.

After 30 more seconds of hugging I thought, "... not a door left open to construe rejection after I leave here ... and he takes this kind of risk to prove it. He's got to know people pretty well, the wrong person might flip out. Lord, they all blubber when they are even near him. He just can't hug anybody who comes along, not with those millions out there." I felt I should weep, but I was just too stunned.

From my earliest days, hand-to-mouth affection invariably made me feel awkward, because I always insisted on holding my own. I noticed then that the thing about mother's boys that always turned my stomach was that they seemed to enjoy being powdered, petted, and stuffed. My reaction as a child when some lady tried it was to push her off, or leave as quickly as possible. I didn't mind it if a girlfriend wanted to hold my hand, but not any mother figures. And as odd as it might be, I was almost feeling this particular flavor of mother's love coming from Baba.

Then I brushed it all out of my mind. I gave Baba one last squeeze remembering that the gender of his body was irrelevant to the deity that filled it.

Baba forecast a glorious future. Baba exuberantly said, "Do not worry. You will be very very happy. It is in my hands. Very lucky, very lucky."

But I wanted to hear more. As I posed the question, I could just see every preplanned model concerning my future for the next decade fragment and change forfever. I hesitated.

Baba responded with a smile that took up half his face, "Do not doubt, never doubt, sir. Time coming soon. No more fear. Very very happy. Bliss." That did it. Baba now moved back a pace or two, and I began to get the signal that my time had run out. But there had been something that I really had to get out, a final validation before signing the dotted line.

"I had an experience, Baba, four years ago..." (the LSD).

"Go ahead," Baba encouraged with eyes widening in enthusiasm.

"I was alone on a mountain, and I took something like Soma...you know, in the Upanishads, Baba."

"Yes, yes."

"My nervous system restructured, Baba, total jump in energy," I whispered loudly as the air escaped my lungs in a rapid tremor.

"Yes, I know," matter-of-factly.

But I had to verify the metaphysics just to make sure I hadn't been misreading all the signposts on the way. "Well, you know how light goes through a prism and breaks into many colors...well in reverse order the colors rejoin on the other side, and turn into white light again. Well, on the mountain, Baba, ego, cells, body structure, mind awareness like broken-down light, before the experience. After a while, I was taken back up through the prism...I went through a pinpoint of light, Baba...very tiny, like atom...I had to turn inside out." By now my eyes were beaming and I was gesturing wildly with my arms.

"Everything was consciousness...Chit...I...fields, trees, grass, pebbles, stars, all pure consciousness, Baba."

Baba quietly nodded and mumbled below his breath in another language while knitting his hand through the air in a peculiar way.

"Everything melted away, Baba, and became God, pure light. I want to go back. This is what I have come for, Baba."

"Yes, I know Rowdie, I know this."

"Baba, did you cause that experience to happen?"

"Yes. That was your due. Reward from the past. Just a taste, you were given a taste until you were brought to me, but temporary experience not good enough. Complete samadhi, Nirvikalpa samadhi, never ends. It is forever bliss. That is the goal, sir."

My faith that had been slowly eroding leaped out of the ground like a phoenix. "I have stumbled upon the avatar of the world," I thought.

Baba opened the door and ushered me out with his hand. And I floated down the stairs and went outside, where I continued thinking over the implications of this life-changing encounter.

Certainly if I lingered on in proximity to Baba, without the crucial faith to submit, I would show as much understanding as the fellow who takes his toothache to the best dentist in the world but never quite trusts him enough to open his mouth. Even if he spent every minute of the day in the waiting room, it wouldn't improve his chances.

The spiritual highways of the world were packed with people who never went beyond the waiting room. They went on through life sacramentally sniffing the disinfectants and anesthetics in the air, while assuming that their ills were being magically cured.

I resolved to stick it out with Baba, and climb the chair. If wrong I might lose a few teeth, but if my heart was still earnestly looking for the truth, at least I would be released from that particular waiting room, which might have been my doom either way.

I looked up from the wall and saw the Lion-man rapidly approaching. For the first time I saw him smiling. Still soft-spoken he said, "You know, the interview was not over when you left." His voice resonated as he began speaking with slow, well-chosen words that took on the classic phrasings of a Lao Tze. His face changed back to a wizened solemnity as I realized that communication was an immense effort.

"I seldom speak, and when I do, it is never for long. So hear me, brother. In a manner of speaking I have to come down from the mountain to talk, and I never like to, it is extremely painful to me and unbalances my whole *sadhana* (path to enlightenment), which is to slow doown, sloooow doooownnnn."

He took a long breath, changing his word tempo. "All I can tell you, brother, is what Baba has done for me, and his nature that I have experienced; his nature is to love. He manifests this patiently and unceasingly. He is not human, so do not mistake his outward form with who he is. He is God manifested in the highest sense and in the fullest embodiment. I have never seen one who gives so completely and continually as Baba gives. Yet his material gifts are only a shadow of the spiritual boons that he can give, when he so chooses. But you have to be ready to receive them, and he will test you to see if you are ready.

"He is very childlike when he gives love sometimes, but don't let that fool you. He is a perfect master. Sometimes his love can seem harsh to us. But he doesn't love your ego, he loves the real you. And do you know who that is, brother? That is God. That's who you are and who Baba is, and he can be spanking you with one hand and feeding you candy with the other, but it is for the sole purpose of waking you up. And that is the secret. That his greatest gift is love. It is freedom, freeeee-dommmmmm, release from being born again and again in this ignorant life of the world. And liberation is the only gift he really likes to give, and the reason he came into the world to free souls and take them back into him."

I was fascinated. I wanted to see into the mystery of Baba from another advanced observer.

"I cannot put Baba into a category for you, he is a mystery. I have seen many holy men, none are like Baba. When an avatar kills a man, as Rama once did, he is released. That is why I ask Baba for death, it is the most complete and immediate means to the void. He first wants you to become weary of this world, and know how it separates you from God. Then he may catch you one day, feeding your ego goodies and trinkets with its defenses down and giggling. That may be the time he takes the sword and kills you forever. What you do not know is that it may have taken him eons of patience to set you up for that one perfect moment. Only a master can operate beyond time like this, so remember, do not limit his love to the tiny acts of this world that you have mistaken for love for so long."

I mentioned the "pinpoint of light as the doorway into God." He registered it but did not show any emotional response. Not wanting to lose the thread, I wanted to find out more about him. "By the way, my name is Tal..."

"Just call me Gill," he finally responded after I had gently prodded for his last name.

For a moment I watched him, probing the blackness of his irises and the range of characters in his features. There were few I met who registered almost zero when you tried to read them. Most were as plain as cornflakes. But when their eyes were mine shafts, that was a totally different thing. Interestingly, he appeared to have difficulty assessing me.

Gill told his story in smatterings, at times almost grudgingly, but nevertheless with resolve. I was fascinated. For standing before me was one of the mystical salmon who had made it up the immense waterfall of life to arrive at this spiritual mountaintop despite enormous odds.

"The time that this happened is not important, but for a two-week period while I was living in a coastal town in California, I experienced without interruption, the state of samadhi, suddenly and by no visible cause, including drugs. I had knowledge, and there was no limit to what I knew. When I saw people passing along the streets, I knew them better than old friends. I knew everything there was to know about them. And complete strangers would stop in their tracks, look into my eyes, and in reverence and trembling ask the questions about the meaning of existence, and about who they were. I would begin teaching. On street corners, by the market, wherever I would be. And by the end of a week, crowds followed me around, many earnestly beseeching that I be their teacher.

"I prophesied, and all that I prophesied came true. Many returned to me, offering to lay their possessions at my feet, but I refused. That was not what I wanted. I loved so much, that it was not possible to love any more, yet many also hated me. I don't know, some of it I can still remember....But the freedom, the bliss." Gill for a time looked away almost dejectedly, with his lion's mane, broad face, and abundant beard standing out against the sandy white of Andhra Pradesh like a sphynx.

"When I would will it, there were miracles, but it was neither my habit nor my interest. They simply occurred spontaneously in my presence."

Longingly he explained being in the absolute center of the flow, the Tao. "Every act was as effortless as moving a hand through the air, as the world tended to my movements and needs, instantly without friction. If I felt hunger, someone would appear with fruits and melons, if I needed clothing, it was there."

A look of torment appeared on Gill's face. I knew the grace period had not lasted forever. "I did not think it was possible to come back from that perfected state. But at the end of two weeks, after knowing God, after being one with the light and without ego, I plunged. I fell into the outer darkness, and all the loneliness and despair of the world weighed on me like an anchor. I was back in the world again, and had my ego and desires, and fears, and it took everything I had for me not to kill myself." He stopped to take a long breath, half closing his eyes and muttering his private plea,"Freeeeedoommmmm," and it sounded like "Aaaauuuummmm."

"I thought that I could go to bed with my wife and remain untouched. I didn't need it, nor did I want it, it was more of a test than anything else to make sure that I was free from attachments forever.

"After that I went into the deepest depression of my life as I tried to find some way to regain my former state. It was then, two years ago, that I knew that I would keep looking until I found it or died. I left my wife, my kids, house, and friends, went off alone to live on a beach, and I meditated, and meditated. I talked to no one, vowing silence. I wore only what I was given, and slept on the ground when I did sleep. But most of the nights I spent meditating." Gill had spontaneously fallen into classic Indian yogic asceticism. How had he meditated?

"The void. But to do that, brother, you've got to Slllllooowwww Dooowwwnnn the mind. It was never who you really were anyway. You've got to be up front all the way with nobody to hold your hand unless he happens to be God." This wasn't yogic play nursery with macrobiotic picnics and coeducational Friday night Hatha yoga class with all the groovies; this was spiritual mountain-climbing on the level of the Upanishads, and separated the trendies from the heavies. Gill was following an ancient path taught in the Vedas 5000 years ago. It was *sanyasa*, leaving the world to go into the forest to meditate and live off of roots until death or liberation caught up. But worldly detachment or *vairagya* was essential.

There was one detail which repeatedly struck a bad chord with me, and that was Gill's sole interest in reaching cosmic consciousness then promptly leaving the scene. He was content to leave his fellow men to flounder in the maze in the same misery he had departed after himself receiving help from a master. It was callous indifference.

Gill claimed to have transcended it all, weary of guru-games and spiritual Boy Scouts, wanting nothing but the void. He deliberately spelled it out, "My sole aim is to enter the state of Nirvikalpa samadhi, in which if you remain for three days uninterruptedly, you proceed into *Turya* samadhi. The body lives for 21 days, all normal functions cease, and then it expires. During this time, the *atma* will have reached the full identity with the absolute, never to return to ego-consciousness again." And how did he hear of Sai Baba? It was another super-natural intervention that had been fairly recent.

"About three and a half months ago, I was in the desert of Tecate, California, meditating at about 3:00 in the morning. I saw Baba in my mind, standing before me and smiling. The next thing was that he was right in front of me. He reached over, touched me in the center of the forehead, the *ajna chakra* and then his face grew bigger, and bigger, and bigger, and started spinning round and round... and I got higher and higher, and higher, and literally soared to the same place I had been when I had been in samadhi, I was free. Just when it got unbearably blissful, and I thought I would be going home forever, Baba pulled me right out of it, disap-peared, and left me sitting alone on the desert, stone-sober and back to normal. Well, the next day I saw a movie about him at the Baba ashram nearby, and learned I could actually get to him physically, and learned that he was really in India. From then on things fell together perfectly: visa, passport, plane ticket, and I was out of the country within a week and sitting right in front of him."

Gill chuckled, "I was prepared for it to all happen the minute I met Baba. He would just reach over, touch me like he had done in the vision, and that would be it. It would be all over and I would be free. I never dreamed I would have to go through what I'm going through now."

He described the initial misunderstandings, favors, and tests from Baba. The ancient books portrayed the path to enlightenment as a titanic cliff-hanger. It was never easy. And the trials?

Gill responded ponderously. "Now and then when I am meditating, I still leave my body for no apparent reason. This started some years ago in California when I would be lying beside my wife one minute, and floating around the ceiling looking down at my body and my wife's the next. Last night this happened again while I was meditating under Baba's window. My body became numb as I found myself staring head-on to a very frightening man-sized creature, which was as real as you standing there. Maybe the moonlight helped me see it, I don't really know... but its skin had the smooth-scaled oiliness of a snake. Its head was humanoid but flattened out, like a man with a nylon stocking pulled over his head, it even had a long flap of skin coming out of the top of its head, like a stocking. The word for it, I believe, is "familiar"; you may have heard about them in Chinese lore. They are a class of demonic spirit beings. Well it scared the hell out of me." Gill exhaled in repugnance, slightly trembling.

"Before I knew it, I was out of my body and wrestling this thing all over the ground. I don't know how long we fought, but it seemed like an hour and it took everything I had. Finally I pinned it against the ground. But when I saw its face close in the moonlight, I knew I couldn't handle much more. I called on Baba and it vanished into thin air. However I have been shaken ever since."

Gill laughed ironically, "Baba had mentioned to me three times that day that I would see a vision. But I wasn't prepared for that. When I saw Baba just now, he explained the meaning of what happened, but I cannot discuss that."

Brightening, Gill said, "By the way, brother, you look a little lighter yourself. Did Baba give you anything?... You don't have to say."

"I never expected it, but he hugged me like a long lost son." Gill's face became solemn, almost ashen, as he said, "That is a considerable gift. Baba, to my knowledge, almost never does that, especially during a first meeting." For a moment this mystic who resembled a Bible prophet looked almost dejected then shrugged as we walked out of the gate.

When we started discussing Baba's central ashram, a hundred-odd miles away, an Indian devotee drove up and eagerly invited us to ride into town. As we got in we heard, "As Baba wills, I am only his servant." I smiled gladly as Gill went back into his vow of silence, choosing not to respond, his face taking on the stony solemnity of Mount Rushmore.

# Chapter 6

# *Greenhouse for an Avatar*

*I*n the first week of February, our bus, an old dilapidated monstrosity, pulled up to the side entrance of *Prasanthi Nilayam*, Sai Baba's spiritual community. It was 4:00 in the morning, pitch black, and dead silent. It had been three weeks since I first met Baba in Ananthapur, and since then I had decided to clear my head out for the long haul by taking a vacation away from India, with its never-ending noise, squalor, and filth, to Ceylon. Green, underpopulated, and clean, Ceylon's shores leapt with tropical growth against a bright cerulean firmament. Its wide beaches and blue ocean were a balm to my wracked body not to mention its substantive food and tropical fruit which all added to my general revival. By the end of ten days I felt ready for the plunge back into India.

The bus trip to Baba's realm had taken over ten hours to go a hundred miles. Each ten miles farther into the wilderness of Andhra Pradesh convinced me that things could not possibly get any more primitive. But they did. The landscape went from desolate to more desolate, knotting and twisting in the moon and starlight into all sorts of weird shapes like giant cryptic writing, which seemed to suggest a supernatural numina within the terrain itself. After 60 miles the road became more of a giant water-buffalo path, crossing rock-beds and streams, dropping sharply and climbing at hideous angles. More reminiscent of the bygone eras of the *Ramayana* than the twentieth century, the final hub of our journey abolished the last traces of civilization as we entered the incredible silence of the night air, and the absolute piercing brilliance of stars above us. Not so much as a cloud could be seen in the arid South Indian night sky to obscure so much as a photon of starlight, lifting us at times, so that we seemed to be veritably perched on the shores of space.

In the dim streetlight, 50 of us unloaded in front of a row of crude little padlocked wooden stalls. As I carried my bags through the large gate, I got my first jolt, the sheer size of the ashram.

From the hospital veranda, where I unrolled my sleeping mat, I could see a large building that rose in height. It was not only the ashram worship and meditation hall, it was also the private residence of Sai Baba. Lit up by the ashram streetlighting, its upper stories and roof resembled the upper decks of an aircraft carrier with different lookouts, ladders, and walkways.

I tried to shut my eyelids that were as dry as sandpaper. Just then a ringing harmonic filled the air like an ethereal freight train coming through the mountain. I listened more intently. It turned out to be a good thousand male and female voices chanting "Om." "AAAA-UUUUMMMM," 21 times, each time drawing out to 15 seconds with a long breath in between. After a silent pause, the faint wisps of a woman's voice floated out above the yearnings of a sitar, beseeching the night air like a minstrel from fifteenth-century Verona. Full of pathos, the voice adored Baba, as Sanskrit phrases floated up into Baba's suite.

Almost completely lulled to sleep again, something far louder started up like a midnight lawn mower. I sat up again. It was a human choo-choo train flowing under

one ashram streetlight after another. Hundreds moved
in a long train singing one song after another, circling in
a caterpillar formation around the entire ashram. Then
suddenly from my wing of the ashram, on the other side
of the hospital, below the hill, shrill singsong voices of
children filled the air. I discovered later that at that
hour, the kids in Baba's school are required to chant so
many slokas from one of the Vedas. Some inherent fascination in the Vedic chants made me tune everything
else out, as couplet after couplet rhymed ending in
"num."

The words cascaded down to the familiar nursery
song tune of "Daddy's gonna buy you a diamond ring."
Only this time it was an ode to the overmind of the
universe, as each word resembled some element or compound on a vast cosmic Periodic Table. And in no time
instead of Sanskrit, I was hearing, "Gall-ium Dyspro-
sium...German-ium, Euro-pium; Lanthan-um, Mag-
nes-iem...Lithium, Molybden-um; Nio-bium, Pallad-
ium...Osm-ium, Plut-onium; Polon-ium, Potass-ium...
Prometh-ium, Rhen-ium; Scand-ium, Rubid-ium...
Stront-ium, Selen-ium; Tantal-um, Vanad-ium...Thor-
ium, Zircon-ium." Somewhere in all this, I managed to
doze off.

By 10:00 in the morning, near the canteen, I ran into
the caretaker of the whole ashram, a six-foot-three
Indian in his seventies named Suraiya. He ambled over
to me and said, "Oh yes, we have been expecting you.
You are the one Baba calls Rowdie is it? Follow me."

As we headed back across the ashram I learned a few
things from Suraiya. He had been a "Baba" devotee in
his youth, during the lifetime of Baba's previous alleged
appearance as an incarnation of God, when he was incarnated as the Moslem-Hindu saint, Shirdi Sai Baba,
in the state of Maharashtra. When the former Baba
"departed" from the previous body in 1918, he told Suraiya that he would serve him again one day.

At the foot of the hill that the hospital was on, there was a long line of suites, usually six rooms in a row with a common veranda, intermittently separated by little gardens in between. There were three of these complexes, and since they were the most sophisticated by local standards, I named them "the luxury suites."

Suraiya pushed open the door of the end room along the first complex, and then ambled off distractedly. This was apparently what Baba had earmarked for me when I arrived. The first room was newly whitewashed, and was stone-bare except for a mosquito net which opened up like an army tent in the center of the room, with a small straw-mat underneath it. On the front and side walls were several bare windows. I threw open the door leading into the next room and found a man with a cherry-red face doing a yogic posture sometimes called "the spider." He grunted and spewed, composed himself, and said, "Hi," forcing an effort to be friendly as he extended a hand while uprighting himself.

After a brief hello I approached the next set of doors fully expecting someone on a bed of spikes. It turned out to be the bathroom. A large terracotta urn held the water supply for bathing and flushing the little cement hole in the floor. The room was dark, damp, and smelly, its walls covered with mosquitoes.

About the length of three football fields away stood the main hall of the canteen where thousands ate meals. It was a large shed with a flagstone floor and a corrugated aluminum roof. The people ate on the floor, sitting on long-woven carpets of jute while eating off banana leaves. As I saw them playing with the food with their bare hands, rolling the rice up into little balls, I began to lose my appetite again. I was immediately guided to an adjacent room with stone tables for foreigners, visitors, and privileged devotees. It was lunchtime and I was starved.

---

For a while I had to hold the walls like a blind man, the room so darkly contrasted to the dazzling brilliance of the Andhra noonday sun. I noticed stone benches jutting out from the walls, front and back, so I slid over to sit at the table next to the door. When I finally adjusted to the 20-watt bulb, I noticed that the entire lower half of the room, which was not a smeared whitewash, was the raw granite gray of cut stone, making the place resemble a prehistoric "Fred Flintstone" snackbar. Smiling down from over the door into the kitchen was a photo portrait of Sai Baba.

The waiter in his early twenties, leaned in from the kitchen with a puerile smile and asked, "Meals, *saab*?"

He returned with a stainless steel bucket of hot steaming rice that had come out of a huge iron cauldron on the kitchen floor, and landed a mound of it on the plate. Next he brought in two buckets of *sambar*, and *dal*, then *bhajee* and *vegetales* after that. The sambar I had to rename pepper water because that was literally what it was, boiled pepper powder and whole peppers with a trace of salt and a few spices. The dal was simply boiled lentils mixed into a soup. And the vegetales were vegetables boiled to the nth degree, and mostly chunks of turnip, rutabaga, carrot, and black pods, resembling scorpion tails. My hand practically trembling from hunger, I greedily spooned a huge mound of the mixture in my mouth, chewing the black pod with a vengeance.

The hottest pepper in the world, so I have been told, is something called the "New Orleans Blue," and is a bluish mutant species growing in the marshlands. Next in line is a black little pod in South India that resembles a scorpion tail—that might well be because the inhabitants actually use scorpion tails. At any rate, those who have ever seen a Chinese air-raid drill will have some idea of how I looked in the aisle after placing the empty spoon back on the leaf. My next mouthful came 20 minutes later after I returned from a short walk. Only this time, I spooned out all the scorpion tails. Now I could safely eat the food without having to walk around between bites. Indeed, all my bodily movements could be done in the stall itself, as I rocked back and forth between bites, occasionally shutting my eyes. My mouth stayed on fire from the pepper for hours after the meal. But it was my initial prelaunch position that got the helpers giggling in the kitchen.

Leaving the canteen, I mused over the fact that not only was one's intake of this type of food limited, but what was eaten had almost no food value. Ninety percent of it was boiled rice-starch and the other assorted overboiled vegetables added up to negligible amounts of protein, minerals, and vitamins. And there was absolutely no meat permitted in this region of Andhra. In short, I was becoming an overnight vegetarian, in an area where the body needed the nourishment of meat more than ever.

By 4:00 in the afternoon, after a siesta, the raging heat had quelled sufficiently for my suitemate and me to go down to the dried up riverbed half a mile from the ashram. I had yet to explore the local terrain.

The path to the riverbed was a water-buffalo trail that felt like burning embers whenever a rock went into my shoe. The sand on it was so fine that it was almost liquid, rich in dried animal excrement. As this was really my first chance to observe the local surroundings, I took note of how pebble-strewn and rocky the rising slopes were on one side of the path. Eventually, near the entrance to the riverbed, the slope became a mountainous ridge.

The white sand of the riverbed itself was blinding, as it stretched an eighth of a mile across and as far as the eye could see lengthwise. The remnants of the river trickled by, six feet wide and a few feet deep, and far from clear.

Herman, my roommate, told me that the river was the bathing ghat for the entire area. He wrinkled his nose disgustedly and said with an accent hard to place, sounding like a cross between Detroit and the Bronx, "Dey come here by da hundreds, bathin in it, washjin in it, brushjin du teeth in it, pisszin in it, garglin in it, washjun da clothes in it. It's unbaleevable why they all don' die tomorrow. I can'd understan." We leapt over the river and headed for the center of the cauldron, as I tried not to touch any moist sand for fear of hookworm or trichinosis crawling under my skin.

"If it's this hot in February, Herman, what's it like in July?"

"Unbaleevable! You notice thu animuls can hardly walk as it is. Ya aughta see em in the summa, they stagger like they was drunk."

The accent, it turned out, was neither from the Bronx nor Detroit, it was Russian. Herman disclosed his story in snatches. He had been an Olympic swimmer in the late 1930s, and soon skipped the country to go to America. I pictured him in some subzero Siberian night crawling under a locomotive, clenching on the bottom with hands and teeth, and hanging on several days as ice welded him to the brakeage system. After that he might have rolled out half-frozen in some ditch, to run on as a fugitive from the secret police.

I questioned Herman about the handkerchief on his head, and he replied, "Sunstroke. You get that and it'll put ya in a coma, and that can kill. Godda be careful in this sun, no kiddin." My mouth was parched. I kept my eye on the ridge over the bullock path entering the riverbed, and was reminded of "God's Anvil," in *Lawrence of Arabia*.

Suddenly there was a loud trumpeting screech from behind us. Looking back, I spotted a tiny man riding an elephant along the side of the riverbed, where the river would soon begin out of a mound of sand. It screeched and blasted several more times, waving its trunk in the air. This was the finishing touch to put us into story-land.

"That's *Gita*. That means the 'song of God.' Thads whad Baba names it. Somebody gave it to Baba, so he keeps the thing. It lives in a shed, right next to Baba. It even knows how to worship Baba. I tell you one thing, it knows a lot, id ain'd no dummy. Baba tellz me in id's former incarnation, Gita was his pet dog.

"When I come to Baba a couple a' years back, he tellz me it's no accident. He bringz me. He treats us real special; me, Cowans, Charles Penn, Indra Devi, Mur-phets, just a handful of older Americans. Then there wasn't so many big crowds. Baba, he talkin to us individ-ually each day alone. Sometimes he come to my room several times a day. But you don' find him doin that now. One day he tell me I was a yogi in former life, that's how come I go to India."

Herman eyed the ground, walking very carefully, and conscious of every movement. His face knotted in deter-mination, as he whispered grimly, "I tell you somethin so you don' make same dumb mistake. Don' blow it like I did. I got big temper. Baba give me a test in doz days when I had it so easy. I begin to doubt him. Don' ever doubt Baba. I start to think I know better than Baba. I get angry at him. Baba still love me though. He tells me before I go that one day I come back, head bowed low. I be sorry for what I did. But it be a little harder next time. Now I keep my big mouth closed, and Baba don' talk with me so much, but maybe he's closer in other ways.

"I tell you, he's got power unbaleevable. He knows every word we're saying right now, just like he knows everything. He's a great mystery that nobody can under-stan."

My curiosity was unquenchable now that we were on the subject of Baba. Herman pointed up to a huge boul-der at that top of the stony ridge above. Its total height may have been as high as a 15-story building, and grow-ing out of it, conspicuously, was a medium-sized tree. "That's called the 'wish fulfilling tree.' You know why? When Baba was a boy, he'd go up there and pick people any kinda fruit they asked for—in season, outa season, tropical, cold weather, you name it, he picked it. One time, it'd be a pineapple, then a mango, apple, banana, orange, grape, pomegranate, watermelon. He even picked cherries that they only find in the Kashmir Himalayas. You even find it written up in some of the old Andhra newspapers.

"One day there's a whole crowd at the bottom here. And Baba tells them he's gonna go up in the time it takes them to blink. Sure enough, one second he's down here, next second he's way up there on top waving down at them. Everybody falls down on their knees. They know, at that age, he can't be just an ordinary yogi and have that sorta power. Well, he yells down to them that he's gonna give 'em special grace. They wait for some-thing to happen. It does! The center of Baba's head opens up, and light brighter than the sun comes out and blinds them for half a day after. He tells them that that's his real form, pure light. His whole head is a ball of light. Well, they fall down again and start worshiping him like God. And that's why he came here instead of the States." We went back to the suites and had a siesta while I pondered Baba's powers.

By 6:00, I was ready to do some more exploring. This time my sights were on the hill springing up in the rear corner of the whole rectangular township-ashram, where the luxury suites sat at its base, and then the hospital on a plateau above them. Two-thirds the way up, where much of the ashram below came into view, I met a tall elegant blonde in her early twenties, standing amid a small grove of trees encircling the famous Tree of Wisdom. Her name was Victoria, she was English, and had the sort of angel food cake prettiness that reminded me of an overgrown Alice in Wonderland. Her speech added the finishing touches to the portrait, as her words flowed in immaculate patrician English. For a moment I felt a romantic twinge for her, but subdued it with the trident of Vedantic philosophy.

She and a traveling companion, Anthony, had come to India on an overland bus tour, presumably because the trendy life of Britain's hip culture was becoming "a bit much," leaving an existential hole. They ran into one of India's minor gurus who was staying near one of the beaches of Kerala. They visited a local Baba temple nearby in the house of a devotee whose zeal and accounts were limitless. When they saw some of the miracles taking place about the house, they were on their way, reaching the ashram about the time I met Baba in Ananthapur. Still they had only had glimpses of Baba so far. He was out of town and due back anytime.

Our talk ended, and she floated down the hill with a farewell wave, blue sari blowing in the breeze. I heard the loud "Om" of the "phantom ghost train" issuing from Baba's prayer hall below. It was the evening bhajan.

During the next day, my explorations continued, as I toured the ashram post office, printing press with three small presses, bank by the side gate, Vedic school, and the hospital on the hill with its two wards, surgical unit, public clinic, and X-ray unit.

The thick stone prayer hall isolated Baba from the depleting elements, much the same way Regents Park Botanical Gardens shielded its flora from the harsh sleet of a London winter night. And with its chlorophyll greens and whitewashed whites, Baba's hall incessantly reminded me of a greenhouse for an avatar.

The building ran at least 90 feet along the front, and 35 feet along the side. Baba's private quarters were two stories along the side ends of the building which interconnected the outside upstairs balcony, where Baba would walk back and forth from his bedroom to his dining room in clear view of everybody.

Welded to the railings of the massive extended front porch were two silver-painted iron sculptures of Siva and Vishnu. Over the roof of the extended balcony were the highest ornaments of the whole building: the Prasanthi Nilayam flagpole, and an elaborately decorated pagoda.

Below the flag and pagoda jutted a carved marble bust of Sai Baba with a perennial wreath of flowers around its neck. It was one of the first things that always caught my attention, each time I glanced at the building, sitting out like a masthead. It looked out skyward with a sunny cherubic smile, with Baba's usual head of hair, only slightly parted this time, as he wore it in his early years. With its Reno, Nevada undertones, this made me wonder whether the ornamentation represented a level of high aesthetics I was unable to appreciate due to cultural bias, or whether it was just plain gaudy.

At about 6:00 in the late afternoon, people shuffled past me, spreading the word that Baba would be back that night. He had been gone three weeks. A car pulled in front of the ashram police station, and several wealthy Indians got out. Then I saw Gill, looking slightly disgruntled, crawl out of the rear seat.

"It's great to see you, brother, how ya doin?" I asked, extending my hand. No answer. Gill looked past me, and headed for the trunk to get his bags.

Continuing to ignore me, he grunted something and led the way, heading straight for the steps of the luxury suites.

Preparing for a long-term stand-off I followed Gill down the porch, passing every door except the one at the end where Herman and I stayed. He entered what had apparently been his room all along, dropping a bag at the base of the mosquito net in the front room.

---

I said to Herman, "Why hasn't Baba straightened this dude out? He's acting like a spoiled child. Somebody ought to tell him that he's a million miles from either compassion or enlightenment, and he's gonna stay stuck until he swallows his presumptuous self-importance." Herman just nodded.

The last thing I moved was my mat. By which time Gill finally spoke, giving ultimatums in the form of disciplinary rules. In turn I gave him a cinder-block stare. Gill shut up, exhaled angrily, and crawled under the mosquito net to meditate.

Within ten minutes, Herman and I were out of the room, and waiting on the road for Baba's arrival. In the long crowded line, I met Vickie's companion, Anthony, whom I immediately liked. Tall, serene, and gentle, I realized that here was the sort of person that Gill needed to take lessons from. Herman could be "heavy" enough by himself, but with me and then Gill piled on top of that, the suite was a potential mine-field.

I felt the excitement in the diminishing evening twilight as a phantasmal trail of dust arose from the road in the distance. I suddenly felt a particular brand of energy that I had experienced only one time before, in Ananthapur. But I could feel it now, a vast sweeping hurricane of spirit flooding across the land where Baba went. Picturing the swirling silvery mass of an autumn storm on the Atlantic I thought to myself, "Forty miles in front of him, 40 miles in back of him, 40 miles to the right of him, and 40 miles to the left of him, the spirit moves like a free-floating magnetic pole."

A wave of dust sped at us in a widening parachute as its nose cone, a little cream-colored Fiat, gleamed in the forefront. A hundred feet away I could see, sitting in the backseat, a red-black figure searching out of the windows. Moments later, as the car was face-to-face, Baba smiled and waved, gleaming radiantly in the backseat, then sped by.

We bolted through the side gate, around the back of the prayer hall to the men's front side (women stood or sat on the opposite front end). Within only seconds, Baba's car sped down the center avenue as shouts of "Om jai Sai Ram" filled the air. It raced around the fenced-in cement lotus, and pulled into the flagstone driveway beneath the extended balcony. Several ashram policemen held the crowd back, while specially appointed devotees motioned the crowd to calm down and remain still; Baba sprang out of the car athletically, and headed to the center of the inner compound near the lotus, amid the crowd's gasps. Baba smiled, made enigmatic hand gestures, blessed the crowd, then turned to walk back to the prayer hall singling me out on the way with a smile, calling "Rowdie." I waved back numbly as I felt the crowd's attention turn to me.

When Baba had gone into his private quarters, I assumed that was it for the night. It wasn't. Bhajans were now beginning, and word was out for everybody to go inside the hall. Those who couldn't fit could remain outside and sing. I leapt inside and sped down the center aisle to a row up front. The crowd funneled in behind me. A Brahmin priest patrolled the aisle motioning the thousand or so people to quickly sit down and shut up, making a hissing sound to quiet them.

Three loud "Oms" rung in the air. Then a male song leader opened the service with a hymn of praise to Ganesha, the elephant god and overcomer of obstacles. Most of the bhajans were either in Telugu, the language of Andhra Pradesh, or Sanskrit, the ancient Aryan tongue of the Vedas. And the songs themselves were usually written by Baba. The pulsating melodies, fired up by a harmonium and little brass cymbals, rolled on hypnotically, but it was no good my trying to mouth the words, they were just too alien for me.

Baba's chair sat in the front mightily, elevating above us on a platform, like an Arthurian throne or something from the court of the Knight's Templar. A teak and silver affair, its only clue with the East was the huge "Om" embossed at the top in Sanskrit. Stretching over it was a huge Bengal tiger skin whose roaring head, glass eyes and all, extended out to Baba's footstool.

The stage directly at the front was an eye-catcher. The central points of focus, like two swirling hypnotic wheels, were two giant oil paintings of Baba. Lit from beneath, they were windows into another world. The left picture I entitled "The Old Man." A wizened mystic staring out into the audience through melancholy eyes, the old Sai Baba of Shirdi, stood in some twilight-lit alabaster room, donned in an ochre robe and characteristically knotted head scarf. The Baba on the right was the present Sai Baba as a young man—handsome, compelling, vital, and innocent—it was an Indian mythical hero smiling out at the women's half in triumphant detachment, like an unreachable god.

A life-sized statue stood between the two paintings. Adorned in silk and jewelry, and shaped and painted in incredible detail, it was Krishna playing the flute. The blue-black god was frozen in perpetual mirthful dance, enacting its legendary skill of captivating the hhearts of devotees. The face with almond-shaped eyes and a coy beautiful sidelong glance, held a reed between the lips in the manner of Giridhara Gopala, the cowherd avatar, more reminiscent of the Greek god Pan than ever. The rest of the stage seemed strewn with items, including a large coiled silver serpent with the Shirdi Sai Baba sitting on it.

Suddenly a surge went through the crowds. Sai Baba had just emerged and was now outside walking among the people. The singing became louder and more frantic.

Without forewarning, Baba appeared in the hall. Walking in quick athletic steps, he mounted the wooden platform and took the chair. His brilliant smile soon faded into routine coolness as though he had never been away. The more heated the feasting devotees became the more indifferent Baba appeared, abstractedly toying with flower petals and looking off into the distance. The women, all eyes on Baba, wheezed and puffed as they clapped their hands and rocked back and forth, transforming into a giant bellows trying to fire up the dying glow of an indifferent ember. Baba would remain the formless fire, dancing with them for a while, but only for a brief season, reappearing in a hundred thousand other places as a flare here and a glow there. Such was the way, they had learned, of the formless Absolute in its ultimate almost brutal impersonality.

On the final note of a bhajan, Baba kicked his stool to the side, and sprung to his feet. The crowd jumped to its feet, lumping toward the front, while singing the closing ceremonial chant. Baba eyed the audience for a moment, while mysteriously weaving his fingers through the air, turned and left into the doors of his residence. Everybody crowded out of the hall as quickly as possible to get a final view of Baba as he appeared on the upstairs balcony.

Baba smiled down as he looked out toward the darkened lands of Andhra Pradesh and up to the black night sky. Then he backed into the portal of his room, like a retreating mechanical figure in a cuckoo clock. The crowd dispersed as the air hummed with nighttime activity. Some went off to meditate, others to eat, others to talk. And the rest stretched their blankets on the sands of the ashram to sleep under a clear starry sky. Truly I was in a different world, an almost magical dominion. Suddenly present was a new presence a new energy in the air and it was unmistakable.

# Chapter 7

# *Forging Bonds in the Desert*

Aquiet sizzling antagonism soon pervaded the luxury suite. Kindling this were such continual nighttime harassments as heavy stifling air that made breathing a physical effort, while the body was under the constant assault of mosquitoes that swarmed out of the bathroom in nocturnal droves. To combat them required a sticky greenish paste that had its own setbacks. Raising the value of sleep even more was the spartan fact that we were without beds. Lying on straw-mats with a cotton spread or two, our ribs and bones were at constant odds with the flagstone floor, giving us a distinctly bruised feeling when we arose from "sleep." However the greatest obstacle of all, the hour of wake-up, was usually the time I would finally drop off to sleep—4:30 in the morning.

The air of brotherly cooperation between Gill, Herman, and myself was about as spiritual as three Oregon panhandlers who have hit upon a gold vein in a riverbed, eyeing each other to make sure no one sneaks out in the night to pan for extra gold; and as everybody seems to be sleeping nice and neighborly, there's a creak from the bathroom door, and three shotguns go off from different corners of the flophouse.

Gill, when he wore his farmer-brown Levi overalls with suspenders and all, became "Shotgun Mountain Bill." Herman reminded me more of "Sammy the Butcher" from Chicago, especially in a self-styled Indian outfit that looked as though its origin had been more from the Cosa Nostra than anywhere else. And the girls much later named me "Marshal Matt Dillon."

As silence became the golden rule of the place, it was evident to me that the particular brand of yoga my roommates followed was a high-octane mixture of mortification of the flesh, ego negation, and yogic toughness, while "love" in any form I knew of seemed to fall away from the picture entirely. Night after night, I could hear Gill's little alarm go off at 2:30 or 3:00 as he would sit up under the mosquito net to do *pranayam*—power breathing—for the next two or three hours, and not sleep again till 9:00 the following evening. Consequently a considerable self-conscious anger, and finally rebellion, hit me each time I was forced to stagger off the mat at 4:30, knowing that Gill in some meditative hypersensitivity could feel every crude movement. The more quietly I tried to slosh water on my head to wake up—so I at least would not fall over in the prayer hall—the more I resented Gill's inhibiting presence. I felt his whole approach was wrong, but I knew I couldn't prove it.

Tired of the "heaviness" of the suite, Herman and I moved our mats outside to the little garden patch between our row of suites and the next. The three of us drifted further apart; Gill forever morose and self-absorbed, Herman more and more silent and distrusting.

At the crowded *darshans*, as Baba walked among us outside the prayer hall, he showered me with attention. In the meantime he would bypass stone-faced Gill, as he repeatedly singled me out to chat, joke, or slap me on the back. If I was sitting on the top step looking out, Baba might sneak up behind me along a crowded aisle of

Indians, then stand directly behind me with his legs and robe pressed against my back. Baba conditioned me to informality in relating to him as my rightful domain. Before long I became the message-carrier and relay station between Baba and the other foreigners.

Herman meanwhile was feeling the brunt of it all. If he wasn't sitting on some strategic step that highlighted him, Herman marched around Baba with a clumsy Rolliflex, awkwardly focusing and peering down the view screen. Herman would next begin elaborate technical maneuvers with the preposterous device. Baba would grimace; those quick enough to perceive, giggled. Phase two of the clowning would continue as Baba paced his movements exactingly enough to elude Herman's lens by a few degrees. Herman never quite tripped over, but he came close to it a few times. Even offstage the Tom and Jerry stigma pursued Herman, mostly because of his apparel, a mutation of the Indian kurta-shirt, with cutoff sleeves. The Cosa Nostra look. As a result, wherever he went, he constantly had his growing paranoia fed by Indians who stared and giggled at him incessantly. Perhaps Herman saw all this as signs of his "heightening awareness." Nevertheless, soon enough we were no longer on speaking terms.

The final cut came the day Herman handed me the keys for our new room. He included ultimatums and entrance stipulations, making the aside that the best thing for me to do was to "stay shutten up." He got a cinder-block stare, as I pondered the idea of making him a cartoon character in my mind from then on. I pointed out the recent strangeness in his behavior and increasing hung-upness.

His eyes burning, Herman resembled a brain-damaged panda. "Um gonna say thiz one time and afta that itz finish. I no talk to you, you no talkin to me. Thatz best policy."

Red as a pimento, Herman dropped the keys into my hand and stomped off, jabbering at the injustice of even having to relate to me. What he needed was a young green-eared yes-man who would follow the orthodox yogic school of a Herman. "Zey would valk alonk and agree, 'Dat's what um saying ... ya just gotta keep shuttin up da mouth and keep de earz outa other people's affairs. And be real careful. Dat's de way to spirtchul enlightenings.'"

The reason Baba was moving us out of the luxury suite was that it was nearing one of the three biggest festivals of the year, Maha Sivaratri, when over 50,000 pilgrims would soon swarm the ashram, converting it to a human termite-mound. Naturally this included those who had financed and built their own rooms, including the luxury suites. The luxury suite owners were the superrich, Bombay shipping magnates, governors of State, surgeon generals, etc.

Our new cubicle was along a row of 30 rooms that faced the luxury suites across the compound. Gill meanwhile had drifted a thousand light years more from either one of us. He moved into Indra Devi's blue Colorado caravan tent, and pitched it in the garden patch between our former suite room and the next row of rooms.

The difference between the new room and the suite was that it was a quarter the size, had a tenth the light with its 20-watt bulb. And as well as swarms of mosquitoes, it also had swarms of cockroaches, some as big as mice. It also smelled. Since all these rooms lacked bathroom facilities, many residents used the path at the back as a lavatory. My greatest fear was having diarrhea, and having to run up a hill 20 times a night, treading on a scorpion on the way.

Two new Americans had just arrived from New York City. And, according to Mr. Kasturi, were to become my roommates whom I would partially oversee until they adjusted.

One was a fairly attractive Jewish girl named Michelle, who seemed self-sacrificing and agreeable... and well built, with whom I envisioned nighttime devotionals. (Yet I knew that to allow the demon of lust to knock me off path would be a really weak way to go.) With lust settled, I knew I was safe with Michelle. With her companion, Jai, I could see that I would have other problems.

When I saw Jai at darshan, it was hard to believe that he existed out of the comic strips. I began to suspect that Baba dragged him across half the world just to blow my mind. He was a Brooklyn Klutz: obnoxious, wore glasses like Coke bottles that expanded his eyeballs in the concentric circles of an onion. And he was interpersonally oblivious to the point of being a social moron. When he talked, he screamed... "like he was yellin' at sum clown across Grand Central station." After two minutes of seeing him make Cherokee Indian "how" signs to Baba, I wanted to take him behind the ashram and quiet him down with a tire iron.

When he greeted Herman, it was my first true glimpse of homicide in Herman's eyes. With Gill, it was even worse. Gill took him to some inward plane of nonbeing and unmade him.

But Jai persisted. In baggy, wrinkled pants resembling diapers, and a bright Miami flamingo shirt, he puttered about blipping nonsequitors to strangers. After several days, I noticed that he neither washed nor shaved. He didn't trust the water supply. He claimed at one point, in the monotonic intonations of Robbie the Robot, that he would probably have 93 days of physical existence left before he expired. After sampling the food, he decided that his intake would be close to nil. He smiled as though we had reached a new level of rapport when I told him he was an idiot.

---

After seeing him grimace and agonize one morning, I also realized that he had problems regarding the bathroom situation—severe problems. He stated that he was a "being" who was "totally modest," and therefore could not use anything during the day but an American toilet, and the only way he would use the great outdoors was in total darkness. I could tell Michelle had "had it up to here." So Jai, with the "forbearance of a true yogi," would have to grip his bowels like the doors of the Kremlin till nightfall. It was a close contest. By late afternoon, he was crawling about the porch as though he were going through labor, undulating his head.

To the dismay of many, Baba was perfectly friendly with Jai, though he passed Michelle for several darshans, as she sat neat as a pin, freshly washed, and sitting like a bunny rabbit in a new Indian silk sari. It hurt but she tried to hide it. But a new fire leapt into the eyes of Herman, Michelle, and maybe even Gill, when Baba came up to Jai and asked, "Hello, sir, are you happy?" And Jai, wearing something like a Polish bowling T-shirt, smiled as though he had just won the double-bubble chewing-gum contest, held up his hand as Chief Grey Cloud, responding with a loud "How," and then dropped his arm limply, swaying back and forth like a baby hippopotamus. Baba gave him a parting smile, then headed toward me. "Tell other foreigners, there will be an interview coming very soon." Everyone cheered and danced afterward, except Herman and Gill.

Back at the room, Jai and Michelle told me how they had met, through a mutual friend, Lila, and consequently through their New York guru, Hilda Charlton, under whose guidance they had grown as brother and sister disciples. Not that it was easy. Their natural animosity for one another was explained by Hilda, who stated that it was a carry-over from past lives together where there still remained a residual karmic debt. But she encouraged them all the same. After all, they were exceedingly high souls, differing only in their individual approaches to God.

Michelle's story was not atypical: communication barriers with her family, rebellion, irreconcilable differences with the norms of society, jobs, college, etc., and finally the arduous pilgrimage through counterculture, hippiedom, multitudes of LSD trips, on the road. And the limbo got increasingly worse, her state of depression shooting down the graph until, when she was "just ripe," Michelle met Hilda Charlton, the only woman she was ever able to really love and respect. Hilda gave her a sense of self-respect, and most of all, seemed to love her abundantly. Confusion left, spiritual purpose was added to her life, as Michelle had a clear goal ahead under Hilda's constant guidance.

Jai, speaking with as much feeling as if he were reciting strings of binary digits, went on to share what sounded like a well-planned tape-recorded autobiography. He had obviously shared his amazing story with quite a number of people.

"I was nevah a hippy, nevah a dope fiend, I was totally straight. I lived a completely Koshah life that made my motha very proud from the time I was a liddle baby. I nevah had an impure thought, I remained chaste throughout my adolescence, always working hard.

"But yogic experiences, that's something I can tell you about. Those I had from early childhood onward." Jai was Alan Sherman as "My Son the Yogi" and "Camp Granada" turned out to be Prasanthi Nilayam.

As Jai unwound, Michelle straightened up the room in a rigid, quiet, self-enforced tolerance. She must have known the facts by heart. She lit a candle in the wall box, then some incense, and finally set up an altar comprised of items out of her suitcase: pictures of gurus, gods, goddesses, Hilda, plus tokens of various types.

Jai's first contact with the higher forces occurred when he was seven. "Night afta night, I had the same

dream. I would be sitting cross-legged on a large river—
it turned out to be the Ganges—whose banks were near
a city, which I also found out was Benares. At any rate,
as I recited the name of my chosen deity, doing a special
type of breathing, something happened that frightened
the heck out of me. A tiger approached from behind out
of the forest, jumped and mauled me, finally killing me.
I'd actually die in the dream. There's no death worse,
believe me. As a kid, I'd just sit up in bed sweating
with the lights turned on. Later on, when I was older, I
learned the dream was a leak-through of a former life,
when I was a yogi.

"In high school, another thing happened. I was in the
back row of my history class. Suddenly as the teacher
was talkin', he changed right in front of me. His head got
huge and gray, his eyes separated, his ears hung down,
and he grew a trunk. It was an elephant head on a man's
body. He talked like that for ten minutes, and I was the
only one who saw it. Not only that, but I heard things
that the class didn't. He told me to read the *Puranas*. I
did, and soon found out that he is a god, one of my own
personal deities. He is the son of Siva and Uma. His
name is Ganesha, the god of overcoming obstacles. In
fact that's how I got A's in high school, through him. He
told me to work super hard. But when I was in trouble,
he'd come to my aid if I invoked his name. During one
examination he told me the answers to each question. I
got an A on it, of course. But one night he appeared in
my room and told me that he wasn't my highest personal
deity and not to worry, since at the time I'd find out, and
know her immediately since she was a goddess I had
been worshiping for hundreds of lifetimes." A New York
youth encountering Indian gods, amazing I thought!

"It finally happened when I was a student at New
York University involved in research at one of the India
exhibits on tour at the museum. I walked into the special exhibit of ancient Hindu gods, and before I knew it, I

was in a corner facing this bronze statue of the most beautiful woman I'd ever seen. I fell at her feet and cried. Suddenly...Blam...from outa' the center of her forehead came a blue ray of light into my face. I saw lights and stars, and ended up dancing around in the room for maybe 20 minutes. Then the statue started speaking. I can't reveal all she said, but she instructed me in practically all the yoga I know now, telling me her name was Lolita Devi. From then on, any time I closed my eyes, I could see her. And any time a major thing came up, I always asked her advice."

Lolita Devi guided Jai into a doctoral history program at Columbia University, until he was later told to drop out. By then he met Hilda Charlton, who was to be his guru and earthly embodiment of the "Divine Mother."

Suddenly Jai and Michelle chimed in together singing a song composed by Hilda called "Divine Mother." When that ended, it was a one-man show again as Jai rattled off song after song he had composed about Lolita Devi. One sounded like a rhumba with strings of complex Sanskrit words, a yard long, following each refrain which he spit out like a computer. He kept timing with the standard baby hippopotamus gestures and idiotic grins. Finally Jai and Michelle withdrew into the silence of their afternoon meditation, sitting stiff-backed against the wall in either the full lotus or semilotus positions.

At 9:00 the following morning, on the one day I had really overslept, I was caught red-handed by Suraiya who stood in the door and said, "Baba has sent me to wake you up. He knows you are oversleeping. Come on, he is waiting for you. He will not start the interview until you are there."

I dashed across the ashram, through the crowd, right up to Baba's door, feeling a combination of embarrassment, guilt, and exuberance. Baba flung the door open, while the huge crowd outside held up its hands in prayer.

Baba chided me with a shaking finger and a smile. This was my second interview since Baba had arrived.

The group sitting on the floor looked up nervously, while Baba still shook his finger at me and announced, "Oversleeping, oversleeping." I carefully eyed Herman and Gill for signs of condemnation. Herman looked grim, Gill disgusted. And I thought, "Okay fellas, he's gonna catch you with your psychic pants down too, so don't gloat." With those two there, it was a real damper on me. I liked to relate playfully with Baba, as a child, and with their constant heaviness, it was a lot harder, as the temptation to become self-conscious grew.

Baba directed me to sit beside his chair, to his left. Then he explained that this would be the last interview for a while until the *Mahasivaratri* festival a few days away, ended. Already 15- to 20-thousand pilgrims were swarming the ashram, camped either around the grounds or under one of the huge sheds.

Baba satirized some of the illustrious people who were coming, and pointed out how men can so easily become bound up by the conventions of the world; aspirants too can be slowed by the number of claims they lay upon the world. "Single man walking has two legs," Baba said wiggling two fingers in the air. "A man and a wife are four legs. Now man goes slowly." This time Baba used four fingers. "Then there are children, then grand-children, nephews, nieces—many legs, go very slow like a caterpillar." He laughed ironically. The gushes of Baba's energized attention proved that our fears of falling away from grace, when Baba was showing the impersonal mode, were unfounded.

It seemed as though my mind had been shoved into a narrower place of constant self-absorption regarding my moment to moment staying in the will of Baba. If my inner "onlooker" sensed an attitude of surrender to Baba, I felt assured that I was on target.

---

For a while Baba spoke in nursery school allegories about love, suns, and flowers. Then things began to tighten up again as we sensed a spiritual IQ test coming on. "God, *Om*, is like a giant current of electricity. It goes through all the different wires and bulbs. Man is like a bulb. Each bulb a different capacity, giving off different brightness. One man is a 500-watt bulb," and Baba pointed to an old Indian in the room—just to illustrate the example, or was he doing more? "Another man is 400-watt bulb." And like an arrow in the heart, Baba pointed to me as all the Americans stiffened, especially Herman. Gill was 300, Jai 200, right down the line until Herman. We still waited for Herman, who Baba finally rated as 25 watts. It must have been a Christmas tree light because Herman turned into a pimento again, at times grinding his teeth.

While Baba bantered with Jai, Herman's eyes still flashed, singling him out. Jai went on obliviously, asking questions and gesturing in the air. Michelle appeared irritated that she was still being ignored, while Jai was allowed to sing a song about Lolita Devi after he had asked whether it was all right to continue worshiping her as his chosen deity. After two frantic stanzas that could be heard outside, Baba halted Jai as Gill impatiently looked up at the ceiling. Baba gave a tolerant chuckle in Jai's direction, then switched to Herman.

With patient chiding, he shook his finger at Herman and said, "Too much talking." Baba flapped his hands making blah-blah quacks in the air. A little exasperation entered his tone seeing that Herman's irritation had not subsided. "Going around talking to everybody, mind restless, very restless like a monkey. Here is some advice: Keep quiet, talk little, and speak only sweet words." As Herman protested in defense, Baba shut him with a tolerant "Ah!" This happened several times more before Herman got the point.

The ripples of agitation in the air were soon smoothed away as Baba dismissed the tiny moods that still lingered. Immediately a waterfall of positive force emanated from him. He kept dishing it out as the final minutes ticked by, adoring us, almost swooning over us with an innocent openheartedness. The old colored mammy in him smiled from ear to ear as Baba told us again, "Love is sweet," with unaffected abandon. For a moment he was somewhere between Ethel Waters and Aunt Jemima.

"You are hungry, want some sweets, *prasadam*?"

"Oh yes, swami," we nodded.

Baba's sleeve went up, and he leaned out over the others. I gripped the arm of his chair, looking closely from his side. On the final wave of his arm, a baseball-sized object appeared in his hand. The same familiar ionized force hurtled through the room like a sonic boom, the instant it appeared.

"Open your hands, Rowdie."

I rose up on my haunches making a bowl with my hands. Baba crumbled the ball up into a soft gravel that quickly filled both hands. "Ladoo. The sweet is called Ladoo. My workmen work very fast." Baba laughed knowingly as he heard a mind-blown "Yes, Baba."

Baba had everybody stand in a circle as he and I went around. Baba would scoop out a fair-sized portion for each person, and then bid them to eat. Then he had me eat the rest, patting me on the back as I licked the last traces off my hands. Another miracle was being eaten I thought to myself.

As we were expecting Baba to open the door and usher us out, he announced "special grace," waving for us to sit down again. He went over to a velvet curtain, and stood halfway through it. "Private interviews." A thunderous "om" suddenly issued from out of the prayer hall just on the other side of the wall. It was the 11:30 bhajan, and we were being held over. A considerable breach of the normal routine, just for us! I smiled at Anthony, and got a merry twinkle back.

A familiar nervous anesthesia filled me as Baba's eyes radiated from the velvet-draped portal. I was the first. He opened the curtains to let me in, then slid them shut. We stood at the bottom of a compact little stairwell that led up to Baba's private suites. The sound of the adjacent auditorium gave me the feeling of being within the bellows of a huge organ.

In my continuum of private moments with Baba, I had thus far made a considerable leap of faith. Especially during the last private interview a week back. So far there seemed to be no ceiling on the limits of his kingdom that he was willing to bestow on the faithful. And both times earlier he unleashed a slightly more dazzling glimpse of his supernature.

A week back, in this same stairwell, I made a bold pledge, spurred on doubtless by every kind of motive. I strongly felt the preciousness of what might be my final ticking seconds with a Messiah who would one day be so globally in demand as to be virtually unreachable. I also felt the remote possibility that I might earn apostleship under him contingent upon my most all-out effort. I knew that if I did have three magic wishes, I had better start fast, and not blow them on trinkets. So during my last private interview with Baba, I took a leap saying, "I want to love you with all my heart, soul, and mind, Baba. I want your will to be mine." He beamed. Then the confession of Thomas: "Baba, I know you are God. You cannot fool me." Baba climbed up on the lower step so our heights would be equal, and embraced me. It lasted 30 seconds, while I constantly wondered what great invisible boons were being offered: cleansing of past karma, purification and opening of the *chakras* or spiritual centers. Clearly some kind of power was at work in the room.

However as I stood before Baba this time, I was far less satisfied about myself. Whether it was my increasing alienation from Herman and Gill or such elementary crimes as oversleeping that morning, I wasn't sure. I felt vulnerable.

"What do you want?" This was my second magic wish.

"Baba, I can't stand the evil in myself. Help me get rid of it and other obstacles, Baba. Anything that holds me back."

"Yes, yes."

"Baba, I really want victory this time, too many failures in the past. I want to be certain."

In patient understanding, Baba abstracted over my sins. "Too many bad thoughts, impure *sanskaras* (traits from past lives). Mind running around like a monkey. Thoughts of material things, anger, ego, jealousy, hate, quarreling, and thoughts of girls. Not good." He wrinkled his face in disgust, in such a caricature of the usual expression, I wondered if the wavelength of the original thought impulse from overmind to avatar had mutated in transit.

Baba mounted the lower step again, as he had done on the last interview. He wrapped his arms about me, hugged tightly, while I pondered. This pondering soon turned into critical reflection where my very survival under Baba was at stake. I was being thrown a "test" I was not sure I could handle. My mind was forced to suddenly make hair-pin turns.

If the hallmark of this session with Baba was my own impurity, then I was presently under a spiritual magnifying glass as never before. And any kind of unexpected key could squeeze open a new skeleton closet. Baba's hug grew tighter. Then that subterranean spider of a thought crept out of some dark abyss. I almost repelled it before I fully sensed it, if that were possible. Nevertheless it got through in an icy quiet, and speculated deep things—notice how his breathing has become a pant, deeper, more intensified. Feel his pelvis twisting. Why does he need to twist his pelvis. Especially in the region of the loins. Accidental? No, not for one who is that conscious. I doubt a detail slips by him. Then, is this some strange divine passion that only the initiates encounter at the higher stages, and could that be some kind of...well...nonspecific pan-sexuality, or bisexuality...or...or...am I twisting something that is innately pure into something that it is not, due to my own suspicions and evils? Yet Baba's pelvis kept nudging and twisting from my abdomen on down. Not hard but gently, almost as though it had the nerve endings of a hand.

Yet if Baba were healing me or opening skeleton closets, it was not without some risk—and you only take risks with things you value. Then I feared that Baba might perceive my edginess—not that he shouldn't know if he is omniscient, but he might choose to dwell on it. And my high sin would be the primal insult to God, blasphemy in the most profound sense. The penalty for which might be expulsion from his presence. Yet, could he in love test me beyond my capacities, knowing I would stumble?

I felt an electric flash of self-conscious anxiety as Baba broke the hug. He held me back and looked penetratingly into my eyes, asking, "What's wrong, you do not like it?" Then I knew that I could not possibly bail out now, or call his cards, for I would hang in space with insufficient evidence to satisfy me either way. And I would go through life without a way of ever knowing for sure who or what he really was, with the perennial question, "What about his miracles?" hanging in mind. And certainly a hug was not as bad a cliffhanger as the least of the initiatory rites of the Himalayan nights of the rishis, or the heat yogas at Lhasa, and probably it all panned out as angels' dreams anyway.

"No, Baba, I like it very much. Great gift, great privilege."

"You are not pulling hard. Very weak hug. You do not like to hug?"

"Baba," I justified, hoping I had some ground left not to back out, "I was afraid to hug too tightly, maybe some discomfort for you."

"No, Rowdie." In an instant we were embracing again until he was satisfied. I really locked in, giving almost a chest-crushing squeeze. His pelvis moved far less, still it moved. I wished I could just shoot the whole area with Novocain and forget about it. Maybe to a saint walking in, it looked like the gates of heaven opening. But to someone without the pellucid heart of a shepherd the scene juxtaposed ironically in my mind, it might look quite bizarre. Where for a second, to the untutored mind, the divine might hinge closely to some incredible scene out of a work by Goddard or Truffeaut.

Baba looked content, and I felt relieved, if not on the brink of a new breakthrough in understanding. The curtains opened and eyes glistened back from the dark corners of the room in ravenous wonder. It had been a long interview. Soon the others were whisked through, and we were let out into the bright sunlight before a massive crowd who sang out and looked at us in awe. To my right, leaning against one of the porch pillars was one of the familiar young ushers, a servant and attendant of Baba's when school was not in session. Frozen against the pillar, he resembled some pristine marble sculpture of Adonis. He gave me a cherubic grin which I returned with a wave.

## A God of Androgyny

Later that day, I decided to go to the old *mandir*, the first ashram where Baba started his mission as a mere teenager. It was a mile down the road toward the actual village of Puttaparthi, and was not much more than a whitewashed adobe building closed into a compound by flagstone walls. I felt pressed to look for clues, yet why and what I was not sure. An inner restlessness prodded me on.

On the advent of one of the greatest festivals of the year and with the day's interview still ringing in my ears, I felt pressed to get my hands into the soil to try for more than just a superficial taste of what was going on.

The afternoon waned into a gray twilight as I stood in the old mandir after two hours of searching, with more questions than answers. The building itself was a ramshackle of rooms that had all been added on to what was originally just a shed. Sandal paste and rose perfume seeped through the masonry, and crept across halls and rooms. Bright red kum-kum powder mixed with other colors which streaked and splotched the walls. Patterns of flower petals mosaicked the outside walkways as similar patterns of colored powder laced under the front porch where sat a large stone siva lingam. Yet artistically it was all bankrupt. There was a certain sloppiness that offended an inbred Occidental sense of orderliness. Then there was a photo exhibit of hundreds of pictures of the young Sai Baba. This pulled in my attention.

A number of old women in the backrooms kept the temple up, making daily sweets, ceremonial offerings of flowers, and going through daily rituals, perhaps hoping that all this would bring their forlorn young Baba back. Why didn't they just walk down the road to the huge community that now stood as a monument to the present Sai Baba?

As I examined picture after picture, some faded, some out of focus, or hand colored, one theme predominated like a pungent nectar. And that was the unisexual godlike beauty of the youthful Sai Baba. "Cultural variable" rang out in my mind, while the more prosaic side of me protested with a stubborn fearful respect for the hard line between the sexes. A line that was a sacred ordinance of God whose violation or perversion didn't promise a new Eden but an abomination of the natural order. I was beginning a deep inner debate.

A philosophic voice of authority answered this gut response: "Among men this cold and hard division is necessary and constant. But if you want to apply such a standard to demigods and avatars, here is where the difference of the sexes is another language of obsolete meanings. Obviously Baba is beyond single gender." The voice eulogized, "He is a composite of the highest attributes of both principles, male and female: strength and beauty, gracefulness and power, aggression and passivity." I finally heard my mind agree, "Ah, yes, Siva-Shakti."

But this argument didn't change the photos on the walls. As I spotted a picture of a dainty long-haired Baba reclining on a couch like Jean Harlow, I mused, "Why is it necessary, and what does it prove?" Maybe this is the way the local Indians could relate with divinity when it came to them on a personal level, I responded to myself.

In another picture, Baba was being carried through the streets of a small village lying upon a large, flower-decorated palanquin. He waved as the throngs showered him with either confetti or flower petals. Another picture was a three-quarter view of Baba with one hand resting on a hip and the other one waving goodbye. It could have been a *Saturday Evening Post* cover in the early 1950s of a mammy in Starkville, Mississippi, waving the kids off to school.

But the most formidable picture I had to contend with was one of Baba dressed as a goddess. This time, smiling as always, he waved with arms bedecked in women's bangles, wore earrings, a necklace, with a red kum-kum dot in the center of his forehead. And instead of his robe, virtually the only thing he ever wore, Baba donned a silk sari, and smiled almost coquettishly.

And this brought me close to the point I was at soon after I first heard about Baba and was reading a book about him on the train from Delhi to Bombay in late November. It was entitled *At His Lotus Feet* and contained 108 pictures of Baba, many of them the very same pictures now hanging in the old mandir. At first sight on the train, my "hang-up" came at about 1:00 A.M. while I was musing through it, propped up on one of those planks they call berths. Finally I saw a picture that was so effeminate that it triggered a portion of my thinking apparatus that I generally label "The area of my brain that thinks in Redneck Logic." I finally had to say it aloud, lapsing into soliloquy that brought me a considerable audience, as I got off the berth, leaned against the wall, held the book out and said, "Either this dude is the most cosmically innocent, unaffected, and pure being I have ever seen, or the most unbelievable drag queen passing itself off as a love child that has ever been perpetrated. Man, this pose sure looks trashy." After that my movements didn't exactly go unnoticed as at least 50 passengers waited for the next proclamation.

A similar struggle was going on now, with different parts of my mind warring: Redneck Logic Versus the Erudite Transcendent Thinker.

Redneck Logic started exclaiming in "boy, oh boy" fashion: "Man, I sure hope that ain't a homo. That looks an awful lot like a fey gesture. Probably just waiting for the troops or some cowboy to come along..."

Then the Erudite Transcendent Thinker countered, "You're desecrating the unfathomable, you spiritual Cro-Magnon. Such thoughts are a frightening index of how far you still have to go to even see the light ahead. You should realize and repent from that whole cancerous level of thought. Surgically remove it before this attitude exempts you from discipleship under what may be one of the greatest avatars in the world's history. Imagine ridiculing Christ's nose."

But Redneck Logic retorted, "You've cut off your gut sense, you transcendental idiot. You've so over-cerebrated around your natural thermostat of right and wrong, that you're calling white black and black white." And on went the inner debate as I walked back to Baba's ashram.

Not 24 hours later, Redneck Logic had been weakened, indeed overwhelmed by the sheer drawing power that Baba had. For acres, extending out in all directions, straw-mats and suitcases lay as far as the eye could see with no more than an inch at the very most between them. The land had become a field of human bodies, where units of people, presumably relatives, would congregate in their own little patches of several square yards. Kasturi, Baba's number one secretary and writer in residence, smiled like a proud grandfather, as he looked out at the masses from his private porch. Awed visitors gaped and saluted him, some trying to touch his feet as if he were Baba. We watched a long black sedan pull in the entrance as Kasturi commented privately to me, "He happens to be a Bombay millionaire. But what does it matter? He too will sleep on the ground with all the others." Sure enough, the Bombay millionaire unrolled his mat on the ground right beside his car.

Nor was it only the Indian elite who had to humble themselves in the presence of Baba. While Anthony ate a *masala dosa*, he told us how John Lennon and Yoko Ono had quietly arrived for Baba's birthday festival on November 23. A delightful sense of destiny filled us as it became clear that neither of the two illustrious pop stars even remotely influenced Baba to seek them out or deviate from his usual course. In fact he had shown far less interest in them than he had in us. They sat and sat in the multitudes, just like everybody else, Baba smiled at them, but that was not enough.

Lennon expected an interview. Gill was about the only foreigner there at the time, so John and Yoko seized upon him. Gill patiently shared what he could with aloof authority, undoubtedly blowing their minds because almost nobody came on to them, John Lennon and Yoko Ono, with that sort of indifference. They treated Gill like an equal; his manner remained unchanged. They may have even become somewhat disarmed by then, and sullenly curious about the authenticity of the place. If they didn't count, it might even be real. But if the ashram had that kind of integrity, where was their bartering power? They were like rich kids in the Olympics where dad could no longer buy them first place. Lennon felt slighted. And this outweighed his curiosity in Baba's miraculous powers.

The following morning, the day of the festival, I was soon caught up in the confluence of people heading for the large metal shed. It was expected that about 10,000 pilgrims could fit into the large structure along the floor in sardine-packed rows. The thousands of other pilgrims were spread across the landscape outside. As I shuffled past the side of the prayer hall I glimpsed someone who looked like an angel. Head and shoulders above the Indians, this walking lighthouse had a flare of red hair that was as much of a shock in South India as the sudden appearance of a Watusi warrior in Grimstad, Norway. He was swarmed by convection currents of people immediately. Then he vanished from view. Truly, we had a fascinating array of Westerners showing up at this spiritual power center, I immediately thought to myself.

Soon a line of ushers let me into the VIP entrance that they were guarding.

As I entered, the view of the crowd was breathtaking. The roped-off front area was bare. It went back 30 feet from the stage, was covered with Indian carpets, and was the equivalent of the royal box at Wimbledon. At its edges, on the other side of the rope, quivered a flowing lava of people. An usher directed me to sit at the very front, right below the center of the stage. Was I about to experience the modern day Indian equivalent of the Sermon on the Mount?

The air exploded in thunderous screams as Karnatic horns wailed, followed by sharp drumbeats. A giant parade was moving from Baba's prayer hall to our auditorium. Vedic chants proceeded a long line of school kids, and then the priests. In the outside brilliance could clearly be seen this human train escorting Baba and moving toward the central entrance of the auditorium. In front of Baba was a gigantic behemoth adorned in mirrored tapestries, braided cords, and saddled in elegance. It was Gita, Baba's elephant. As wealthy Indians filtered in quietly beside me, tiptoeing up from the VIP entrance, I learned that by Baba's side and holding his umbrella was Governor Dharma Vira, the diminutive Governor of Mysore State. The umbrella shone over Baba's head as the classic Puranic sun-umbrellas seen in the traditional captions of the gods and avatars—Krishna on the chariot, Rama with a drawn bow, and so on. Baba's gown shimmered with a brilliant red, as his hair, more voluminous than ever, encircled his head like a halo as the sun ran through each strand of hair. He was less human and more godlike than ever before. The crowd inside and outside surged in hysteria as Baba passed by. People raised hands in prayerful *namastes*, and many lunged across on the ground to touch his feet. The elephant caravan and the Vedic boys parked by the side of the auditorium, and the hall fell into a dead quiet as Baba entered. Karnatic horns still screamed eerily away in the background.

Baba suddenly entered the rear of the hall. Baba was in the impersonal mode, scanning the audience and smiling out at generalized quadrants, rarely if ever singling anyone out. I turned around and looked up just as Baba was behind me, a wave of force rolling down the carpet, his eyes shining like two discs. He left the impersonal mode to whisper to me, "Special seat, special seat," mounting the stairs with gymnastic leaps.

Mr. Kasturi picked up an amphora-shaped vase—the size of a large flowerpot.

Songs rolled by as Kasturi raised the vase upside down directly over the Shirdi statue. The singing became louder. Suddenly Baba thrust his hand up into the vase, making the same circular motions inside the vase normally associated with all of his materializations.

Immediately a steady fountain of gray ash cascaded out of the vase, on and on and on, through several songs. The only break in the flow was when Baba stopped to change hands. A small mountain of powder rose around the silver statue, waist-high, and higher as clouds filtered out over the stage across five or ten front rows of the audience covering everybody in a light frost. Out of the waterfall of ash came little hailstones bouncing off the figure and onto the carpet, occasionally rolling off the stage. The women would scramble to get them: gems, cardamom seeds, and crystals of rock sugar. A round green bloodstone rolled across the stage and right into my lap. I was in the best seat in the house, the very front row on the aisle.

Baba yanked his hand out of the vase, spun around, and left by the rear stage. The volume of powder was several times that of the vase.

Eyeing the fourth row back, I flinched automatically as I locked eyes with the angel creature. The face was strange—pale, sensitive, and almost feminine in a Raphaelite sense. Within the chestnut-auburn eyes lay distant enigmas, oscillating from melancholy to impish glee, cherubic innocence, then Mandarin wisdom, and finally sheer amazement. Still not entirely sure whether this being was some very tall unusual girl who had stumbled obliviously into the male section, or was a male after all—which was beginning to look the case—I nodded as though to say, "Isn't this whole thing more incredible than any storybook?"

He nodded with reddening tearful eyes, this time resembling the Dicken's good lad, mistreated by the world, the fugitive of brutality, but forever gentle and innocent. A magnet behind me turned my head back around. Baba had returned to the front stage wearing a clean new robe.

While he had been gone, the priest and Kasturi had laboriously cleaned off the statue and urn, collecting the vibhuti on a number of silver trays. It was now apparent, however, that the ceremony was not entirely over.

As Kasturi poured a milky liquid over the figure, Baba washed it with his hands, resembling a midwife bathing an infant. My thoughts wandered to a conversation with Vijaya Laxmi, the ashram number two doctor, who told me, "I could spend days telling you all the miraculous healings Baba has performed." She and Kasturi had mentioned Dr. Thathachari, Professor of Dermatology at Stanford University Medical School, who had an incurable carcinoma. Here he was a staff member at one of the most advanced medical centers in the world, and even his colleagues gave the hopeless prognosis of his being a terminal case. Since modern medicine was powerless, the Stanford physician took a leap into the unknown and flew to India to see Baba. Baba called his name, identified why he was there, materialized vibhuti, rubbed it on the doctor's back, and then told him to go back home to America. Doctor Thathachari came back from India healed. He electrified his colleagues because no matter how many tests they ran on him, there was no trace of the malignancy at all. And when they heard that a little man in a red robe massaged him in the area, and he started to feel better, there didn't seem to be any textbooks around with any explanations. This was a recent case.

Baba rotated his hand. Casually he held out his fingers as a brilliant ruby appeared. Then holding the gem, he pressed it into the metal where the third eye is allegedly located.

Baba left and the morning session ended.

# Chapter 8

# *A Fork in the Road*

*T*he moment I flowed with the enormous crowd out into the side compound, I saw "the angel" and a girl sitting on the steps outside my old luxury suite. We connected eyes and drew one another like magnets as I sensed their awe and urgency.

Shaking his head with introspective profundity "the angel" proclaimed, "He's God. The minute I saw him I started crying, and all I could say was, 'He's God, He's God. He's God.'" Baba had summoned an interesting apostle, the nephew of the famous thinker and globalist, Marshall McLuhan. His blazing mane of hair reminded me of a fusion of the Archangel Gabriel and the Spirit of Ireland. His name was Kerry and his wife was Janet.

He spoke of Marshall McLuhan as an enzyme of our generation who had predicted the effects of multiplex media on global unity, but who had failed to pierce the spiritual barrier. Kerry guffawed knowingly, "He's still got his ego invested in being an armchair academician." There was a wry brilliance speaking behind Kerry's down-home jargon.

"Well, how did you get from what... Winnipeg?... Canada to here?"

They looked at each other as if to communicate that it was okay to talk. Janet, Kerry's wife, struggled for a starting point. "Well, we didn't exactly hear about Baba, we were guided here."

"How?" I asked hesitantly, sensing that it was only revealed to few. It turned out that Janet was a very powerful channeler!

Kerry explained. "Well, since Janet was around five years old, she's been psychic. She often sees things through an area in her upper visual field, around her forehead. And it can be anytime, anywhere. It's like she had an invisible screen in her mind. In fact we call it the Screen. And these things appear superimposed over the things she normally sees."

Janet broke in, "It really used to scare me sometimes when I was a little girl." She giggled reassuringly. Then proudly held up her head like Judy Garland marching to see the Wizard of Oz. "But I got used to it."

I quickly established common ground, "You know, we've all had to brave an awful lot alone. Everyone tells you you're wrong, but you go ahead anyway following that spool of intuition—maybe that's why so few get through in the end."

They nodded, beaming with smiles. They were also impressed with the fact that I had sporadically astral-traveled from the age of 11—when I got the mumps in London.

A context of innocence colored the dialogue between us. They were apparently "soul mates" who knew it instantly when they happened to bump into each other in London. Theirs had not been a normal marriage as they were attuned to all sorts of spiritual frequencies that intersected their minds. Speaking of their meeting Janet said:

"Well, hmmmm. To start out with we met a few years ago in a London tourist office. It was a close call though. There was a five-minute interlude, and that was it."

Janet's eyes twinkled, "Something just gave Kerry the impulse to step off St. James Street and go in. He wasn't even planning to go into the tourist office. That's all it took. When I saw him and he saw me, our destinies unraveled just like that. We knew we were soul mates immediately."

"After we were married we knew we had to go into the wilderness, and find out who we were. Which also meant extricating ourselves from the psychological game-patterns, and hang-ups of our folks. In all we spent seven bitter cold months in an abandoned cabin in the mountains high above Vancouver. We just stocked up on grain and vegetarian supplies that we got at a surplus depot. It got so each knew what the other felt anytime of day or night. But it went beyond that—Janet and I both had a number of major psychic breakthroughs."

"Then suddenly we were told one day to leave. And that was it for the isolation phase."

One of them would utter something, stop, and the other would continue the sentence on. Kerry continued for a while, "Yup, within several weeks of the order to move on, we were on the way out of the country. We just packed, took care of a few details . . . went through some psychodramas with our families, who've never understood us . . . ."

Janet went on from there, looking up and rolling her eyes with a sigh, "Yeah, never try to play by their ground rules or you lose every time. If you're firm enough, after a while they learn you really mean it."

"At any rate, within several weeks we were in the Greek Isles living in an abandoned house that we got for next to nothing."

"Not to sound like an idiot, but what did you do for money?"

"Oh," they looked at each other as Janet pointed her head at Kerry and said, "He inherited $10,000."

"Finally we were moved on. And that's when things really began to happen. Most of all, we met our spirit guide."

"You see," Kerry interjected, "Janet's kind of a medium. I guess it runs in her family."

"This guy's a spirit. Apparently he has been watching me since I could walk. I guess the best way to describe him is to say that he's an astral master."

"In fact," Janet chimed exuberantly, "He's a full-blooded Cherokee Indian. His name's Red Hawk."

"Well, the real breakthrough was in London when we met this highly developed psychic woman, well known in the inner circles. The upshot of all this is that she finally got some key people together for a secret meeting, all psychics and some of the greatest channelers in England. Conditions apparently were perfect for me to go into a full trance."

Kerry described the rest. "All of a sudden Janet stiffened, the muscles in her body changed, and she looked completely different, like a giant hand in a small glove. She seemed twice the size. Her face was transfigured, she sat up proudly, just like an Indian chief, and when she started talking, it sure wasn't her voice. The whole room shook. It almost blew me under the table. It was the deepest voice I'd ever heard. The lady asked it to identify itself and it said, 'I am Red Hawk.'"

"Well, Red Hawk announced that we were to go to India. That he had been guiding Janet all her life, and that there was someone in India who was higher than a perfect master. But he could not talk about it."

"In one or two days we found a Ford van for about a tenth its market value. We furnished it, and that was our wheels." Kerry chuckled good-naturedly, "Like clockwork we got shots, permits, you name it—we had everything except the route we were supposed to take." Even the smallest details of the trip were channeled through Janet.

"We just started driving. We went through France, Germany, Austria, Yugoslavia, Bulgaria, across to Turkey...then to Iran, Afghanistan. And that's where we were ordered to sell the van, in Kabul. It was almost impossible to get a car permit for India anyway."

"We were told 'turn there-take a right—keep on—stop for the night.' Whatever Red Hawk said to me, we did."

"You were lucky one of the roadside gangs didn't turn you inside out, especially in Afghanistan."

"If something was rumbling up ahead, or if we sensed bad vibes, Janet would usually see a fine spider-web of high energy threads of light, sort of a tent, sitting off the road. We'd just drive right into the enclosed area, so none of the car stuck through. Only Janet could see them. Then we knew we were safe. And in fact nobody ever did bother us, or even appear to notice us for that matter. That was another one of Red Hawk's riggings."

As we were talking suddenly Baba stepped out onto his rear balcony and that ended our talk. Janet gasped, apparently seeing something that she was unable to talk about. She looked up in quiet wonder for a long time, perhaps as a native islander would watch an erupting Krakatoa. When Baba receded, we left in silence, looking for a bite to eat.

## Materializing the Cosmic Sphere

By 4:00, the crowd stretched out along the ground going out a fifth of a mile in front of the Shanti Vedica, Baba's specially built six-sided festival enclosure that resembled a giant Iranian bird cage. It stood in the main compound right out in the open.

Baba then entered the hexagonal chamber from the rear and came into full view. Baba's giant chair glistened with a large silver embossed "OM" ॐ on the upper third of its back. The enclosure was full of wreaths of flowers. Sitting to the right of Baba's chair were the three honored speakers: Sri Nakul Sen, the Governor of the State of Goa; Dr. Gokkak, Chancellor of the University of Bangalore; and one other luminary. They droned on, one at a time, as the crowd waited for Baba to take over.

Baba with absolute poise and control arose and looked across the audience with a broad smile. Someone flicked on the fluorescent tubes, electro-luminescent signs and all. Suddenly the rapidly approaching darkness leapt back from Baba's enclosure. The hexagonal chamber transformed into a celestial arcade.

Tonight, all over India, throughout ashrams and holy cities, the followers of the great Hindu god Siva would be paying homage to him. Siva was the god of destruction and was often portrayed with a half moon in his hair, a trident, sitting ash-covered in the full lotus, and eyes shut deep in samadhi as he sat atop Mount Kailash. Countless millions across India would hold all-night vigils, fasting, meditating, and repeating the names of God. But those across India who realized the avatarhood of Sathya Sai Baba, would dwell on his name and form, singing bhajans to him in family halls, and meditating on him. He was considered to be Siva and Shakti—the male and female principles of the universe combined.

The estimated 20-million-plus devotees of Baba all over India from Assam to Kerala to Simla, all hoped that tonight would bring the greatest boon. That Baba's miracles on this plane would accompany invisible transformations, and bring them across the ephemeral dungeon to eternal life, the Upanishadic *sat-chit-ananda*—the being, consciousness, and bliss of the Absolute. Freed from their painful tragic existences, they would emerge like the monarch butterfly in spring into a state of awareness infinitely more ecstatic than the legendary paradise planes.

Baba's miracles could come anytime, like the uncontrolled spasms of childbirth. And devotees were on the edge of their seats because of this. While either singing, speaking, or just sitting, Baba would exude either one or several egg-sized spheroids from his mouth that had been "growing" inside him, made of precious or semi-precious stone or metal—gold, silver, ruby, lapis lazuli, emerald, topaz, moonstone, or opal. Certainly their size alone would make a normal man unconscious from agony, if pulled up from his stomach and out of his mouth. Years later, America would view such sacred stones in the famous film, *Indiana Jones and the Temple of Doom.*

The Siva lingams were not just breathtaking stone Easter eggs, adored for aesthetic value. They were loaded with significance to every Indian in the land, regardless of caste or sect. They represented the seed-spores of the universe. They were also those muddy little stones around which the ancient nomadic primitives had danced near smoldering embers. The bhakti devotees worshiped them as divine concretizations, touching them as perennial fertility symbols—reciting Vedic hymns of praise dating back thousands of years at any one of the 11 ancient hallowed sites bearing lingams, allegedly planted by Siva himself. But for the Jnanis, rishis, and sages of Advaita, the significance of the lingams jumped from static points in the realm of dualism to causal principles. And Baba had stated this in speeches of years past. They symbolized that point in space-time where all aspects of "relative phenomena" go in and out of physical existences: on one side of the barrier is the illusion of multiplicity—physical, astral, and causal. But through the elliptical creatrix is the vast silent "Static-Eternal." Westerners who were advocates of Martin Buber called it "The Ground of Being," Gill called it "The Void," And Herman called it "Dat Place."

In the yearning adorations of a forlorn lover who has too great an abundance of love to contain, and whose mate is separated and tentative, Baba's voice filled the night air in resonant power through speakers all over his realm. Baba chanted a sloka from the Bhagavad Gita (XVIII-66), stretching his arms like a bird of paradise: Sarvadharman...parit-yajya...mem-ekam...sarnam...vrja. Aham...Tva...sarva...papebhyo. Moksha-yisyami...Maaa...Sucaaaahah....

The melody of the verse resembled the same wistful tune I had heard while in Rishikesh at the Maharishi Mahesh Yogi Ashram. Kasturi later translated the verse as saying, "Renounce all *dharmas* and take refuge in me alone. I will liberate you from all sins; grieve not."

Then Baba began a monsoon flood of highly charged Telugu phrases. Battery after battery inundated the audience. Baba's tone rose in power; at times it resembled snatches of the voice of Hitler in Leni Reijhenstahl's famous propaganda documentary, "Triumph of the Will." Baba "the Lover" had become "the Teacher and Mighty Counselor."

After the speech had extended to 40 minutes, Baba paused, looked at the audience, then fell back in his seat. He looked away, as though hiding great pain. Labor had begun. He convulsed several times, still trying to be as graceful as possible, took sporadic sips of water, and constantly wiped his mouth and forehead with a handkerchief. He hiccuped, winced, held the arm of his chair, and when possible, smiled reassuringly. The smile would then be interrupted by a hiccup or a sip of water.

Raja Reddy, an inner circle disciple who resembled Clark Kent, took over. With crystal presence of mind, he came from behind the scenes to shepherd the crowd by leading the audience in bhajans. He bent forward, only feet away from Kerry and me, eyes squeezed in intense concentration, and vigorously pumped his harmonium in front of a row of microphones. The hand organ rang out and droned, suddenly filling the air of the entire ashram, which was wired from end to end with speakers. Raja flawlessly chanted the opening Sanskrit phrase of one of the bhajans. Then with admirable grace and control, he sang like a speeding charioteer—nonchalant and joyous, yet coiling his energy into a powerful spring, as always, guiding it with great self-discipline. One song praised Baba as Siva, and after each refrain, the audience repeated it with absolute fervor, eyes glued to Baba the whole time.

On the third refrain, the song was barreling along, *Siva, Siva, Siva, Siva, Parti Pureeshwara, Shambho Shankara Sada Sivaaaaa.*

Several songs later, Baba gracefully stood up. Raja immediately brought his songs to a halt, and readied his harmonium to follow whatever Baba was to sing. In sweet, almost defenseless tones, not nearly as demonstrative as the previous opening Sanskrit sloka, Baba chanted the opening of the song. He reminded me of a delicate flower as he sang about Krishna, almost mouthing the words in baby talk, *Chita Chora Yesoda Ke Baal, Navanita Chora Gopal.* The voice was quite beautiful and provocative. That sweetness of character that I felt coming through the songs forced me to repent some of my impressions of Baba the day before in the old mandir. It was suddenly obvious to my now enchanted mind that my suspicions had been a clear case of cultural projection.

Fifteen minutes later, halfway through a refrain, Baba abruptly gagged, as though hit by a sudden wave of uncontrollable peristalsis.

Baba's head jerked in spasms, then he leaned back against the chair to control them. It seemed he was trying to hide the pain, perhaps intense pain. More heartrending were his numerous smiles of reassurance that gently told us not to worry. For us, the beneficiaries, this indestructible man of steel was taking on the infinite torments that we deserved. His grace was covering our "karmic debts."

In a concentrated thrust, Baba pitched forward as though to vomit holding an open handkerchief before him. His head recoiled like a 120-millimeter cannon, and in an explosive gush a brilliant stone, larger than an egg, shot out of Baba's mouth on to the handkerchief.

Finally Baba held the object high so everybody could see it shine and glisten, then set it down on the table in full view, arose, spun around, and quickly left, disappearing into the night. Many of our Western contingent were up most of the night contemplating this act.

## Turning Point

Four days later, in early March, right before Baba was to leave for Whitefield, his other residence in the neighboring state of Mysore, he granted us one last interview. I didn't expect it, but longed for it more than ever. I was completely split down the middle on where to go. With my large suitcase and typewriter in storage at the Kendra in New Delhi, and charter ticket about to expire, I was still going through the motions of leaving the country by the six-month visa deadline.

By the morning of the interview, Gill had already left for Whitefield to reclaim his old cottage where he could meditate in the absolute quiet of a semibarren farm. Herman also had left, by Baba's command, to wait in Whitefield before returning to the "householder's" duty of business and family.

The minute I walked in, Baba grabbed my shoulders, and sat me down in what was now my customary place, to the left side of his chair. Baba addressed many of the stories directly to me, as though we were having a private conversation and were the only two people in the room. Then he would look up and share it with the others. He often slapped me on the back.

After an hour and a half of interview time, we had already been given much. Baba's oozing ecstatic force had surrounded us in a lake of honey, and we were almost reeling from intoxication. Just as we were about to get up and leave, he looked me in the eye and asked, "Private interview? You have questions?" And I did, because I was starting to panic about where to go.

The dark velvet drapes shut behind me and Baba looked searchingly into my eyes. "What do you want?" The question came with the force of a psychic whammy.

On a high precipice of choice, I automatically went through several gearshiftings of awareness.

The problem of staying in India had now disappeared. The priorities were suddenly totally different. I had entered the spiritual marketplace set to bargain over tables and chairs unaware that I had entered an exclusive arena where bids for cities and towns go by almost unnoticed as kingdoms, empires, and dominions balance, then shift, and dance as assemblies of concentrated thought move them across the board like shuffleboard plates.

Something helped me talk. "Baba, I offer you my life as a son, as a servant, for your direction, to have completely and do whatever you will."

As though a covenant had been made, "I am also your property, sir. I am also your servant," Baba replied.

Still nosing up a waterfall like a Canadian salmon, my quest cannot end until the full tribute is consummated. I must acknowledge my deepening faith. "No, Baba. You are *Mahapurusha*, the Lord of the Universe, within that body. You can't fool me. I am your property, your servant. I am you. I want to be an Arjuna, Lord."

We embraced automatically, his wiry cloud of hair surrounding my face. I wondered what kind of deep soul-cleansing was going on. Then huge force surged from Baba to me, almost visibly sparking. "Guru *kripa, shakti paat*, power purification," I thought.

I stood hugging that same unreachable Messiah who stood atop the pagoda, whom tens of thousands came to

see, who often wept, just for a glimpse of or a touch, or a
smile. The same one who sang with such incredible
compassion before miraculously creating the seedpod of
his creative love. A still, musing voice entered my head.
It spoke of great things in the tables of fortune. A prince
is being crowned into life and glory, a once and future
king.

Baba broke the embrace and held me back. "Do you
want a wife?"

Here was one of the truly great pitfalls that had
thrust great seekers and adepts far from the prized goal
of liberation, back, back into the timeless spiral of *maya*.
You were trapped once again and bound to another, as a
householder. What a pathetically dull and ordinary fate
when you have glimpsed the mountain of eternity. To be
bound down financially and emotionally, a slave for yet
another life. And in the next life, would you even remember the wife of your youth in this life? She too would
disappear into the winds of time, spiraling into nothing-
ness with your billion other former wives. Besides, I had
already tasted the fickle transience of romantic love.
That no matter how powerful, given enough time, would
disappear as though it never existed. And you were still
alone.

"Baba, I don't need to get married, do I?"

"No, Rowdie, there is no male or female. In the end,
there is only God."

In accord with each time I had been in the stairwell
with Baba, the "Om" in the neighboring prayer hall, one
cinder-block's thickness away, struck the hour in the
explosive rush of a jet during takeoff. The discussion
about a wife resolved abruptly. Baba had kept me beyond
the magical hour. While 5,000 remnants of the festival
waited in the sun just for a glimpse of him, he was
pouring over me.

Baba reached out to embrace me again, pulling me in
strongly. The musing voice pondered Baba's comment,

"There is no male or female." The embrace of Radha-Krishna, the avatar of the *Dwarka Yuga* and his lover, was the highest resolution of two polarities. And since the avatar was transsexual, his embrace of Arjuna when he appeared as Krishna was roughly equivalent, with everything but the basics taken away. Tradition, the voice reasoned, made Radha-Krishna lovers—it also made Arjuna-Krishna like brothers, or father and son, or teacher and disciple. Arjuna and Radha were both polarities, Krishna was forever the "changeless One without attributes." Now the musing voice likened the embrace with Baba to the meeting of God, and God, breaking the wall of *maya* to merge.

Baba's nudging pelvis stopped. Then suddenly a hand unzipped my fly, with the facile smoothness of turning a doorknob, and went into my pants, as though it knew the location of each stitch of cloth and each zipper stub. Then, like an adder returning home at dusk, the hand burrowed into the mouth of my underpants. I froze, a lump in my throat.

If Truth required these kinds of impossible labyrinths, I had already made my vow to see it through. Some day I would see the overview one way or another. I stood my ground, and tried not to noticeably flinch hoping this touching would end soon. My mind now raced trying to go up the escalator of possibilities of what was really going on.

The voice of reason was getting a little rattled. It began to summon every scrap of my accumulated knowledge and latent intelligence. "When they line you up in an army physical, and check each draftee for hernias, is the doctor trying to homo you or the other draftees, or is he busy trying to make sure that you don't get killed on the front lines? And if Baba is who he claims to be, it is inconceivable that he would stoop to anywhere near the impurity of the average army physician. Obviously if you're not getting married, he may be helping to close up some rather old troublesome doorways. And he may even be sublimating the energy to higher levels. And that can take some Hatha yogis 50 years of concentrated meditation."

Baba's hips continued to shift again as he squeezed an unresponsive organ that had about as much interest in rising up as it desired a bath in liquid helium. It was frozen out, and not even a legion of nude Middle Eastern belly dancers could thaw it out at this point.

Baba's rapid breathing did not exactly register lethargy or unexcitement. The voice of reason proposed, "He's cooling your heat center, and purifying your lower chakra," However Redneck Logic also sat on the judiciary board, mumbling subsurface before I could censor the embarrassing thoughts from leaking out. "Man, I sure hope all that squeezing is purification because if it ain't, Jack—and that's a strange way to be purifying it—you've picked the wrong guy. It'd be a lot easier if you'd just radiate the thing from outside my pants. Somehow it just looks bad the way you're doing it."

With a surge of willpower, rather than blow it by panicking, jumping to conclusions, and consequently pressing the wrong button at critical mass, I let my autonomic system take over, "relax, and float downstream." It can't last long.

But my mind was reeling at a lightning speed. I sensed that part of the test was not merely that I comply, but know positively, and see, the holy in Baba's act. The Indian scriptures had declared repeatedly, "anything done in total purity is without blemish," whether it be wiping a nose or opening the gates of the most holy. Therefore Baba was bearing this out by showing this essential nondifference in all actions and things. Once this teaching was truly believed, one would see the body of God behind a patch of fungus, a dead fly, or a brilliant sandy shore. Parallel to Crane's *Red Badge of Courage*, you still had to be on the front line to finally know what your reaction to killing would be. Otherwise you might armchair philosophize forever, and yet, never know. Baba could ask me, "Do you trust me?" And I might reply, "Of course," forever. But until I was given a wide-open chance to suspect him or question his integrity, the depth of my faith would remain an uncertainty.

A minor voice interceded before it was quelled. "If there is no absolute standard to judge by and anything goes right or wrong, how can you ever fully discern the genuine from the counterfeit? Other than a tenuous airy faith or a look of 'knowing,' what concrete evidence can you ever go by? And how do you know that what you safely label a 'test,' to preserve your faith, is not a slip by the counterfeit spiritual Master?"

Interrupting at top volume in my mind was the voice of an advocate, defending the accused with authority. "Baba himself is the final evidence. His love, his patience, and . . . his miracles. He has consistently demonstrated an innocence, a goodness, and a purity regardless of the audience. Mightier than any president or king, he has not been too proud to feed you or pat you on the back. If you call yourself his property, and he has already told you that he is your property, why do you gladly surrender an arm or a leg, then recoil in horror when he chooses to take an ear or something else? What boldly spoken yet shallow faith. You might find the rigorous demands of discipleship eased, if you don't try to use rational analysis on the inscrutable mind of God. That is treading on hallowed ground." I was checkmated, and in a torrent of confusion.

I knew that even if I were given a thousand years to stand here in the stairwell, I still might not be able to resolve the present dilemma with its delicate balance of facts. Yet it seemed that all eternity rested on this one crucial moment, the moment of my verdict—to either believe in Baba far more than ever, or fall away entirely, and perhaps, remain confused for the rest of my life.

And this made my mind boggle. It was nearly an impossible situation. But suddenly there was a clue to the answer. An impossible situation. Impossible in the sense that it was almost perfectly designed to the last atom to short-circuit my mind. And was this sheerly coincidental? Or was it the ultimate *Zen Koan,* the supreme illusion, contrived by an omniscient cosmic mind, with all the perfect variables lined up, to stretch me to the limit, and break me of numberless habits of belief—of which one of the most fundamental, as basic as salt in my blood, was the conviction that good and evil were absolutes. The eventual critical situation brought about to dispatch this would require the touch of a neurosurgeon, otherwise I might end up like the frog, "at the bottom of the well."

In Zen Buddhism, it is taught that the ideally timed Zen Koan dropped on a pupil by a Zen master, by creating the perfect paradox of contradictions, brought about satori or enlightenment in the disciple by initiating a chain reaction of self-consuming lies. The last lie to short-circuit was the ego, the sense of separateness, and finiteness, leaving nothing less than the infinite to take its place. But now that I was balancing on a high-wire the risks seemed enormous.

I would either see the impossibility and contradiction in the very idea of Baba's having homosexual lust—the leap toward liberation—or the old habits of belief would win in the end. And I would dismount on a desolate halfway point of metaphysical confusion, perhaps doomed to wander into deeper spiritual labyrinths, with not a reference point on the horizon. Indeed, the stakes were frightening.

But the agitation remained. Baba showed every pant, every tremor of arousal. Why?

"Part of the props for the total existential dilemma," came the answer. How else, other than by the perfect situational dilemma, an art-work of circumstance to the very last stage prop, could my most ingrained beliefs be challenged? My thoughts flowed quickly through a breaking stress point; the situation here is a contradiction. He's using the thorn to remove the thorn. Good stacked over evil like a staircase to walk beyond them, where opposites merge, the new reference point.

The impasse breaks more; my belief in Baba's deity begins to overweigh superficial appearances. Too much at stake, too much to forfeit ... it can't end in a shoddy little stairwell with a queer, not after all this, the years, the pieces stacked up. He can't be a queer ... impossible ... impossible. I have got to believe in him. The only way is forward, I have to follow him in blind faith. That's the answer.

The balance tips faster; of course—blasphemous accusations fading—lust contradicts Baba's nature. Therefore it does not exist in him. He cannot sin, because it is not in him to do so. Blind faith, a new generalized optimism enters the horizon. The verdict—

Baba is innocent. A mounting sense of victory replaces the mental weight that had almost overwhelmed me with stellar force. After my decision, I feel changed in some way. Altered. My will, reason and emotions were at war, they all had to be unified. Somehow they worked it out. "What's the fastest thing in the universe," Mephistopheles is asked. "A thought," he replies. "When the will turns from good to evil."

The boundary around my personality or mind no longer feels impermeable, like a protective shield or a one-way membrane. Something has been pierced. It is semiporous; a sensation akin to fasting, or a fever, or an alkaloid hallucinogenic, or a lung full of Acapulco gold. Partially gone is that vestigial thermostat of duality, the puritanical conscience, forever hung-up on two-dimensional interpretations. In its stead, a heady sense of freedom, a mellow exuberance. I am not more alive, necessarily, nor particularly more lucid. In fact gone is some of that former sharp edge of emotional sensitivity, or hypersensitivity. But there is now nothing to fear. My legs continued to shake nervously. I had not responded to Baba. Baba removed his hand from my pants and zipped my fly. The entire dilemma had lasted about half a minute. And I had not responded. It wasn't so bad, I thought, echoing those first words after once bravely receiving my first hypodermic injection as a very small child. This moment I would lock in an inner vault deep in my mind not to be opened for a year and a half.

Smiling proudly, slightly flushed, Baba said, "Very happy. Go now." He waved with familial informality. And I passed through the curtains, stone-faced as 20 eyes, consumed with curiosity, looked up.

The rest of the private interviews with Baba were just token meetings, the curtains half-open the whole time. They sped by in about five minutes for everybody.

As the others filtered outside, I remembered, "Oh, Baba. Do you want me to go to Whitefield?" realizing the absurdity and needlessness of the question.

Amazed that I could think otherwise, "Of course, sir, of course. You stay with me in Whitefield. You are near and dear."

Consistent with my pledge of turning my life over to him, "But Baba, my stuff is in New Delhi. It may take several weeks to go there by train and get my bags..."

"Go tomorrow. Then come to Whitefield, Brindavanam. Then many interviews and lessons in sadhana for all foreigners. I will train you."

Baba's car left that night. That next morning, Jai, Michelle, and I left on the 5:00 A.M. bus to Bangalore City. Both of them had diarrhea and mild fever. I was deep in a new level of silent contemplation. Our parting agreement, once in Bangalore City, was that they were to find a house which we would all share together, and I would join them in late March.

# Chapter 9

# *Choosing the Kingdom*

After a 50-hour train ride from Delhi to Madras on one of India's huge steam locomotives, I felt like a character in a Rudyard Kipling novel in old British India with my feet out of the window. Coal-dust and smoke blew through our train car, fiery hot curries were served by turbaned waiters, monkey packs roamed village stations, and we clickety-clacked along a stretch of track in Maharashtra that transformed the train into a cast-iron oven on wheels. My mind went deep into the mystery of Baba as India's timeless terrain passed by. After a brief night at the Madras YMCA, I was on the final hub of the journey on another train, the "Brindavan Express," India's fastest, most modern train, which sped from Madras to Bangalore. "Where's Whitefield? I asked the conductor, hoping the train might stop at this local town only 13 miles from the city of Bangalore. "We are coming to it just now.... No, the express has no stops on the way."

The terrain of the state of Madras was parched and arid as ancient temple stupas periodically loomed into the sky. But Mysore was shining much greener, true to its reputation. For over a hundred miles, we had passed Mysore rice paddies, verdant thickets of palm trees in lush semitropical settings, wells, and primitive rural villages with water buffaloes and bare-chested peasants. I pressed my face up to the glass as Whitefield blazed by in a flash. It left only scanty afterimages in my mind of mango sellers kneeling in the road, a nondescript rail depot, scant trees, dirt paths and roads, monkey packs, a walled-in compound on one side, and a modern factory on the other. "Sai Ram," somebody uttered. We had just passed near Baba's compound, but I could not remember anything standing out. Technically, neither it nor the "Whitefield railway station" were in Whitefield. They were in Kadugodi, a tiny village. The old British farm community of Whitefield was several miles down the road, vacated of its days of glory since independence.

An hour and a half later I was back, riding in a three-wheeled auto-rickshaw from Bangalore, India's most modern and upbeat city.

Contrasting with the primeval wilderness of Puttaparthi, the Bangalore region exuded the spirit of contemporary progressive India. Meanwhile, Baba's residence had once been the summer home of the king of Nepal, and was quite impressive. It was called "Brindavan" and had several acres of well-kept garden in the rear. Within it, and separated by a gate and drive, was a two-storied stucco house with the distinct architectural flavor of a rambling oceanside home in California, complete with circular frosted windows of colored glass, a front drive-in porch, bougainvillaea and all. The remaining half of the compound was divided between the school and the public. Trees were plentiful, providing comfortable shade for devotees sitting on various walkways.

The minute I left my bags with the Gurkha guard at the gate, Sai Baba came out for morning darshan. In fact he had already been by the main Banyan tree, and was heading back to the house via the school. As he was inspecting a wing of the academy, Baba saw me squatting playfully behind a hedge. I was testing him, humorously.

His rasping voice joked with a few who closely followed him. The rest of the crowd stood back 40 feet. "Come, Rowdie." I felt a trifle embarrassed as I stood up in sudden plain view, walking out into the open sunlight where he stood.

As hundreds looked on, he grabbed my shirt sleeve, and said in my ear, "Tell the other Americans that tomorrow there will be a private dinner and a school-day festival. Krishna play, singing, and speeches. You are invited, sir." Before I ran off in exuberance, Baba tugged my sleeve again. "Invite fat man with glasses . . . and . . ." He went on to name or describe everybody except Kerry and Janet.

Later that afternoon, a pensive Kerry and Janet told me that for the past two weeks Baba hadn't been paying them much attention. He had held morning interviews with Jai, Michelle, Herman, and a small middle-aged group from California, who had flown in for several weeks, but no one else from our group had been included. I told them to persist, and that the tide would change.

By the next afternoon, the tide hadn't changed. They came to Baba's house along with the rest. But I wondered if it hadn't somehow been a bad gamble to encourage their coming. It was a fascinating event, and again, Baba singled me out for attention.

From March 20 until late April, we went to the daily darshans, heard a few words from Baba, and then went home till the afternoon darshan. Our days became like clockwork, as we relished each word spoken by Baba and every little intuition, dream, or psychic experience that any of us had. The program of gradual consciousness expansion was underway. We had all come for enlightenment, and we were in the presence of the most powerful figure on earth, as far as we were concerned.

As I told our whole group, even a single word from him was "extra gravy."

Meanwhile the days lumbered by at our little house as we arose at 5:00 (the guys sleeping in the walled-in stone courtyard and the girls in a room inside), fixed tea, meditated, dressed, and by 8:30, headed toward the ashram. The hut was without a stick of furniture, so cooking was done by kerosene stove on the floor, as was eating, sleeping, and sitting. Water was hauled up out of the local village well down the path, and kept in a large earthenware storage bin outside in the courtyard. Some of it was used for cooking, some for bathing—(the old rusty tin-can routine), and some for cleaning our toilet, a cement hole in the floor of the courtyard stall. For those of us sleeping outside, the courtyard latrine didn't really matter because the rest of the neighborhood smelled so bad that we really couldn't tell the difference.

As we entered the Bangalore summer in April, the tin-can routine no longer worked. So we stopped for a cold shower on the way to darshan at the railway depot, and on the way back. Even this didn't prevent sunstroke. Vickie, the tall pretty English blonde, had it on and off for weeks at a time, and I came close to getting it several times. Walking that half mile became a painful chore. We would cover our heads with white cloths and dance in and out of the shade to avoid the burning rays of South India's merciless equatorial sun. There is nothing like it.

At the same time, my body was not adapting to a vegetarian diet very well. I felt hard put to do almost anything physically. And to subsist on the food that we cooked for ourselves was no pleasant thought. It was all bruised, tiny, insect-wasted vegetables that had been irrigated with open polluted drain water. Anthony and I bought these vegetables in the hot, dust-swept village market, where people missing eyes and hands crouched in the dust, and haggled over stacks of stuff on burlap rags dirtier than the garbage cans of New York City. And after we boiled these things, to kill anything from amoebas to tapeworm eggs, there was nothing left but tasteless mush.

Kerry and Janet, renting a decrepit room in the row of rooms across from Brindavan, solved their food problem by hiring a manservant to do the cooking, which was a common practice in India.

Understandably, our one big relief from the squalor of Kadugodi was the hour-long bus ride into Bangalore, the famed progressive capital of Mysore with its unlittered streets, wide roads, and modern storefronts. Along Brigade or Mahatma Gandhi Road, there were all sorts of Indo-European restaurants. Our favorite was a snack bar called Nilgiri Dairy, a modern, inexpensive milk bar where the educated middle class and the college set hung out.

What inevitably followed our Bangalore trips was an ensuing interest in bookstalls and shop-windows, like the proverbial line of crumbs before a chicken. It usually took about a second in the darshan-line on the driveway for Baba to look into our eyes and know where we had just been. "Enjoying tourist trips? Too much sweets is not good."

Gill was the only one who roughed it through all the way, hanging on with the willpower that would pale a lobster. He almost never went into town except over visa matters. He lived alone in a cabin several miles down the main road from Brindavan toward Whitefield. Which meant a four-mile walk in the fierce sun to and from Brindavan. After walking for a week, Gill rented a bike. The cabin itself was down a long winding path on what was once an English farm, but was now as bleak as something out of *The House of Seven Gables*, belonging to an old Anglo-Indian woman named Mrs. Blake. When Gill wasn't at darshan he was meditating all hours of day or night. Since no one cooked his food, and he didn't trust "restaurants," and didn't want to bother cooking himself, his diet was restricted to fruits and melons that he bought along the road on the way to and from Brindavan.

Even if the heat made me delirious, and close to nausea, after walking less than a mile, still Gill's ghostly form in headdress and wraparound could be seen shuddering in the distant heat waves far off down the main road as he walked in sandals on the scorching tar. Early April was one of the hottest times even for the elevated Bangalore district which was known for its relatively temperate weather compared with the rest of South India. Soon, though, the monsoon rains would come, cooling everything down to the seventies and eighties and filling Brindavan with aromatic smells while thoroughly washing the tired arid ground. We couldn't wait for them.

On April 20, Baba called a halt to our obvious agony of adapting to village India in the heat. In one of the few interviews we had en masse, Baba revealed what happened the previous night to one of our people, a German, who couldn't even open his mouth he was so amazed that Baba knew. As Baba told the story in detail, Benno's eyes opened in amazement. Referring to the fact that India, Marsha, Hans, and Benno (who had arrived at Prasanthi Nilayam at the tail end of Mahasivaratri) had spent the last few weeks sleeping under one of the large trees on the main road outside Brindavan, Baba said, "Not a good idea...too many dangers, thieves, beggars...sometime rain coming down. No place to leave luggage, no privacy, not good." Indicating his pleasure in the spirit of their persistence and self-denial, Baba nodded his head with pride and commented, "Not even my Indian devotees take such chances, put up with hardships, they are too attached. And you come from much higher standard of living."

Then Baba revealed exactly what had happened the night before.

"Last night he loses some money. All that he had, 93 rupees." Benno shook his head in amazement. "At 3:00 A.M., thief puts hand in money purse, and quietly takes. Then he wakes up and looks around, but it is too late." Baba went on to tell details of the story. At the end, he had Benno as a permanent disciple. "Don't worry, I will get you your 93 rupees. Whatever is mine is yours, your property . . . this house, these gardens, anything." And Baba looked to all of us and continued, "You have personal needs, just ask, that is why I am here. Don't be afraid, you need money? Ask."

"Now too many foreigners; foreigner means fore-near . . . near and dear. Now, school is closing, you come and stay here at Brindavan." Baba looked down at me and said, "Living in Kadugodi! Dirty, noises, smells, not good for meditation. Now I will open two large school rooms, there you stay. Males in one room, females in the other. Now 17 Americans, too many people. After interview, get all your belongings and come here tonight."

After a month and a half dry spell for the group, as far as Baba's attention went, now the flood was back on again. Both Gill and I had already had two devastating interviews. One, a private one, was so mind-boggling that I didn't talk to anyone about it. I just knew with a quiet assurance that with Baba I was more or less equivalent to a first-century apostle of Christ. Gill wasn't around for that private one—I was in line after him, and the last one to leave, and the only one totally alone with Baba.

I could now feel my annoyance at Gill mount as he moaned at the mention of having to move in with the group. Somehow it was beneath him. He protested several times, and Baba had to finally tell him sternly enough that it was his will that Gill move in.

———

Baba whispered something sweetly in his ear, and Gill muttered an obscenity. I wanted to smash him so hard in the face that he'd never be able to move his mouth again. Baba apparently didn't hear the comment, or allowed it to go by him through sheer divine mercy, I wasn't sure which. Later I found out from Anthony, since he was the only one Gill confided anything to, that apparently the night before he had had another frightening fight (while disembodied) with a demon from the void, and that it almost killed him. He was scared and wanted to know when it would end. Baba uttered, according to Gill, a pat meaningless phrase in his ear.

The air crackled in silent hostility toward Gill as the group began to wonder if he was anything more than a large spoiled baby putting on some kind of a tremendous show. The others, like me, were ignorant of his astral heroics with the demon.

Baba for ten minutes talked about the divine reaching out for man, and man, the *jiva*, reaching up for God during his spiritual evolution. He likened it to a stalagmite and a stalactite in a cave growing to meet one another in the middle to form a column.

"I'll show you." The air began to hum. Baba leaned forward with his sleeve rolled up, and spun his open palm around in giant circles. There was a huge flash of power. All 17 of us in the room rocked, as Baba's hand began to quiver like a tuning fork. Then as something flickered into visibility in the palm of his hand, he closed his hand to catch it. He opened his hand, holding a large smooth stone about an inch and a half long. He passed it to three people to look at. Then Baba asked for it again, held it up to his mouth, all the time holding it between his thumb and forefinger, then blew on it, and turned it around for all of us to see. There was a large hole where he had blown. As Baba passed it around, he explained that the two cones almost touching in the hole, was like his relationship to us.

Baba gave the stone to Gill, who accepted it in apologetic gratitude. As the interview ended, Baba materialized a large lump of *Mysore Pak*, a type of Indian fudge, and handed it out. Then he brought in a box of mangoes, and gave one to each of us.

For the next two weeks, we felt the full force of undeserved grace as we went up to Baba's house almost every day to have a group interview. This was a total of over ten interviews, averaging two hours apiece, an unprecedented rate for anyone, considering that this well surpassed the average quota of interviews per lifetime of even the closest devotees. Afraid of our squandering such a gift, I got into the habit of recording key points as I sat next to Baba's chair. Later I would type them up and hand out several copies.

Now that the faucet of grace was on again the days soared by. We got more attention each day than the entire previous month. Accentuating this was the recent quiet within Brindavan. The compound was locked up with the mid-April school holidays in effect, which left only us, Baba, Baba's staff, and the Gurkha guard. We were beginning to feel as though we owned the place, especially since we had been given free reign over the entire grounds, except for Baba's house inside.

We arose each morning at 4:30 or 5:00, washed under the cold taps in the public lavatories, then meditated on the porch. By 7:00 we cooked breakfast, a porridge called *soojie*, and tea, in a bare room next to the Gurkha guard's quarters. And by 9:00 most of us were out waiting for morning darshan. Some of us in the male section lingered behind for Baba's room inspection. The usual three of us who weren't so blown out by his private appearance as to be incommunicado were Anthony, Gill, and myself. Baba would often spend 15 or 20 minutes with us, revealing facts about the various "holy personages" on our puja table, or telling puns and jokes, stabbing us in the belly with a finger. Or he might tiptoe in to catch us off guard. If Gill was meditating, Baba might tweak his ear making him jump. Gill's enraged face would then discover the embodiment of his meditations, Baba, and his face would soften. This exclusive clowning was the envy of the crowd outside which would stand motionless, all eyes and ears.

## Baba Reveals Hidden Truths

On May 7, Baba gave us our tenth interview within two weeks to "recharge batteries" since he was going to Bombay for a few days. He said May 7 was an auspicious day for us to be with the world savior.

Sai Baba hadn't called in the rishis or the pundits of India, but the foreigners camping out in the school building. He was revealing occult secrets that went back to before Nimrod built the tower of Babel. We were hearing it all from the Power Source, infinitely more powerful than any leader of an esoteric group or channeler. The sort of stuff that one day would drive Shirley MacLaine wild with amazement wouldn't even qualify as a door opener here. MacLaine and other New Age leaders might eventually talk about Baba in *Out On a Limb* and other well known books, but we had made it to the real source in person and now lived in his presence.

Baba spoke as I rested my arm on the armrest of his chair and looked up at him. "The position of the earth, the orbit of the sun, the stars in the heavens now converging for the first time in many thousands of years. Some seven thousand years. Today is the day of the seven rishis, the seven oceans, the seven planes, the seven rays of light."

We were deluged with the mysteries behind numerology and astrology and references that were fleeting and hard to interconnect.

Gratitude alone brought mercy and grace from the God-man, not austere works. Gill was used as the reference to an impatient yogi whose remaining lives were as the leaves on a neem tree. To the gracious yogi a spiritual master could give him the special boon of picking the leaves off the tree. The aspirant would not need to go through all those lives. We hoped Gill got the point.

Then Baba spoke of the secrets of meditation such as visualizing fire at the third eye, then going beyond form altogether. Those who were still hung up on images could meditate on his own form or that of Rama or Krishna, it didn't matter. Village India was full of such dualists. But beneath it all were the parallels of physiological transformation within the body to prepare it for the high voltage of enlightenment. When this happened the secret *sushumna* passage would open within the spinal cord sending the ancient Kundalini Serpent power through the seven chakra power centers along the spine as one became enlightened; here was the mysterious secret of the ancient Sekurati tree, the tree of wisdom in the Kabbala. For wasn't the nervous system like a cosmic Banyan tree? And have we not fallen from our neurological estate, misfiring our engines and thinking like toads? We were like primitives hauling around a rocket car hitched to a bullock cart when all we needed to do was turn the key.

The mystery of the Kundalini had always enthralled me. In it lay the secrets of yogic power and miracles. Baba illustrated the reality of what he had been teaching. We realized that perhaps none alive in the world apart from Baba were in a position to do this. Baba materialized rings for all the ladies then metallic pictures of himself for all the men from his cosmic dimestore. For truly, as Kalki might do, there was indeed a

dimestore quality to these items, all part of his *leela.*
Leela is the Sanskrit word for God at play in his realm of
created illusion. On leaving, Baba tossed out the best
golden Bombay mangoes imaginable. No one could
doubt that we had been to Vaikuntha, or Brahma Loka,
all ancient Sanskrit words for heaven.

Baba stood at the door to teach us a Vedic prayer. In
the same sweet yearning refrains, Baba sang into the
night air of Brindavan, just as he did before the thousands at the Mahasivaratri festival, using different
words as we left the interview.

*Asatho maa sad gamaya* (from untruth lead me to
truth). *Thamaso maa jyotir gamaya* (from darkness lead
me to light).

*Mrythyor maa amritham gamaya* (from death, lead
me to immortality).

When Baba's Fiat, driven by Raja Reddy, pulled out of
the compound the tempo of things slowed down. I was
amazed how dead things were in comparison now that
the faucet seemed off. Yet how could Baba's spirit in any
way be localized, I pondered?

Many of us headed into Bangalore on protein binges.
Jai always managed to make himself scarce as we got to
Brigade Road. Jai finally unburdened his heart and
revealed where he had been going on the sly for some
time now. "There's this fat guy on the otha parta town
called Siva Bala Yogi, and he's a Kundalini power yogi,
who meditates all day long. Well, since it's respectful to
give homage to enlightened beings, I decided to go by
and see him. Anyway . . . ." The story went on like a CIA
tape as both Michelle and I raised eyebrows, now com-
prehending why Baba had looked strangely at Jai in the
interview. I made my disdain for Siva Bala Yogi no
secret.

Baba had been molding me into the position of being
the leader of the Western contingent. I felt responsible
for Jai. I told him, "You go after meditative zap-outs like

an eel sucking on a broken power cable. And you've got the brains of an ant when it comes to discerning the relative values of all these things." Jai had just informed me that one of Bala Yogi's miracles was to sit in samadhi, and generate such mind-warping power that he could say nothing, and within five minutes have a garden of 300 people dancing around and babbling, some hanging on branches like "Hanuman." Jai was choosing a small-time local guru over a global avatar and with contempt I could see the writing on the wall as far as his future with Sai Baba went.

The only hassle with Gill occurred at 4:30 A.M. in the men's dorm. Gill, who almost used to howl if a fly made too much noise, finally began raving at Jai for doing his most complex and elaborate power-breathing—a seven-stage affair that sounded like a locomotive—taught to him by Hilda Charlton who, in turn, learned it from some avadhut super-yogi when she was in India. Jai finally moved out on the porch, but could still be heard a block away. Meanwhile, I was looking for Gill to slip, so that I could jump on him.

By the time Baba's car returned on May 20, we were ecstatic. During the days, the schoolboys who comprised the school band filled the air with wailing trombones, tubas, cymbals, flutes, and fluttering drums (the same squad that marched the procession down Baba's drive on the school-day festival). Their rehearsals drove us close to the edge at times as we tried to meditate in silence. The more ambitious they became the more hideous a cacophony filled the air, as they progressed from Sousa Marine Corps marches to Midwest high school football rah-rahs, from fox trots, and romance songs from *The King and I*, to "The Stars Fell on Alabama." It became "cosmic high camp."

Now that Baba was back, the band tried even harder, creating impossible flute solos that fluttered in the air, then fell with a gronk. Ultimately the scenario was

perfect for a confrontation between Gill and me. At
10:00 one morning, while I was writing, Gill yelled
something in the air about the way I coughed (I was
plagued with recurring tonsil trouble). The room cleared,
and five minutes later, there was a "roar-out" between
us that could be heard a block away. At first I let him
blow it with a rapid-fire dialogue fit for the Santa Barbara "Angels." I stared at him with a cinder-block gaze.
Then, still holding my cool, I told him that the very fact
that he could curse betrayed that beneath his usual look
of austere reverence was a fundamental twist in personality that indicated that he had lost sight of the true
path light-years back—that he was playing games with
himself, and copping out of the responsibility to love by
going through all kinds of yogic heroics—better he
should start anew and learn humility, love, and self-
control. He started yelling again, and finally I snapped.
There was a standoff, eyes glaring, nose to nose, and I
swore that if I saw his arm move I'd blast him so hard in
the center of face, he wouldn't know what hit him. After
another minute of twitching deadly silence, "Shotgun
Mountain" Gill snorted, turned around, got under his
mosquito net, and continued meditating, as though
nothing had happened. I took a long walk, immediately
coming face to face with the girls scampering around the
kitchen area, pale-faced, and talking in whispers. They
seemed to sympathize with me the most, knowing that I
was usually the cheerful peacemaker. I told them that
somebody had to keep Gill in line, knowing that his
sensitive system had gotten a dose of aggression that he
hadn't seen for a long time, and that it would be simpler
for him not to insist on living by the gun.

The next day Baba came by for room inspection and
informed me that we should all go up to the house after
darshan to hear about his tour. We were electrified as we
sat around Baba in his large living room. Baba's story
was so impressive that we wondered what he was doing

even spending a minute of his time with us. After giving us a photograph album given him by the press, he flipped through the pages and recounted the main events. He also gave us a large stack of glossy photos, some of them of himself before crowds of 70,000 as at the Bombay stadium. Instead of talking down to us, as practically anybody would with a reception like that, Baba amazed us even more by speaking with the unself-conscious joy of one family member to another, never allowing the conquests to get in the way.

After chartering a private plane to Jamnagar in Gujarat State, and being received at the palace of the Rajamata of Nawanagar with a full honor guard and police band, Baba proceeded on the next day to Dwarka, the legendary birthplace of Krishna, where thousands awaited him at the famous Krishna temple. After blessing it, he drove back to Jamnagar with a huge motorcade, stopping on the sandy shore of Kuranga. As the crowd followed him, he collected shells, walked along the water's edge, and finally sat down.

"Krishna temple, too much peoples, very few have darshan of Krishna, so give special darshan." With a crowd of many hundreds looking on, Baba described how he sat on a completely foreign beach, heaped up a cubit of sand, flattening it on top, and then drew a pattern on top: first a three-slanted line, then a circle on top, a small triangle over that, and then a short line across the circle, symbolical of Krishna. After announcing, "It's ready," Baba stuck his hand in the mound, and pulled out a sparkling 15-inch solid gold statue of Krishna. To be sure, the picture of the miracle was in all the local papers, announcing that the idol was far too large for someone as tiny as Baba to smuggle, and the chances of finding something preplanted on a beach he's never been to in his life amid a giant milling crowd was highly unlikely, especially the way he had moved so freely across the acres of faceless sand. As they were about to leave, Baba asked the awe-filled chauffeur his favorite god-form. As he mentioned "Amba-Bhavani," Baba waved his hand, creating a gold plate with the picture of the deity on it.

The second great event was a visit by Baba to one of the most hallowed grounds in India, the Somnath temple, established in 200 A.D. and, at one time, the richest temple in India. After many foreign invasions, the temple was rebuilt a number of times. The final building was started in 1947, and called Mahameru Prasad, the Hindu equivalent of Saint Peter's in Rome or the Blue Mosque in Istanbul.

Before a titanic crowd, Baba mounted the inner sanctuary after being received by the temple trustees and high officers of the district and state. Then amid Karnatic temple horns, Baba went along a red carpet, opened the silver door, and proceeded along the festooned pathway lined with banana trees toward the main shrine of Someshwar. There is no other figure or guru alive in India today who would have received this sort of honor, not by a long shot. And this included Muktananda, Rajneesh, Maharishi Mahesh Yogi, and virtually every other famous Eastern figure in the West.

As Baba entered the "holy of holies," while Brahmin pandits recited Vedic hymns, Baba directed that a silver tray be brought to him. He opened his empty palm, held it over the plate, and instantly materialized a stream of 108 silver bilva leaves, and then 108 gold flowers. In turn, Baba poured these upon the three-foot lingam of the temple (inaugurated by the Indian president, Rajendra Prasad), to revitalize the "new" lingam; the original lingam, as mentioned in the *Skanda Purana*, existed thousands of years ago, an egg-sized object, as bright as the sun and self-originating. And, according to legend, was originally installed by Brahma himself and worshiped by the moon-god, as well as being the first of

the 12 sacred lingas of light that every Hindu is expected
to learn and recite.

Before some of the highest priesthood of the land,
Baba waved his hand to fulfill his promise that before
he left, he would restore the original "Sowrashtra So-
manatha." Instantly there appeared a brilliant ball of
light in Baba's hand. Baba claimed that he had brought
it up from its ancient hiding place underground (as it
was never to be seen), under the shrine of the present
linga. Later the priests and trustees confirmed this fact
regarding its legendary location. Then Baba materialized a solid silver stand, gave it to the chief priest,
and announced, "Let it remain in the full light of day for
pious eyes to worship. The avatar has come to remove all
fear." Before leaving, Baba unfurled the temple flag
that towered over the central shrine, as the huge crowd
shouted "Jai Bhagavan" ("Victory to God"—*Bhagavan*
being the highest name...far above Rishi, Mahatma,
Avadhuta, Shankaracharya, Swami, Paramhamsa, etc.,
...only given an incarnation of God, an avatar).

We left the darshan room in dazed wonder, as I flipped
through the photo-album Baba had given me. Later we
got to pick and choose the glossy photos between us,
feeling luckier every moment that we had sustained this
casual relationship with Baba. All this privilege while
his countrymen were aware of his unapproachable splendor.

Several days later one of Baba's Indian servants ran
up to me. The youth strained to pronounce an English
word. It turned out to be a name, "Gill Locks." Baba
wanted to speak to Gill Locks. Arming myself for another roar-out, I went up to Gill and informed him. The
response was amused incredulity, "Baba's never known
my name, everything else, yes, but never my name." I
defended Baba's "omniscience," yet all I could recall
tangibly were Baba's descriptive reference to people,
never names. With the older American devotees, yes,

but I had never heard one of our names mentioned before except maybe mine. A message soon followed saying that Baba wanted to see all of us the next afternoon.

After an hour with Baba that next afternoon, Baba briefly left the room and returned with a computerized card, and handed it to Gill who exclaimed, "Good God, Swami, you couldn't have done that...there's no way that thing could have gotten here by now. Why, I just mailed off my claim a few days ago. How the..." Then Gill noticed that the card from the San Francisco branch of the Bank of America happened to have "today's date stamped on it!" He then exclaimed, "There's no way that thing could have gotten from San Francisco to Bangalore City, South India, within an eight-hour stretch." Not even a private Phantom Jet F-104 hijacked from the Strategic Air Command could clock that sort of time. In fact by ordinary air mail, Gill's claim should only now just be arriving at the San Francisco Bank, and then there is usually up to a week's computer back-up to go through, at least according to the Bangalore branch, which was unable to replace Gill's stolen traveler's checks. This was something that a stage magician could not do, not with the technology of the day.

"Baba, how'd you get it through the computer so fast?"

Baba replied, "I have the whole world in the palm of my hand. Divine will, space, and time are no obstacle to Swami."

After handing out a basketful of prime Bombay mangoes, Baba broke the news that there would be no need for interviews as we were to start coming to his house for "private bhajan" when he had them. It wasn't possible, we knew, for devotees to get much more intimate with Baba, short of being actual houseguests, and almost nobody had ever done that. Before we left, the girls had a surprise that they thought they would spring, a dinner invitation to Baba. Which he accepted!

During the dinner Baba pointed to Gill and me, who sat in the very center of the circle right in front of him. It was time to iron out some group chemistry. Perhaps Gill and I had some "bad karma" from past lives, maybe a shoot-out in Dodge City somewhere in the spirals of time. Baba described Gill and me, "Mutt and Jeff... the team captains... the lion and the tiger... like an angry couple." Baba threw a few more jibes our way, making me feel embarrassed, amused, and complimented. Then Baba went on to build us up in the eyes of the others, saying that we were basically two yogis, very sincere and dedicated, indeed, two very high souls on the verge of reaching the final goal.

As Baba casually arose to leave, he dropped another bomb on us on his way out the door. "The school principal will need classrooms. School holiday ends in a few days, then school starting. Where to put the Westerners?" As we stood with mouths dropping over the bad news, Baba answered his rhetorical question, "Kadugodi not a good idea for meditations, too much noise, too much dirt. I know," his eyes lighting up. "Starting tomorrow, all Americans move into my house."

# Chapter 10

# *The Cost of Privilege*

*I*n mid-June we moved into Baba's private residence. At night, the girls either spread their bedding on the back porch or on the floor of Baba's private bhajan hall.

The males were given a large room for private quarters. We also had a downstairs side-room off the living room where we could read, meditate, store luggage, and sleep. Most of us chose to sleep on Baba's rooftop patio where at night we could gaze into the mysteries of the black heavens above and feel the cool aromatic breeze from the gardens and orchards, all as cosmic reminders of the unique privilege and mystery of being allowed to sleep only yards away from the rooftop domicile of the world's living God-on-earth. Who millions sought a distant glimpse of we encountered casually as members of his household.

As we had been attending bhajans for over a week, prior to moving into Baba's house, some of the Sanskrit word patterns of the ancient hymns were beginning to be identifiable to me. Those of us Baba insisted should sit along the front row would be picked randomly by Baba to sing what he had memorized so far of any given bhajan. After one of us had led a phrase, the others would repeat it after a brief pause.

Any mistake made by one of the singers was invariably seized upon by Baba as an object of humor, where the accent, the tempo, or the manner would be mimicked. Gill once said in Ananthapur that when Baba is at Brindavan, he's more like Krishna but at Puttaparthi you begin to see his power and awesomeness, as he becomes impersonal again.

Baba let the ladies battle it out as to who would sing. When Baba himself starting singing, the girls would sigh, as he would carry off the most complicated voice warbles. At one time he did a highly skilled 20-minute ballad of Ram's wedding—interchanging the parts of the characters, and singing with remarkable speed and agility, while defining complicated beats with the clackers. Not only was it flawless, but the melody was beautiful, with dashes of regal splendor and long romantic refrains. By the end of it the women's side was leaning forward starstruck, like the "Girls of Saint Trinians" watching Rudolph Valentino.

Through the the rest of the week, we continued to have bhajans with Baba every night.

As the days passed there was a mutual reconciliation between Gill and me. On another occasion Baba met us in the side room, joked for a while, and suddenly asked, "Where is that fat yogi?" Jai had missed several bhajans as well as a number of private meetings like this and my patience was wearing out. "Baba, Jai is in Bangalore." Baba replied with irritation, "Very confused, looking here, looking there—hurting himself." Baba introduced us to his tailor who was sitting in our side room at a foot-driven sewing machine and making scores of Baba gowns.

Suddenly Baba commanded everybody, including the tailor, out onto the front porch. With hands on hips, and chewing a betal leaf, Baba told the tailor jibingly, "Measure all the Rowdies." By the end of the day, Baba called out our numbers, and we marched up to receive a pair of striped pajamas. We put them on and stood in a row to be inspected by Baba—as Gill remarked, "This is the funkiest thing I've seen yet." It was an old maxim that the humor of a perfect master is free to break any convention or boundary anytime. It can seem silly, even perverse.

A couple of days later, I was alone in the side room sitting on the couch. While the tailor was humming away making bright red Baba gowns, I read a Bible that I had picked up from one of the Bangalore bookstores. I was into Saint John's Revelation, but managed to carefully avoid the rest. After just having read about "Faithful and True" wearing a "blood red robe" and riding a white horse (a lot of us had discussed Baba's being the Kalki Avatar, tenth incarnation of Vishnu who would appear in the Kali Yuga (age of wickedness) riding a white horse and wearing blood red), I focused on chapter 13.

Then I saw another strange animal, this one coming out of the earth, with two little horns like those of a lamb but a fearsome voice like the Dragon's. He exercised all the authority of the Creature whose death-wound had been healed, whom he required all the world to worship. He did unbelievable miracles such as making fire flame down to earth from the skies while everyone was watching. By doing these miracles, he was deceiving people everywhere. He could do these marvelous things whenever the first Creature was there to watch him. And he ordered the people of the world to make a great statue of the first Creature, who was fatally wounded and then came back to life. He was permitted to give breath to this statue and even make it speak! Then the statue ordered that anyone refusing to worship it must die! (Revelation 13:11-15).

Around the time I got to the number "666," the key to the identity of the Beast, I saw a flash of red, and Baba walked in. Feeling a peculiar significance in the moment, I decided to ask Baba, since he was omniscient, what it meant. Emitting a soft playful aura, Baba practically swaggered over to me, took the book from my hands, and started reading where I had my finger. He could barely say the words, in fact much of it was word skipping and word blending. Baba gave me an odd smile, made a silly grimace, and then blew me a loud kiss, turned around and exited, saying something like "the great and the small, will be all in all." The playfulness of the perfect master?

Later Kerry, Janet, and I were talking, after I had mentioned this, and she looked bothered. We moved back to a rear fountain, and Janet said that the day the girls moved in, Baba gave her a similar test. "He just walked into the bhajan hall in a straight line, no facial expression, right up to me, and clicked his fingers with such force that it sounded like a firecracker. He almost looked wrathful. His face relaxed, and he walked on. Boy, he was telling us that if he wanted, he had the power to vaporize us. I mean, it really scared me."

On one of our final meetings with Baba before he was to leave on a day's tour to Madras, and we were to leave for Puttaparthi, there was a strange incident that broke up our meeting. After an hour of stories, a servant ran into the interview room informing Baba of something. Then Raja Reddy stood in the door and verified it.

Now in a flash, Baba was up from his chair almost yelling nervously and apparently giving instructions.

After a few minutes he reappeared in the doorway, speaking with assurance, but still seemingly shaken underneath. "Five minutes ago the small child of one of the servants was kidnapped and smuggled out in a truck...." Suddenly there was yelling again, and Baba disappeared for the evening. After five minutes alone in the interview room, we gathered it was over and left, some of us worried about the child, others were smugly confident that Baba had everything under control. Trying to sleep on the roof, some of us wondered in whispers— "Why didn't Baba know of it while it was happening? or why didn't he foresee it? Why did he appear nervous, since that seemed to indicate that something was at stake? Why couldn't he rematerialize the kid? Besides the crying of one of the servants indicated lack of faith in Baba. How could someone have the privilege of working in Baba's house, and yet doubt him even now?"

The morning we were to leave, Baba gave us a brief session. All smiles he described how Raja Reddy, following his instructions, had managed to track the thief down in half an hour and recover the kidnapped child. Baba explained that it was an ill-conceived plot to expose him and extort money for the child. With a pitying laugh of triumph for that particular category of fools, Baba stated, "Nothing and nobody can oppose my mission. I have come to establish dharma, the laws of God, and no tricks can slow down my divine mission."

That evening, at 7:00, our bus rolled into Puttaparthi in the neighboring state of Andhra Pradesh. We were shaken to bits from the 12-hour ride and had no idea that we would be in Puttaparthi for a seeming eternity—five months till November 25. That is, some of us in the group. Others would not last. I looked up at the ragged skyline of rocks and jagged hills in the sunset and thought once again that if anything had ever reminded me of God's Anvil, that bleak and tortuous desert in *Lawrence of Arabia*, this was it.

Because it was so hot, all 17 of us laid our bedding right down the 20-cubicle stone porch in a long row, the males in one strip, the females in another.

Before the elements began to eat away at us, the newer people had time to run around and buzz off the novelty of the whole place. They were amazed at Baba's huge hall, the hospital on the hill, the press, the ashram canteen, and the weird, almost volcanic landscape. This was India's wilderness with its enchanting quality. It seemed we had access to the ancient world 3,000 years ago, and any century in between. But the novelty went away for many when they bit into their first bite of food. There were no more easy trips to any city, much less temperate upbeat Bangalore. The wilderness would get old. This was Baba's laboratory on the soul, the impersonal aspect of his love.

When only a few of us had been here we didn't draw too much attention. But now we stood out. Our size, shape, color, and habits were obviously different. And some of our dress was unmentionable to the Indians. Not only that, but like all Americans, we did something that is unthinkable to an Indian. We immediately befriended all the local dogs. "We" meaning just about everybody but me. I couldn't complete the transference. For one thing, these things were two-dimensional instead of three, and had the dispositions of desert rats. And when they were shown even an iota of affection, never seeing it from a human before, they were as hard to pull away as a large octopus. And they smelled, and they had sores and bleeding lesions, and bugs of every description, and all types of internal worms, and I feared, some of them had the one disease that you don't fool around with, foaming at the mouth disease—rabies. And so should one nip you at 3:00 A.M. because you rolled over, you might sleep through it and wake up one day a few weeks

later, foaming at the mouth and screaming. And everybody but a doctor would assume you were enlightened,
and had entered Turya samadhi.

By our third night all the dogs had names given to
them, most of them originating from either Bruce or
me—"Dying Dog," "Boscene Dog" (later changed to
"Boscenes'a Doggies," with a Mexican accent), "Tinker
Toy Dog," "Reindeer Dog," "Desert Demon," etc. And
anybody with a grain of intelligence went to bed in the
great outdoors with a club by his side. The dogs would
sneak over, flop right on top of you, and if you smacked
them, they would go away for half an hour, and go
through the whole routine again. The thing was that
they could afford to stay up all night, we couldn't. If we
did, we were shot the next day. And sometimes we would
wake up at 2:00 A.M. amid a sound that was like a game
of "Hot Potato" in the center of hell, using a hydrogen
bomb for the hot potato, as a swirling mass of dogs
howled and fought.

They would be about three inches from our faces
snarling and twirling away, fighting over who's going to
flop down on your mat. My main problem was the compassion of the girls. I told them, "I know it's pitiful. But
if we start here, we'll have to borrow a billion dollars to
really make a dent in the problem, get a fleet of helicop-
ters and fly over all of India dropping tons of bones. But
then we'd have the problem of starving people, and
that's even more tragic." The group consensus of the
males was that the kindest thing to do would be to go off
and get an arsenal of 44-magnums and AK47s and blow
them off the face of the earth to put them out of their
misery.

Like many things, they kept on reproducing and suffering the consequences.

Baba appeared within a week of our arrival, stayed
two days, and promptly left until the Guru Purnima
festival in late July, weeks later.

On the first evening of Baba's arrival, Kasturi came over to me and said, "Baba wants to talk to you and Bruce privately, as well as Michelle, and one other." Feeling the secretiveness of it, I ran off to the front of the bhajan hall as quietly as possible not wanting others whom Baba had not specified to come along.

It was for a special letter to the authorities to grant residence permits. As it happened, a large number of the "American bhaktas" were not American. Kerry and Janet had Canadian Commonwealth passports that exempted them from visas, the same with Anthony and Vicky, Sandy and Zolt, Peter and Martin, and several Germans. A residence permit was extremely rare for Americans.

The ones who were put to the test by this were Jai, Howard, Tony, Bob, Gill, India, and Marsha.

Once inside, Baba grabbed my arm talking softly and said, "See, I am writing you a special letter for residence permit to stay in India. I want you to stay with me. Special trainees." He gave us a sheet of paper to sign with our complete names.

He also instructed us not to be afraid, but to go ahead and begin leading bhajans in the big hall at the two daily bhajans. That he would explicitly authorize it to Kasturi, the temple priest, and Kalyan, and make sure that everyone understood that it was his will. Ten minutes later we left with butterflies in our stomachs. This was another historical precedent in the Baba mission.

Before Baba left the next day, he gave one of the harmoniums that he had in storage to us to practice with. Kalyan, a Bengali singer, was then instructed to teach us. The girls too were given permission to work with Vijaya, and use a harmonium; Michelle and Vicky being the final obvious choice.

Another group activity, after Baba left, was a daily reading by Kasturi, who had been given the official title by Baba as "the mother-in-law." He was an elderly

Brahmin intellectual who resembled the wise old school-teacher.

One of the people included in the listening was a disagreeable stumpy little woman, Dr. Vijaya Laxmi, second in command at the hospital, who seemed to have a competitive sore spot for foreigners, and pressed her authority as far as she possibly could. Now and then Kasturi corrected her like a little girl, or told her to be quiet, and she obeyed implicitly. She had been with Baba from the very start, part of the old guard like Kasturi, that had become enchanted with Baba before his world mission in the early 1950s, when he was in his twenties. The problem was that Baba had really not spoken to her in years. The same problem would soon plague some of the foreigners as well. Baba's selective attention could be painful for those not on the receiving end.

Jai came back from Bangalore to get his bags after several trips. "Look, the Indian authorities are the most difficult people I know. My visa runs out in a couple days, and if I don't leave the country then, they can expel me forever. That means no guru and no enlightenment." The way Jai had solved this problem was to run straight over to Siva Bala Yogi and ask for a letter. He got it, but it was conditional. Now he had to be a full-time 100-percent disciple of Bala Yogi. Jai gulped when I informed him that this was it, as far as Baba was concerned for this lifetime. Howard was in the same position, but had decided to throw everything in for Baba.

Howard came over, looking a little more positive since I had given him a pep talk. He explained to Jai, speaking English with affected Indian mannerisms and accent, "Swami will come through in the end. This is just a test. Before I had many doubts, but now that he sees my faith he will get my visa." Howard was the latest incarnation of "the woodpecker" whom I left at the gate at Maharishi's in Rishikesh. What I hated was the feminized sweetness. The latest self-serving term for me, by a certain minority, was "homophobic." I would have put it differently.

Jai left for good, and Kerry, Janet, and I were amazed that this much weeding had started so soon. These were people who had paid high stakes to get here. That chosen, privilged fraction of humanity. Believing as we did in reincarnation, perhaps it had taken hundreds of thousands of lives for them to get here in the very presence of an avatar.

Kerry finally summed up his view of this weeding process, "Baba works at a remarkable speed. You go through more changes and have to work through more crap when he's gone. I can't believe he's engineered this thing with about six different people." Janet finally predicted, "India and Marsha are going to make it through but I don't think Bob will." She was right, after a few more weeks, following the coming festival, as I myself had suspected, Bob was on the way to complete his world tour, as was usual, never conceding the possibility that he was capable of error. He just boarded the bus, and produced the most sickly sweet knowing smile he could muster.

Yet it was Jai who worried us (everyone except Gill, who by now had pitched Indra Devi's tent again and was off by himself and getting by with the minimum number of words to any of us). Michelle felt a certain degree of responsibility as Jai was from the same generation of Hilda disciples, and she had come to India with him. I chalked the whole thing up as a huge spiritual lesson and finally said, "To have Jai shot down in three months is a serious omen." Here was a fellow who talked to Indian gods as a child in New York, who had gone through enormous obstacles to get here. He is then given more access than he envisioned in his wildest dreams, even living in the very house of the avatar, and he wanders off into the fold of another guru, like some of his forefathers' Israel defecting to Canaan. I told him he was a fool but it didn't get through. At least half our group under me, like Jai, was Jewish.

Another serious omen was something that crawled by my nose one morning after scratching in the vicinity for half an hour. When the shadowy grays of around fivish started disappearing, I heard a yell. One of the girls was pointing at my mat. I sat up, and spent the next three minutes watching a huge black scorpion march and skirmish in the area, occasionally raising its tail and dancing, and then lowering it, so that the whole thing was over six inches long when running. I recalled a Hatha yoga pamphlet in Rishikesh on how the ascetic in the forest should deal with a scorpion sting, since it was not only deadly, among certain species, but by far the most painful sting in the world. If the ascetic is stung on the chest near the heart, it said the thing to do while in semiparalytic agony, is try to survive the next 12 hours by totally regulated breathing, while lying on the forest floor. Do not move, but conserve all energy in order to breathe.

As I was deciding how to kill it as painfully as possible, fire being my old favorite at least as far as ticks and bedbugs were concerned, Zolt came over with a box, and escorted it in with a stick. Then making a peace sign, he informed me that he was going off to a hill to let it loose, that killing it was out of the question. And I said, "Yeah you do that, that's a real spiritual idea just loaded with divine compassion. Let's see how you feel when you squat down to defecate, and sit on one of them or one of the local cobras." This episode did succeed in giving some of us second thoughts about running up the hill at night barefooted.

During this rather arid spell between our arrival and the coming festival in late July, there appeared two new people out of six to come on the scene. They were a young couple from New York, another batch from Hilda's meditation group. The guy, Eddie or Ed, was to become one of my close friends. Chris was almost the complete opposite of Ed who was short, talked out of the side of his mouth by a thick Brooklyn accent, and came off at times like a con-man at a racetrack, or a one night stand "sick" comedian at Vegas. With curly hair, widow's peak, and sharp ears, his appearance at times suggested a devilish strain. He talked in rapid testy sentences that resembled extracts from gangster movies or some character conceived by Billy Crystal. Yet I saw in him quite a soft spot.

They were put in the luxury suites since they were man and wife. In no time Kerry and Janet had befriended them and moved in, and practically all of us had access to a lavatory once again. Soon after that, many of us moved up to their screened-in porch to sleep unhampered by the dogs, and have "rap sessions" by candlelight.

Ed's first day at the ashram he had come loaded with pictures of gurus, tapes, stories, and messages from Hilda to various people. He was in fairly low spirits, because he had just come from Nainital where the guru he wanted and had dreamed about, Maharajji, the guru of Ram Dass, had sent him on his way simply stating, "I am not your guru."

Ram Dass, ex-coworker of Timothy Leary (whom I had met), had met this guru about the time I came to India. Since then his name had been changed from Richard Alpert to Ram Dass, and he had toured the States extensively, giving darshans and proclaiming the esoteric teachings of Vedanta and India's chain of gurus. He himself had quite a following now, many of whom, like Ed, had become friends. When Ram Dass was in New York, one of the places where he stayed was at Ed's. But Ed was warned, "Maharajji is funny, unpredictable.

He doesn't want a lot of followers, he doesn't want streams of turned-on people coming over from America. He's a quiet hidden-away little Master who looks like an ordinary fat old man wrapped up in a blanket, who happens to be merged with the cosmos. And if he hasn't called you as a disciple, he'll be quite blunt." This Himalayan guru was now quite hot in America among the growing cognoscenti of pre-New Agers.

Maharajji had been incommunicative with Ed on the whole, making occasional cryptic or puerile remarks, and then leaving Ed to puzzle them out. One day he ordered Ed and Chris to go off and see the new Hanuman temple. Then another day he ordered them to go and visit the fruit-market in Nainital. When Ed would offer him an apple, he might hold it up to his eye as though looking through it, or polish it and hand it back. Finally after Ed and Chris had been hanging around for a week or more, he called them into his house to chat with them. After "playing" with them for an hour "like a little kid," laughing and chatting about things, playing games with the fruit on the floor, and telling them things about themselves, he suddenly told them, "Go, I am not your guru. Your guru is in the South—he is greater than an avadhut, his is a great mystery. Most yogis are one- or two-rupee notes, he is a thousand-rupee note." Ed described his dilemma with pained humor, "Whadya supposed to do when ya hear that, roll over and die? I felt like I had my head kicked in. I had my heart set on this guy as being my guru, for months I meditated on him, people gave all kinda assurances, and I get there, man, and he doesn't knowya."

By the evening of the day they arrived, my future friend and I had a head-on run in. I went off like a bomb, fighting fire with fire, and I held the floor for ten minutes once I had started. Though Eddie was still making the expected background noise, he had been silenced. He knew it, and I knew it, as I knew from elementary

**Tal Brooke, the year before going to India.**

The prayer hall, a small portion of Baba's domain (ashram).

**Thousands adore Baba at his residence/prayer hall.**

**Baba at the Festival
being worshiped by thousands.**

**Pilgrims awaiting Baba at the Festival.**

**"There is no force, natural or supernatural that can stop me or my mission." —Sai Baba**

Gill and Tal on stage with Baba
at a public singing.

**On stage before 40,000, celebrating Baba's
incarnation as the World Avatar.**

**Tal and Gill with Baba
leading the crowd in ancient hymns.**

**Tal, meditating.**

**Ex-Harvard Professor Ram Dass with Tal
visiting Baba at the end of Dass' world tour.**

Approaching the point of no return.

Reverend Ivan and Winona Carroll
in South India.

school days at recess that unless you made a stand, this type of guy would never get off your back. But if you did, he would accept it once and for all, and end up respecting you. I was right. By the next day, Eddie and I went up on the hill, and had a heart-to-heart talk.

Eddie had a "super-rough childhood," incredible problems with authority figures, especially after his mother died when he was about five. The only "religious guy" in his family was his uncle, who was a mystical rabbi and the intellectual of the family. Eddie's dad was mainly interested in money. Being extremely perceptive about getting on "the system" bandwagon for its own sake, Ed couldn't see doing anything until he had some basic answers. Life grew from bad to worse, and by his teens he had dropped out of school, was hustling on the streets, and waiting for the "bird of paradise to flop out of the sky on the table" where he could see it. This didn't happen, so he went from psychedelics to army jails, which he broke out of several times, to Ram Dass, and finally to Hilda.

Conveying that his toughness was not that of a mindless brute, but a necessary mechanism to cover some hidden area of tremendous pain, Ed shared with some sensitivity what he had come to realize: "Coca-Cola machines weren't makin it, groovy hangouts weren't makin it, orgies weren't makin it, nothin was, and nobody had the answer. Finally I met Ram Dass, and I looked into his eyes, and he knew something. He told me about this guru in the Himalayas wrapped in a blanket who was the embodiment of love. I just about cried, because I saw the compassion in his eyes or somethin. Then I met Hilda, and she began to straighten me out. And I knew more and more that what I had been lookin for all the time was the divine mother. I began to realize that the divine mother was in her. I just put my head in her lap one day and cried."

The next day, someone who was presumably not the divine mother entered the stage. And as I saw this tall carrot-topped woman loping along, I looked at her pale scrawny son, and said to myself almost without thinking, "Mechanical-repetition, verbigeration, emotional refrigeration, and retardation." There was a lost terror in the boy's eyes as he seemed mysteriously guided to do impishly compulsive things without letup: throwing stones in the air, pushing her, making weird howls, yanking away from her with sudden force. And I recognized instantly that it was an autistic teenager, as a battlefield of contradictory schools of thought welled up in me. One emitting encyclopedias of clinical theory very authoritatively (Freudian, Jungian, Adlerian, Frommian, Bernian, or the expert of them all, Bruno Bettleheim). On the other side of the wall was the metaphysical-spiritual schools of thought, whose propounders all blamed such things on karma. Another suggestive impulse stated flatly, "There's a demon in the boy."

When the lady opened her mouth the environmentalist argument gained in credibility. I suspected that her deepest fear was of her incompleteness and her own sins of omission, because she seemed to be cloaked in the old familiar defensive garb of, "I'm not dirty, you're dirty."

Rambling on, and doing the work of two people by asking questions then answering them June introduced her background. "After several years of marriage to a guy I had gone to college with in Indiana, I had had it, and we divorced. At any rate I met a few supportive women, and after that, for the first time in my life, got involved in spiritual things, and I knew that here was where my inner searchings had always pointed. Someone had the *Essene Gospel*, and then I saw the *Aquarian Gospel*, and got to know some of the deep things that are only traced over in the Bible. Well, I had Terry to take care of... Terry come here!... anyway I had Terry to take care of and so moved to Santa Barbara, and I began teaching elementary school. Well, it's been a long haul. Well, one day I ran into Indra Devi, and saw so much wisdom and compassion in this woman I just wanted to cry. Later on she told me about Sai Baba, that he is here in this world, and is the same as Jesus. Well it was just too incredible to be true...."

Terry was now grabbing handfuls of sand and rocks, and spasmodically throwing them up in the air in all directions, but mostly right over his head. I had estimated June as being around 45 and Terry 15. I asked her when she first started to note things abnormal about him, wondering if his tormented pale face had always been that desolate or whether she always had been as hypertensive, speaking as though she were in the middle of a bomb attack with air raid sirens droning away, never in calm reassuring words, but staccato bursts loaded with hesitancy and anxiety.

"I guess around the time he should have been speaking. I just noticed that he had stopped developing. And I only got glimpses, because Terry was always in a nursery as I had to be away teaching. In fact it has cost a fortune." At that point I asked her what the long weird-looking instrument was that she had been holding.

"Well he gets so out of hand at times, that I have had to resort to using this. I was terrified that on the airplane he would cause commotion. And you know he's grown almost bigger than I am now, and he's really quite strong. Why, not long ago I was going down the freeway, and he started strangling me and grabbing at the steering wheel, and I mean he doesn't realize it, but that could have killed both of us. So I figure a few good jolts will keep him back, he's really quite terrified of this..." coming to the point of the question, "Oh, it's an electric cattle prod. Somebody gave it to me, and said it would work. The batteries go in the handle here, and the current is..."

"Yeah I know," I replied, "it runs off a bank of capacitors, and can emit several hundred volts in a fraction of a second...."

June suddenly remembered something. It was the moment that some kind of spiritual "thing" made entry into the boy: "You know there was an interesting incident connected with Terry's problem. It goes back to when he was a little kid, around the time I first got to the Los Angeles area, and had to find a house. My new house, it turned out, had belonged to Yogananda's Spiritual Realization Fellowship, used as a retreat and a monastery, and I heard that Yogananda himself had slept there. At any rate it was suffused with a spiritual feeling. Well one day, a very strange Indian, who I believe had been a sadhu, walked up to my porch. Perhaps he still thought the house belonged to the Yogananda people. He had the strangest eyes I have ever seen in my life, dark and powerful. The next thing I knew he was holding Terry in his arms, and staring intensely into Terry's eyes. He then gave me a curious look, and said, 'The spirit in this body has been a longtime enemy of mine. I have just defeated him,' and he handed Terry to me, and left. Within a year or so I began to notice funny things about Terry, like his slowed-down locomotor control, and lack of response to holding." Obviously one of her reasons for being here was for this Christ of the New Age to heal her afflicted son. Soon she was off in pursuit of the boy as he trotted off.

By the time of the Guru Purnima festival of July 19, 1970, more Americans had arrived, and the older group were shuffled around like cards in a deck. I was always attentive to our group chemistry knowing that this was a domain where Baba invisibly worked. You could even see it in the people as crises came and went. Which salmon would make it up the waterfall? I kept wondering. My own resolve to weather any obstacles that came in my path became steel hard.

Meanwhile there was a growing parting of the ways between a fellow bhajan singer and me that had emerged during our daily practice sessions under the Bengali, Chowdri Kalyan. Yet I knew this disagreement was wrong.

The minute Baba returned before the festival, he called the two of us in to speak with him. By his very kindness and forgiveness, he convicted us of our sin of being so small-minded. But there was no mistaking that he had been aware of our feud. Rather than sit above us on the chair, he sat with us on the floor of the interview room and taught us several new songs to illustrate technique.

This unexpected act of graciousness of Baba's toward us thrust us into the spotlight before the entire ashram community. Baba then ordered us to come back the next day at the same time. Baba himself would be our teacher, on the very day before the Guru Purnima festival.

And indeed Baba did sing with us, as we felt even more patently undeserving. Baba was noticeably pleased at our reconciliation. He told us a story from the Chandogya Upanishad, about God being smaller than the smallest grain of mustard seed that resided in everything. I grabbed his feet and lowered my head, and vowed to "surrender to the guru." An apt statement on the eve of the festival throughout India celebrating the guru as God. Baba's eyes dazzled with luminous pleasure. He patted us on the backs on the way out, and mentioned that a surprise was coming our way.

# Chapter 11

# *Center Stage with God*

*I*magine the feeling of sitting in front of tens of thousands of adoring devotees right next to the throne of their God-on-earth, singing some of India's most ancient hymns and all this after having crossed the world on a thread of intuition to get to center stage. Indeed, maybe the center stage of history.

Minutes before the start of the great Guru festival, one of the many badged ushers ran up and said that bhagvan had reserved a special seat for me. When we got dangerously close to the front, I began to get nervous. The audience surged up to the very front steps, and was so packed in the middle that I would need a crane to find maybe a place in 15,000 people.

Only feet from his elevated throne, side stage, sat Gill and two others, with a space for me in the center. I looked up, and Baba whispered to me, "Singing some bhajans."

As I gazed back at the brilliant chrome of the microphone, I thought, "I'm too stunned to be really nervous." Baba gave the signal, and whispered, "Govinda Krishna Jai."

Immediately our voices filled the ashram, sounding not bad at all. There was safety in numbers, because if one strayed off the rest could stabilize the tune. But there was something else going on as well.

I had felt Baba's force many times in interviews, especially so at the private interviews, but the cloak of sheer power that I was feeling now was almost a semi-visible electric aura, resembling the impenetrable force fields in *War of the Worlds*. And it seemed to both electrify and numb me, arching over us in a protective sphere, shielding us from the noise and consciousness of the crowd. In the web of energy, I felt a single-minded concern for just singing songs and nothing else, almost as though I was transforming into a mindless musical instrument, beckoned, guided, and finally played by an entity in the force that was not sheerly mindless. And later I reflected on a simple metaphor of Baba's, "Your body must become like Krishna's flute, the senses and ego hollowed inside for the divine hand of God to play."

Baba lifted his hand on the final beat, and we stopped after the fourth song. As though surfacing from a long scuba dive, the web disappeared as the usual sounds and movements of the outside rushed back, like the crashing waves and spray of the sea-air. I was stunned, but still attentive to what was going on.

Baba began his discourse, after a brief introduction by a high magistrate from Bengal, who was to become a comrade of mine on a future project. Baba's voice filled the ashram for over an hour like a powerful thunderhead. Though none of us could understand the Telugu being spoken, there were familiar Anglicizations dropped that suggested we were being used as examples and models for the Indians. "Perfect *raga*, perfect *itala*, just like Indians...American bhakta devotion, pure, egoless...called from around the world, 12,000 miles," etc.

Though it had seemed like a dream at the time, a little uproar had occurred while we were singing. There was a bestial canine howl that pierced the air—it seemed distant then, but now, while Baba was talking, it started coming back clearly. The autistic boy, sitting with June in the women's section, began flailing about, knocking some of the women aside, throwing something, possibly June's purse, and finally just scrambling all over the place with extraordinary energy. Humiliated and teary-eyed, June had to go through the agonizing ordeal of marching the boy from a place that, had she used any foresight, she wouldn't have been in: the absolute sardine-packed center of the giant crowd of women. After treading on saris, stepping on legs, arms, and what not, and bumping into heads, June and Terry broke from the crowd, she clutching his shoulder, as they walked with a fast bouncy gait, reminding me of two giant sandy-haired kangaroos bouncing in military step. From behind she resembled a giant-sized "Little Orphan Annie." The large cylindrical springy red curls of her hair bounced up and down in exaggerated quivers. Dr. Vijaya Laxmi gave her a cold look of disdain, as Vijaya, the girl bhajan-singer, leapt to her aid.

## A New Test of Faith

The festival continued in tempo, during which we even managed a Baba interview. Prominent in the minds of the Americans was getting permission from Baba for a residence permit. This created interesting problems.

There was only one problem left for two devout girls from the States named India and Marsha. Even if they had Baba's written permission to stay, they had to account for at least half a year spent illegally in India, when they did not have extenuating visas. And they also had to account for the fact that one of them didn't have a passport. When they were in the far northeast of India, perhaps Darjeeling, India was so caught up in the spiritual idea of vairagya, or detachment, that she either gave away or sold her passport. These were mere material items then, and it simply did not matter. It was also reported that the passport had found its way into a local museum exhibit, via the notorious Indian black market. Their next Herculean task was to "explain away" the missing six months, explain away the fact that in the Bombay vicinity they had been declared *persona non grata*, because they were accidentally busted in the company of a hashish smuggler, an American who carried *Chittral*—a powerful Pakistani hash—in empty watchcases, among other things. And it was already established that the Indian government had genius in one area, nitpicking and red tape. If the loss of passports and the other incident were somehow correlated, both women faced a minimum penalty of being expelled from India, if not legal proceedings. They loved Baba but a legal impasse hung over their heads.

Baba sat in his chair grinning from ear to ear as I saw something rolled up like a white scroll in his hands. Presumably India and Marsha had been in communication with Baba for the past few days, with Kasturi as the go-between, and Baba knew of their dilemma.

With beneficence and sweetness, Baba announced through Nanda, an articulate aristocrat, what he had done. He explained and pleaded India and Marsha's case, giving the details. And he told a heartrending story of two sincere seekers of truth coming to India alone, and running into one difficulty after another through adverse circumstance. But that Baba was always with them, and had guided them to his physical form. I had a special affection for India and Marsha; in fact, you couldn't help liking them they were so sweet, and I used to think that anyone who didn't like them ought to have his head examined.

Baba then proceeded to read the letter in Telugu as Nanda faithfully translated every word with a luxuriant erudition that put many of the Americans to shame. She enunciated every word as though it were a final exam in elocution. In the background were enthusiastic outbursts that sounded like something out of the "Beverly Hillbillies," "...Aw gee Baba, that's incredible." Which it was! It was a white lie to protect them, and a risk on the part of Baba.

A few lines later, Gill, who had been groaning and squirming around, finally let the steam blow out, interrupting Baba midway in a sentence.

"Baba, that's a lie." It hurt him to say it, and his tone, wounded and bewildered, seemed to say, "Aw, why do you have to make me say this. I don't like it, but I haven't any choice."

Nanda's face twitched, and she was no longer able to speak. No Indian had ever pulled this on Baba, at least around her. It was certainly rough medicine for such gentle sensibilities, and for so aristocratic a constitution. But for less cultured folk, truth was not always like a subtle hors d'oeuvre on a plate, it was something that even coal-miners have to pick at in their own crude unapologizing way. And it almost came like a voice of some Midwest pioneer calling the cards, straight and to the point, "but that ain't no spade." It wasn't delivered in delicate metaphor and distant hints, as an obsequious earl might speak to Henry VIII.

As keenly as I was now watching for it, and as much as I hated to admit it, Baba appeared to manifest a human reaction when I had anticipated a transcendental leap into divine equanimity as being most logical. The scroll in Baba's hands was shuddering visibly, as Baba wound and unwound it "nervously." His face seemed to twitch, and although he continued to smile compassionately, there seemed to be a contradictory surge of emotion beneath this.

His voice quavered just a bit as he spoke rapid English.

---

"Not a lie," Baba replied, awed that Gill would say such a thing. "Not a lie! Your mistake, your misunderstanding."

"But Baba, the fact is that India and Marsha were not with you in Whitefield all that time they were in Darjeeling and lost their passports. Couldn't ya have done it another way?"

"Small mind, not understanding. God is everywhere, I am everywhere, I brought them to me. Everywhere is in me. Darjeeling. Whitefield. Prasanthi Nilayam, is all with me."

"I know, I know that Baba, but the facts were interfered with. The fact remains that you told a lie.... India and Marsha were not with you *in Whitefield*."

There was so much concentrated energy in the room, that I wondered if we were going to have lightning. I was strangely divided down the middle: I greatly wanted India and Marsha to get through the obstacle course, but Gill had a point, was this the right way? And that particular question had been trying to enter my mind. Yet Baba was being loving and sacrificial, and what he was doing by helping them was ultimately good. And I should after all defend him. Meanwhile there continued in me this ringing fear that we were all treading on very dangerous ground, that if we challenged him too far, we would, once and for all, turn the tables of his favor, and be cast aside. And that this eventuality was nearer than it looked.

Hovering at some faraway antipode of my mind came a discernment just too strange to be true. That unbefitting omniscience, Baba had been caught off guard, that this had hit him suddenly and unexpectedly, almost as if he hadn't seen the lie until it was pointed out, and then perceived the error.

I interrupted Gill, absolutely shaking with "caution" signals.

"Hey Gill, you've made your point, now why don't you listen to what he has to say. You know as well as I do that space to him is a joke. They've been waiting for this letter for months, what are you trying to do, deprive them of it?" My intensity was mounting.

Gill flapped his hands and said, "Aw be quiet, you don't understand what's going on." Unfortunately, I did.

As Gill sat in pain, swallowing the pill that he elected to take in full knowledge, Baba extended my remark. "I wrote this letter out of pure love, divine love. Not a lie, sir. My devotees want to stay with me, not break their hearts by leaving." India and Marsha nodded helplessly. "Your misunderstanding, unable to see divine love because of jealousy—you want a letter, so when I give extra grace to make a special letter, you are jealous."

"Now Baba, that isn't so. I'm not jealous..." And then trailing off, "I had to say it, and if the situation repeated itself a thousand times over, I'd still do the same thing."

Perhaps sensing that he may have gone too far already, and that he might as well get everything out on the table, that there might never be another chance again, Gill unloaded another gripe that had obviously been eating away at him.

"And Baba...the food in the canteen. You've told us for months that we must eat satwic food, pure food without spices. Yet the food you eat is so hot that it burns my mouth to pieces. And the food in the canteen is so hot...I mean full of peppers this big...," indicating with his fingers, "...that it physically torments me to eat it."

Baba explained, "For Indian peoples, there is special nourishment in pepper, source of special energy, vitamins and minerals. You American not understanding. Pepper diet the same, all over India."

"But then Baba, why do you tell us to avoid spicy food or food that is *rajasic* or *tamasic*? Isn't it the same for everybody?"

"For Indians, it is all right, but for Americans, it causes wrong desires and wrong thoughts." That ended the subject. Gill continued staring at the floor looking puzzled, as Baba laughed understandingly at his ignorance.

Before closing the interview, Baba said, "Faith is very important for sadhana, for spiritual path. Doubts are evils and enemies—doubts come from ego, envy, jealousy, hatred . . . all bad qualities." He looked down at Gill as he said this, and it seemed like Gill was going to get his biggest test of faith, though I wasn't sure how. I also continued to feel apologetic for Gill's outburst that turned what was to be a sweet grace-filled interview into something so strident that almost nobody could swallow the ill feeling. And though things had blown over, the memory of the jarring attack hadn't blown away one iota, nor the tiny imperfections in Baba's explanations.

Baba shared a final piece of Indian scripture as what he termed "a faith-building model." It was from the Bhagavad Gita, the poetic account of India's avatar predecessor of Sai Baba, Lord Krishna, the blue-black miracle worker who lived thousands of years ago.

"One day Krishna and Arjuna were taking a walk together. Seeing a bird in the sky, Krishna said, 'There is a dove.'

" 'Yes, a dove,' responded Arjuna.

" 'No, I think it is an eagle.'

" 'You are right, it is an eagle.'

" 'Well, now I can see that it really is a crow.'

" 'Then beyond a doubt,' says Arjuna, 'it is a crow.'

"Then Krishna laughed and chided Arjuna for always agreeing. But Arjuna replied, 'You are the lord of the universe, whatever you say it is, it is. For your words are truer than what the eye sees.' "

Baba dismissed us smiling. But I knew that a bubble had been broken, something spoiled, resulting in some kind of irreversible damage. The group left quietly, people going off by themselves and huddling, taking walks on the mountain, and staying to themselves. I felt like the peacemaker, and wanted to talk to Baba with such urgency that my chest physically ached. Meanwhile the lucky few were joyous at the letters, and "mind-blown" over Gill. Baba and I talked privately after the others left and I petitioned him to persevere with the Western contingent while vowing my own implacable fidelity.

Gill heavily paced up and down the ashram all that afternoon, and into the next day, not eating, and probably not sleeping. He seemed to be in a total stalemate, as though arguing over every facet of the affair again and again, and then coming to the same conclusion. That given the same circumstances, he would have done the same thing all over again.

The next day, Baba, on a post-festival inspection of the ashram passed by Gill, and paid no heed to him. Gill had tried to get Baba's attention, walked near him, but was avoided each time, as though cut away. Baba handed those of us still left, those who had not gone to Bangalore, cups of ice cream from a visiting magnate. But he didn't hand one to Gill.

In a climax of pain, Gill finally told Anthony that he was leaving until he settled a lot of things, and might be back in two weeks, two months, or never, that he had to do it. He gave Kasturi a formal letter to Baba, put away Indra Devi's tent, and started packing.

I was still worried about the standing of our group in general. I spent hours sitting on the steps at darshan. Meanwhile more of the others were leaving in order to get their legal status straightened out. They all knew what I was trying to do, and in fact looked to me to do it, perhaps feeling that I had just about the only chance of approaching Baba.

When Baba came out at dusk, my feelings had become so strong that I used that special status he had given me—an auxiliary covenant, so to speak.

Baba walked over to me. "I need to see you now, Baba," I said very quietly. He smiled, patted me on the back, and said, "Go inside, very happy."

There were three other people there, all close Indian devotees, but there was no doubt about the fact that the interview was between me and Baba. When Baba asked me in, Eddie's and Howard's mouths dropped, as they ran off to tell the others that "Tal made it in."

I immediately went from one of my peak depressions into absolute jubilation.

I sat next to Baba cross-legged on the floor, and held his hand as was the custom in Indian families. In truth very few Indians had ever done that with Baba. I was so moved by strong feeling that I was oblivious to the wide open stares of the Indian devotees, who were taken aback at my intimacy with Baba. Later this would only add to my special status among the hundreds of long-term Indian devotees around the ashram.

And then Baba and I explained together, to an older devotee sitting there, the implications of misunderstanding God through lack of faith. It was one of my key moments with Baba, I reflected later, yet I was hardly even conscious of it.

"Baba, great misunderstanding. All the others know it, Baba—only Mr. Freedom is confused, the others have great faith in you. Instead of thanking you for those letters, you had this problem, and I am sorry, very sorry. Great lack of appreciation."

Baba imitated Gill, "Too much serious, too much sadhana like this, always tapas, but no love..." suddenly assuming Gill's yogic posture of meditation, with a severe face. "His mind now is very confused, and his faith is very weak. And also jealousy, some jealousy for the letter to the two *gopikas* (term denoting the female adorers of Krishna). I have given him very much, but he always wants more, always asks for more. He is spoiled, that's right, like a spoiled child. He will now learn a very hard lesson. Before it was much too easy for him, now it will be hard."

Baba then told the others that I was his "nearest and dearest," and his best Western disciple. "Always happy, cheerful, and with much gratitude, not like Mr. Freedom, a spoiled child." Then Baba told them something in Telugu about my future with him, and their mouths dropped as they were told not to convey it to me, but merely act as witnesses.

Still holding Baba's hand, I described to the Indians the gulf between the common understanding of Baba that most people had, and his transcendental reality as an avatar, equal to Ram or Krishna.

Baba gleamed, talked a while longer, and then we were let out into the night after being with him an hour and a half.

I broke the news to the others. They were in light spirits again, and much more joyful about leaving for Bangalore on the morning bus. The real shock remained that Gill, of all people, was getting weeded. Kerry and Janet had always "kinda wondered" if this would finally happen.

## A Strange Departure

By 10:00 that night, out of the blue, Gill came up to Anthony and me, and invited us to spend what he hinted might be his last supper, for all time, in Puttaparthi. He was looser than I had ever seen him before, as though a great weight had been taken off his shoulders.

He put his arms on our shoulders, and almost danced as we went out the ashram and headed for one of the local lit-up tea-shacks on a timeless village road. Whether he was retreating into an unreal lightness or not, I

wasn't sure. It reminded me of the times at University—
when someone busts a course that has meant everything to him, he falls into a real "hang-loose" optimism.
Some of Gill's hidden humanness crept out briefly.

"Do ya know that my son's the cutest little thing in
the world?" Gill announced to us and the surroundings.
"That's right, he's got so much talent he doesn't know
what to do with it. Why I used to take him to the park
near Golden Gate Bridge, and walk him around...you
know, around the time they used to have the first be-ins.
He was hipper and more 'up-front' than they were...."

"Where's he now, Gill?"

"Oh," suddenly cooling down a bit, "he's living with
my wife and daughter somewhere in Marin County. I
don't know where, but I reckon he's okay."

By the time we reached the restaurant, Gill had told
much of his life story over again—his father shooting
his mom, then himself with a 38, the funeral; the
Marine Corps for Gill, confusion and violence; going
straight with the insurance company that he started;
marriage; psychedelics; his genuine nondrug two week
mystical experience...then his fall; the mental wards;
the divorce...and his rising; "up-front" communes;
hitchhiking down Route One, till he met a guy who was
his first true father.

As we sat down at a crude stone table, under a 20-watt
bulb, Gill told us about his surrogate dad, while he ate
chapatis, and Anthony and I got hot coffee in crusty
little stained glasses.

"This man was one of the few people who ever genu-
inely cared about me," Gill said gravely. Then lightening
up, "Why, the first day I walked into his tree nursery in
Marin County looking for a job, he said, 'I've been waiting for you.' He was a giant of a man, six feet six, and all
muscle. Used to be a lumberjack. But he knew plants;
why, he could make 'em grow just by talking to 'em. In
fact he taught me how to hear plants grow. Have ya ever

heard the trees growing in the early morning? That's something ya both gotta experience.

"He was so kind to me. Why some mornings he'd walk up to me and say, 'There'll be no work today, we're going to have fun. Come on, we're going into town.' He'd walk me through the fruit market with his arm on my shoulder. He wasn't afraid, he'd talk so loud the stalls would shudder. 'Now what dya want today?' he'd ask. He taught me how to pick a ripe melon. Say, do any of you know how to pick a ripe melon?" Gill asked Anthony and me like a gleeful Rumpelstiltskin.

"When it sticks to the bottom of your hand, then ya know it's ready. That's because the sugar begins to leak through the rind."

By the time we left the restaurant, Gill was roaring obscenities, which embarrassed us. We didn't want the local Indians spreading the word on Americans. Besides I wondered if Gill was off-limits to me as far as Baba was concerned. Gill was telling us about one of his last experiences in the States before he became a sadhu, the time he was a road member of "the living theater."

"Ya heard about it?"

"Yep," came my answer.

"Why we used to blow people's minds to pieces. They'd walk in off the streets, uptight, straight as an arrow, full of roles and ego games. And we'd break 'em down. Living theaters interact with the audience. We had one girl who was so wild she'd.... And we had a soul brother who'd been in the 82nd Airborne. He was seven feet tall, and his tongue was as thick as raw cow liver. And when he used to talk, why he'd talk 'jus lik dis, yeah, muva!' and their brains would fall out on their laps."

Anthony and I knew that it was time to go. By the time we saw him off at the bus, where he was going to spend the night till it pulled out in the predawn hours, Gill was singing us a song, which sounded like old Farmer Oakey's truth song—

Doooooo (low pitched) what chya Doooo (falsetto), Beeee whatd Jya Beee (low again),

Doooo whatd leya dooo, beee whatjya beee.
Do what ya do, and be what ya be (reflective,
slogmatic),

(Le grand Triumphale)... Doooooooo What
Chya Dooo (screeching falsetto) and Beeeeeee
Whatd Jya Beeeeeeeeeeeeee (full bass).

We all gave each other "up-front" hugs, said "take
care and see ya later," and left. There was no doubt about
it, I was concerned about Gill and wanted to see him get
it together. I liked him more now than ever before, and
was just plain sorry that this had to happen. He said to
me, "Now, brother, you take care of the others, you're the
strong man... and I'll see ya sooner if not later." This
would become strangely true a year later.

A week later, a lot of the group came back from Bangalore with news that Tony finally "freaked out and
split," Gill had gone on to Udipi Taluk to meditate on the
beach in a hut, and that Jai was now more "spaced-out"
than ever, begging for food, standing on street corners
with gray ash smeared all over his head, and as usual,
talking at a hundred decibels about Kundalini yoga and
what a powerhouse Siva Bala Yogi was. On the other
side, Jai would pump Michelle for local ashram news,
what Baba was doing, what I was now doing. And both of
them wrote Hilda for advice, receiving in return, transcendental slogans of supreme loving optimism.

At the ashram, all the way till mid-September, Baba
had been gone, leaving us to battle it out with the heat
and desolation. I spent most of my time with Eddie,
Kerry, and Janet, and continued singing in the large
prayer hall leading hundreds of Indians along with two
or three other bhajan singers. Meanwhile many of the
new people were having their first really painful battles

with dysentery, sunstroke, general debilitation, and assorted unknown miscellaneous diseases. A growing problem in our group, common in India but shocking to Westerners, were sores and dripping lesions that would form on the arms and legs, get larger and larger, and drip more and more as the days went on. If they were unbandaged, flies would constantly swarm around them and crawl on the open sores. Then you were really in trouble. Some were infected mosquito bites, others we thought were due to the bad diet. It might take months to heal, leaving craters for scars.

## Special Status

By October Baba continued to shower me with attention, greatly singling me out from the others, as usual. Our flock of Westerners was considered very chosen. One has to fully appreciate the value of a look or a touch from Baba (people like Kerry and Janet could count the times he had spoken to them on one hand). And when you are repeatedly singled out to walk and talk with him, at times before thousands, that is a potent sign. One day the red figure of the avatar would be halfway up the mount at the octagonal building. Crowds in the thousands would stand at the base looking up in wonder. I would be summoned to his side. Then he and I alone would descend holding hands. Then there was the time Baba stood with me and one other, blessing our new room which he had built for us to the side of his large prayer hall. Then it was just Baba and me walking from there. Or the time a few of us helped him throw away paintings he had done in his early twenties. An awesome task. Then there were the long hours with him as he visited us while we painted large granite signs for the ashram. Baba would usually talk to me, the others would be nearby. He would talk about Gill, or "my spiritual brother" (Ram Dass) en route to India. Later he gave assurance to Anthony who suddenly left to be with his dying father in Malta. Indeed, a volume could be written about these countless hours.

But no one outside of Baba's closest inner circle went to the upstairs private quarters atop the prayer hall. I remember often looking up in silent wonder. Yes, I had lived at his house in Brindavan, but this truly was the final mystery of access to me. Till one night it happened and even this barrier fell away as I was given one more key to his kingdom.

I was just ambling around the village feeling very ordinary at one of the local tea stalls. The next minute I would learn that Baba had summoned his entire force of Seva Dal volunteers who were out looking for me, hundreds of them. They had seen maybe a handful of people go up the forbidden stairs into Baba's private quarters and now I was one of them. This was like being invited to a private tea with the Queen of England, and from the viewpoint of the peerage, you are never the same afterward. Status accompanies privilege.

I entered Sai Baba's upstairs bedroom over the prayer hall which fed out onto the giant upstairs veranda where thousands stood beneath to catch a glimpse of him. What stood out in that electric half hour, in that red room, was a dazzling certainty of privilege. That I might one day be the Western equivalent of Baba's absolutely top Indian disciple, Raja Reddy. And that I was being carefully groomed for the role. As it turned out, Raja was there and he and I spoke as Kasturi, Saraiya, and the temple priest stood at attention against the wall. Baba sat on the edge of his bed joking with us. The ostensible reason for my visit was to hand out saris to the Western ladies. Baba had stacks of them.

But did anything else catch my eye, something unusual or special about Baba's room? Indeed there was. At the focal point of the blinding red was this very large bed where Baba reclined. It was shaped like a lotus pad, the traditional seat of India's ancient gods. Arching over the bed, indeed part of it, was the ancient Serpent, Seshma. With its monstrous seven hoods, ruby-red eyes, and darting tongues, it formed a looming canopy over Baba. It was carved out of the finest woods, inlaid with ivory or stone, but what made it alive was the rich gold leaf which gave it a lifelike glow. It seemed to tower over everybody, ready to strike. This was part of the symbolism of the highest planes of Vishnu, the secret of his avatars. The serpent was also a potent symbol of Wicca, the Druids, and one other Being in the crusts of time.

Raja and I would sit on the floor beneath the snake and Baba, playfully counting saris on the plush red carpet. This moment was the envy of India's rishis who had spent millennia just to sit at the feet of the avatar, the kind of scene that would one day be scratched out in the epics of Baba—as he and his Western Arjuna counted saris under the seven-hooded serpent one night in South India. An electric presence seemed to perpetually hang in the air of that room.

The afternoon of the next day, Kasturi came up to me matter-of-factly, and said, "Oh, by the way, be ready to give a speech to the All India Sathya Sai Seva Dal and Seva Samithi in front of Baba in the main prayer hall on October 3. Baba wants you to address the assembly."

"How many members are there?"

"Oh, I would say at least 1,500 to 2,000. And since the Seva Dal is nationwide, in all the big cities, most of the members are prominent citizens: doctors, lawyers, engineers, and the like."

Chapter 12

# *Sharing the Throne*

*D*uring the long months when there were no festivals, we longer-term residents on the ashram lived in an almost primordial wilderness. Suddenly, Puttaparthi was an ancient village again. It was during these quiet periods that we entered the perennial ebb and flow of village India, getting our water from wells, cooking soojie, chapatis and curry, walking the mountains. We passed water buffalo on the roads when we went off to swim in an irrigation well by a field. We could feel the soul of ancient India. But it was also a time of isolation and tedium. The road within could get dull at times, stale. So festivals brought excitement and novelty.

Now the sky was a silver gray from the parting Andhra monsoon season as armadas of buses were beginning to pull in at the beginning of October. The coming Dashara festival would last two weeks. Pilgrims were claiming patches of ground and I knew that soon the side compound in front of our new quarters would be a field of human bodies. We all partially dreaded the ordeal of managing the essentials of living in the ensuing chaos. The ashram canteen would run in supershifts, long lines of badged volunteers ladling out tons of rice to thousands, production-line feedings of potboiler hot rice, bone white and practically devoid of protein, but for traces of lentils.

Some of the girls, headed by India and Marsha, volunteered to get a food line going so that most of the foreigners might avoid the canteen. They would cook enough for 15 of us on kerosene burners in their small cubicle (by now, there were 28 of us altogether).

A general in the Indian Army had brought a small division of troops, now encamped on the outskirts of the ashram. They were spraying the area with DDT. Presumably, the army was also instrumental in collecting the 30 or so local stray dogs—already a constant menace of howls near the kitchen area. They packed them in the back of a flimsy open-ended truck, and drove them 30 miles off into the hills.

That afternoon, word soon spread that Baba had called a meeting for the ashram residents in the large prayer hall. Not ten minutes into the family gathering, we had a glimpse of Baba as the wrathful God. He was chiding a number of key rumormongers, old women who had had feuds of jealousy for decades. Now the subject matter of their vindictive little notes to Baba had switched to lambasting the most recent additions to the fold, the American women gopikas. It was human nature in all its tininess, even in the presence of an avatar.

Baba then pointed a stabbing question to one of the Veda schoolteachers. There was a whining reply. Baba seemed to bring him to tears, then adeptly forgave him. He sank back down relieved. Now Baba was chiding another school official.

Baba addressed all. Heads sank in shame. They must become beacons to all the visitors and pilgrims of the festival, and to the world in general. They must be becoming of him, and of their true natures. The storm was over, and repentant nods came from the audience.

Baba's tone was consoling. Then he taught. And finally his dam of bliss broke again as he laughed and mimed, and made light of their inner darkness.

When we entered the large stone prayer hall the next morning, and were handed the agenda, everything was according to schedule. I was the only one of the Americans listed to speak, and my talk would follow the address of the chief guest, the Governor of Goa, in the afternoon session, after which would follow the "Divine message to delegates by Bhagvan Sri Satya Sai Baba." In other words, I would talk to the delegates, then Sai Baba.

However after about three hours of hearing regional delegate heads, there was a sudden change. Kasturi leaned over and whispered in my ear, "You are next, Baba says you talk now, not this afternoon." I looked at Baba and he nodded.

I sat down, and started scratching down an outline on one of the spare agendas. Looking for a connecting theme, I decided to listen to some of the interminable ramblings of the different representatives up front.

But there was little, as each tried to outdo the other in pedantry, and irrelevant details, in hamming around for as much personal recognition from Baba as he could muster. One man had brought 20 typewritten pages that shook in his hands as he strained to read them. Baba said, *"Bas, bas."* And papers spasmodically shifted as drops of sweat hit them. The man sank in his place after getting through half a page.

Finally a motion hit the floor that taxed credibility so much that it had to be repeated. Indulah Shah, a Bombay magnate whom I knew, smiled apologetically toward Baba as one of his regional underlings put a motion to the floor. He was a gesticulating, stuttering, winking little man in the back of the hall, who talked at top volume. His idea—that Baba devotees all over India should have detachments whose jobs would be to act as sentries at bus stops to assist all people getting on and off buses. And during the rainy season they should stand there with umbrellas forever ready, to shelter those disembarking from the sudden harsh traumas of rain.

At the end of the pandemonium, Kasturi gave a little introduction, and I walked to the microphone.

Baba had walked halfway back into the hall, and looked at the rest of the audience, leaning against the wall. He was smiling from time to time with enthusiasm as I made point after point. Again a cloak of energy gave me a bold abandon as I extemporized. It was my chance to get a certain revenge on the elitism of the Indians, especially the Brahmins. What if we from the West were the more evolved souls who had incarnated in the West for the coming spiritual transformation!

I criticized the attitude of small-mindedness in the delegates that had put some of the motions on the floor. They did not do justice to the God-man and avatar of the age, Sai Baba. What we needed was an overview—a look at the contemporary world on the eve of technological catastrophe. The blindness of the West was always a sore point for me. A world of smug atheists and God-denying materialists, who had worked themselves not into a utopia, but an impasse.

If the volcano of civilization was about to be ignited by the technological time-bomb, it was because people had given up their search for truth, and were living the lie. We needed a new fusion, East and West. I took it from there.

The inspiration had been bold, almost magical. My talk made it hard for them to glibly typecast us with the usual condescending cliches. I stepped away from the microphone and walked back to my place.

The Governor of Goa, Nakul Sen, might now be up-staged and he knew it. Not by a learned Indian but by an American mystic and that made it all the more humiliating. He had to fend for the honor of Bharat by thwarting this danger of having some young Western disciple outdo a thousand educated upper-class delegates: doctors, lawyers, engineers, architects, industrial magnates, and yes, governors too. Baba was still smiling. This meant the gem performance of 20 years of political rhetoric.

The chief guest speaker, as he was billed, waxed long in his oratory, as much of the audience settled into a slump. Everybody was now waiting for Baba to make the formal inauguration, and bestow his divine blessings. And of course he did, thrilling them with a thunderous address in Telugu or Hindi.

We stood up while Baba left out of the side door, walking right by Kasturi, Raja Reddy, and me who stood together. He stopped in front of me with a dazzling smile, poked me in the stomach affectionately, and said, "Very good. Very, very good. I'm very proud." Soon I would be well known by name, as I became, almost overnight, a disciple of great promise in the public eye. My desire to be the American counterpart of Raja Reddy seemed to be materializing. Long-term Indian devotees began to view me in this light.

That evening Kasturi approached me and congratulated me again, informing me that a copy of my talk was to appear in the next month's ashram publication *Sanathana Sarathi*. It would come out just in time for the November 23 birthday festival, and would take up most of the magazine—20 pages of center spread with articles by Baba accompanying it as well. It was one more considerable privilege.

Inaugurating the festival was an even larger parade than the one at the Mahasivaratri festival. Covering all available land was an ocean of heads, neatly roped-off from the various festooned and flower-decorated walk-ways. This time we were part of the parade with me and one other person leading our group.

For a full seven days, from dawn to dusk, the famous Mantap took place on the stage of the auditorium. This was the high priestly adoration of Vedapurusha, involving a handful of relatively well-known Vedic scholars across the land who had come especially for the honor of being able to participate in the sacred *yajna*, or rite of worship. One thing they did involved making what looked like mud babies or mud dolls. A background chorus, so to speak, was comprised of lesser sastris, the Veda schoolboys, and several instructors. The principal of the Veda school, a man who resembled a tiny Tolkei-nien gnome with an almost piercing glint in his eyes, took full part in the yajna, reciting one entire Veda after another by heart. The Veda sastris were in full ceremonial attire of gauze dhotis, bare-chested, except for a scarlet tunic and the sacred Brahmin thread. Most of their bodies were smeared with ash.

Anyone doing what they did in the West would have been institutionalized. To the ignorant observer these great men of letters appeared to be babbling with exaggerated mouth-movements, each in a self-styled sandbox or play area, while making what looked like mud pies or tar babies by the thousands. A little lingam would be rolled vigorously on a rock board, bowed to, decorated, babbled to, worshiped, held up on the air, and then rolled into the mass of clay to be remade again. Again and again.

Kasturi in his magnum opus on Baba, *Satyam Sivam Sundaram*, shared the deeper meaning behind this apparent buffoonery with no loss for words. It was the monist rationalization for idolatry that so often follows right behind monistic/pantheism:"The fire is adored as sacred, for it ignites and illumines; it destroys and purifies: it burns and burnishes; it spreads and shines. It moves fast from one victim to another. So it is praised and fed hymns of praise. The sun is the giver of life, and energy; it nips a day off from our allotted span of life, with every sunset; so, it is worshiped by continuous prostration, repeating each time, hymns of extolment. Others can visualize God in the expansive Banyan tree, timeless, self-propelling...thus, hymns are uttered to the spirit of trees, as incorporated in the Vedapurusha."

One way to deal with the Mantap was to consider it a nifty anthropological sideshow. Yet it did manage to capture my imagination with the fascinating singsongy melodies in the early morning mass utterances of everybody involved on stage. They would come over the loudspeakers building up to energized peaks.

One of our group whom Baba had shown a lot of "grace" but who would later be thought of as "the doubter," was talking to me in front of Baba's garage. He wondered how, if Baba never accepted donations as he so often said in his speeches, he could have a brand-new, air-conditioned Lincoln limousine station wagon with tinted windows. It was shimmering from the brand-new shine and wax as was Baba's Fiat and Land-Rover. Impressive cars for even the wealthiest Indians with the massive import duties put on them. Just then Kasturi came to him with news about his residence permit. "Baba says you're on your own resources. If your faith is sufficient, then I am sure the Mysore police will grant the residence permit." If Kasturi had been more like a relative or a friend before, now he was distant, the schoolteacher handing out the failing mark. Anguish clouded this fellow's face, he moaned in incredulity, then walked off sulkingly. Kasturi as an extension of Baba brought the painful news at this fellow's moment of doubt. One more lesson for the group.

Kasturi came into the male quarters one evening announcing, "This festival celebrates Baba as the divine mother aspect of God."

"Dashara celebrates *shakti*, or power, as victor. For the first three days Mahakali or Durga is extolled. She is the facet of power, worshiped mostly in Bengal. Ramakrishna adored Kali. You know this Tal. She can be frightening: anger, vengeance, adventure, and destruction. This is the tamasic aspect of the *triguna* nature." Kali was the goddess who wore the wreath of severed human heads.

"The second three days adores the divine mother as Mahalakshmi. Here you have the rajasic nature of power—wealth, authority, imperium, prosperity. In Punjab they worship her to bestow the boons of wealth.

"The last three days are devoted to worshiping the divine mother in her higher or satwic aspect, as Mahasaraswati. Here you see divine energy in its highest sublimations—self-control, vision, value, knowledge, virtue, purity, justice, and equanimity." It was a triune-goddess fest. The only problem was that I was never into the goddess.

Like a 70-year-old Missouri farmer who starts to get the rhythm in his feet after hearing the first riffs of a ukulele at the local square dance, Kasturi's eyes lit up in reminiscence. "In the old days, around 1950, when I first stayed with Baba, the crowds were sufficiently small, and Baba enough like a relative to permit us to adore him personally as the divine mother. Sometimes he would appear wrapped up in sari and bangles." I recalled the faded pictures at the old mandir. "The women put sandal paste on his feet, and the men would carry him about the villages atop a palanquin. Baba became the divine mother for all to behold. Sometimes devotees would see the very Goddess they were worshiping transfigured on his divine features. Baba would just smile at them knowingly."

# Chapter 13

# *Ripples in Our Mood*

$O$n the way to get something to eat that evening, Ed, Kerry, Janet, and I felt a light drizzle. We decided to have a late snack outside at one of the lit-up restaurants. A carnivalesque feeling pervaded the streets, as though another type of festival was going on independent of the festivities of the ashram. On the way back, sure enough, gongs and heavy drumbeats pursued us down the deeply worn dirt road. We loitered by the side gate as it passed. A small procession of peasants who resembled gypsies, carrying torches, and wearing nose-rings and turbans, carried a large platform on their shoulders. On it was a miniature altar and a rather sinister-looking god that glared out into the disappearing road ahead. The procession looked defiantly at the gate and went on. A local Indian told us that we would be surprised to know how many of the peasants in this locality of Andhra Pradesh were involved in magic, occult arts, and dark ceremonies. "They are going to perform a sacrifice out on the mountains somewhere. Who knows where?" The Indian walked off into the crowded road as June approached us at the ashram gate.

June spewed out the last report on the autistic boy

whom Baba sent to a clinic in Madras. "And he's beginning to make a few word sounds. The doctor said a number of times ... oh boy they had problems with him at first ... at any rate, the doctor said a number of times that Terry was able to form several actual words. He's a lot less antisocial. When Baba sent him away he told me and the doctor not to worry, that Terry was in his hands, and that the atmosphere of the clinic was the best place for Baba to work on him from afar."

We all stood there trying to work up great faith in Terry's healing. That was the secret. As Christ had said, "Thy faith hath made thee whole." In front of the Nazarene, even lepers became unblemished before entire crowds of onlookers. It was instantaneous. As was the instantaneous healing of the mentally tormented, deranged, and demon-possessed. Christ would utter a single word, and it was done. Terry just took longer, that's all.

Halfway through the festival Baba looked down at me from the stage and said, "Foreigners ready?" The next thing I knew, he was beckoning all 28 of us up on the stage before thousands of onlookers. Raja Reddy passed up a harmonium and Baba had microphones adjusted in front of "the doubter" (who didn't get Baba's second letter for a residence permit) and me who sat leading the others, in the center front of the stage. Baba walked down where we had sat in the audience, and signaled us to start. "The doubter," taking it all in with a forced philosophical calm, turned with the usual ready signal, and said, "Quick, what song?"

"Nataraja" I said as an ocean of faces looked up at me center-stage before the microphone which Baba was straightening. Then off we went before the 10,000-plus, harmonium and voices surging across the speakers all over the ashram. Baba sat smiling, and I was satisfied that it was up to standard. We were wearing special gold threaded garb that Baba had especially made for us as of late.

But "the doubter's" mood underneath had not been appeased. All this had come too easy.

At one of the events Baba asked me where "the doubter" was. He was annoyed. Several hours later that evening outside the men's quarters, Ed and I saw "the doubter" come down the hill. As he approached he did little dance steps and jigs. His rich repertoire of routines I had learned to read as warning signs of hysteria and depression.

Resembling a crosscut between Vincent Price and Donald Sutherland, eyes swollen like poached eggs, "the doubter," at the 20-foot mark did an imitation of the chorus line kicks of the Rockettes at Radio City Music Hall, Times Square. His Lawrence Welk "Da-dee-dee-do" version of "Mississippi Mud," mutated, behind a brief perverse grin, into a spontaneous nasal falsetto warble of Gill's swan song his last night in town, "Do Whad Ya Do, Be What Jcha Be." That ended at the four-foot mark, and "the doubter" oscillated between mock guffaws and flickerings of indignation and anguish. Then he produced a modulated mock-hysterical scream from "The Haunted House on Skull Mountain." "You wouldn't believe what just happened. It's the final straw ... it's ..."

To the tune of okay-what-is-it-this-time, Ed and I put in our cue, "What happened?"

A groan of cosmic betrayal. Flustering, "the doubter" told us how he had been in the men's quarters suddenly experiencing the familiar hypodermic-needle-in-the-abdomen pains of dysentery. Without a moment to waste, he gritted his teeth, held it in, and ran up the hillside barefooted fighting time bitterly. We all knew what he was up against. It was not an uncommon ritual. Before he could totally disappear from public view on the hilltop—the pains in his side were like skewers—he abruptly scrambled to a steep, jagged pocket of boulders, nettles, and thorns, and he defecated. Suddenly halfway through he lost his balance and rolled down some 15 feet of sharp edges and thorns right over his own excrement. A world-class sadist could not have invented a more unique scenario. The latest degradation was too much. This couldn't have been an accident. Rage against Baba. Why was crucifixion unavoidable on the path to enlightenment? "The doubter" held out his arms as though on a cross.

"You're gonna do penance anyway, you don't need to invent it," we told him.

But "the doubter's" problems brought up some issues that we all had to face. That though we were all brothers, we were also passing strangers on our own roads that at times went into puzzling netherworlds. Even though we could each extend an arm, we were truly alone when it came to working our own way out of the maze. We were all one, yes, but nobody could walk our particular tortuous path but ourselves. As Raja had told "the doubter" and me, it was the most sublime and subtle surgery to cut the roots of the ego from all the projected phenomenal universe; one had to implicitly obey the inner voice of the atma, or its concretization, the Master. Ed and I knew that "the doubter" had to resolve his problems with Baba, persevere with the guiding inner light, or sink. He was an object lesson in the making.

But "the doubter's" root problem was a faltering faith in his own spiritual guidance system, in himself, in Baba, and even the guiding inner light. He needed someone he could trust to meet his perfect standards. Too many contradictions about the festival had fallen short of those standards. Could he really throw his soul on Baba?

But wasn't Baba Christlike in many ways? Why he was known to feed thousands in mass feedings.

Starting at the crack of dawn the next day, the festival practically over, came a constant waterfall of human movement. Literally drifting in from nowhere, from pockets and crevices in the neighboring hills and mountains, as far as the eye could see, along obscure bullock paths out of nearby rice paddies, which in turn, ran head-on into banks of arid, stark mountains, and from the riverbed of the Chitravati River, regions as bleak as a planetoid, came ant trails of the starved and the destitute. How far they had come, or how they had gotten word that today was the day for feeding the poor, was just another of an endless series of puzzles. They shuffled in—hollow-eyed, toothpick arms, limbless, atrophied, noseless, fly and dung-covered, bruised, tortured, swollen, and baked like prunes—and a Seva Dal member, almost crossing a thousand layers of inbred caste repulsion, but now realizing the unity of mankind in a leap of faith and a desire to please the Master, would resist holding his nose, and direct each zombie to his place on the ground.

By 9:00 in the morning the magnesium-white glare of the equatorial sun was back. The long compound was layered with rows of the poor, running the entire length of the compound from the Veda school at the far end to our room, and its mirror image connected to us, the "town hall." The thousands of destitute were awaiting Baba's arrival. It was sunstroke weather, and I could already feel the powerful beams penetrating the granite whitewashed walls of our room. The room was empty except for me and "the doubter" who was lying down still suffering from diarrhea and depression from his degradation the night before.

The gale of human voices outside, my weariness from lack of sleep, and my certainty that half an hour out there in the sun's rays and I would feel fever quelled my conscience about not being out there. Besides, Baba had a mammoth enough problem out there, and my absence

would have such a low reading on his gradient of awareness that it was doubtful that either "the doubter" or I
would be missed.

Half asleep, a sonic boom, and then a dead quiet
alerted me that Baba was approaching the compound
from the side. I closed my eyes again. The screen door
quietly opened, then shut.

My eyes opened. It was Sai Baba quietly coming in the
room.

With years of boarding school, "the doubter's" autonomic system went "ten hupt." He was up in a flash, and
ready to start apologizing. I figured I didn't have a
chance in the world to start rationalizing.

Baba looked around at the room in a shambles and it
didn't faze him.

In a note of things-as-usual Baba chided, "Come on
Lazies, service is needed. Too many peoples. What is
wrong, some ill-feeling?"

"No Baba, feel great. A little earlier felt bad, but now
feel fine," I volunteered.

"Get ready and follow me," Baba said and then left.

Three minutes later we emerged before the watching
world, scrubbed, vital, and wearing freshly starched
and ironed kurtas and cotton pants, resembling white
sailor's uniforms. We joined Baba and Raja Reddy in the
adjacent garden near Nanda's porch, ten feet above the
compound, and handed down stacks of saris to the Seva
Dal below. Every ragged peasant woman would be given
a new cotton sari. There were thousands of them. Not
only would there be a "feeding of the 5,000" but they
would given clothing as well. Some of the Western women
joined in handing out saris. So did Governor Nakul Sen's
wife, a tall elegant woman, as well as June who was now
wearing a look of unbearable compassion along with a
brand new silk sari of her own.

The men ladled food from huge hot cauldrons dragged
from the kitchen area in front of thousands of kneeling

peasants. The primitive food was served on plantain leaves. The virtue of the moment and the good works satisfied some internal quota within "the doubter," and he momentarily cheered up. Not exactly the five loaves and the fishes to feed the 5,000, and not necessarily any overt miracles of sudden increase going on, nevertheless it was a welcome sight to see the giant brass cauldrons lugged down paths from the canteen area.

On the final night of the festival, "the doubter's" mood was a disaster. A number of people were troubled, even Kerry and Janet, and I myself, usually positive and brimming with faith in Baba, was taxed in making an effective case on the Master's behalf.

The parting scene in the auditorium was an unveiling of Baba's fuller glory as the embodiment of beauty and truth, coinciding with the eve celebrating the cosmic mother in her pinnacle of glory, as Mahasaraswati.

As the mother aspect of godhood, Baba shimmered and dazzled, smiled and reclined on a large silver-plated swing couch. Swaying the *Jhula* to and fro was an invisible row of boys whose crossed legs could be seen under the couch. Baba was wearing his once-yearly, silk-embroidered "Om" and "Sai Baba" monogrammed white gown. To the side, so Baba could be entertained, and so we could be entertained watching Baba being entertained, was a series of singers and minstrels, each successively worse than the preceding.

At the side gate, we all deliberated. "The doubter" had been cheated, and was shaking his head plaintively. A pathetic laugh, "All I can think of is Jean Harlow." He wasn't the only one.

The charge of "cultural variable" was always the best counterargument. Some of us had been burned by a chain of sick media associations. "If you're pure enough," I justified, "you don't see all that garbage. Clean 20 years of TV out of your head, and you'll be back in the batting."

The side-show productions hadn't been much easier on Eddie. Indeed, if the truth be known, they had even depressed me a little. I retorted, "Okay, when is it ever good enough? Get Ralph Richardson, Olivier, and Alec Guiness doing 'Henry the Fifth' as a side-play, and it's still substandard. Or get the best production of Bach's 'Magnificat,' and it still falls short of saying it."

Eddie did the Harlem shuffle while announcing, "Yeah, or get Stokely Jackson doin' Oh, Dem Bones." A pained chuckle issued from our small gathering.

# Chapter 14

# *The Wilderness Proclamation*

*B*y the November 23 birthday festival a month later, many of us could feel the toll of being in the homestretch of over five months out in the bleak wilds of one of the poorest and hottest states in South India. The "chipper" days of the Whitefield Brindavan estate seemed in the far past. And what accentuated the duration of our stay even more was that, due to the heat and hostility of the terrain, our actual free movement was very limited, confining us to a monotonous few acres here and there outside the ashram itself. I figured out at one point that I had not left the ashram for over a month.

During the time between the mammoth Dashara festival and the birthday festival, the Westerners seemed to be going through their second phase of weeding out. Each drifting along his own privately tailored, internally reinforced route to higher awareness. Often strangers to one another, we pursued doggedly the complex beckonings of the strand of intuitive thread within each of us. True, some of us compared notes, had heart-to-heart talks, but our courses were sealed, each balanced on a slightly different ledge up the awesome granite slope of the mountain of truth. The Hindu's called this Mount Himavat.

When Baba left the ashram immediately after the last festival to flush out the myriad pilgrims who otherwise would have hung on indefinitely, we were faced again with the reality of backlogs of unworked-through hang-ups and problems. They stuck out like sore thumbs in the post-festival quiet. Also in the wake were two almost dry wells, brown with sediment, and each with its own family of large turtles. There was also the physical depletion. For five months the diet had been rice and pepper water with traces of vegetables. I had lost weight and stamina. And for five months before that, I had still been a vegetarian, though the diet was more varied. Altogether ten months without meat, milk, fish, eggs, and only a few samples of cheese.

Between the two festivals, "the doubter" spent much of the time in Bangalore ostensibly to get a letter for a residence permit, but also to settle deep-seated doubts and unarticulated complexities of thought. A number of others also used the opportunity to go to Whitefield for the change of air, more intimacy with Baba, and for settling visa problems. They were all but ignored. "The doubter" moved to Bangalore to a westernized guest lodge called the Regent Guest House on Brigade Road, an oasis for transient Westerners, with piped rock music, hamburgers, and waffles. We all knew that "the doubter" was flirting with dangerous territory. When he came back to Puttaparthi just in time for the birthday festival, he was in miserable spirits. He had broken some of Baba's prohibitions we suspected.

At one point, unannounced, the Canadian High Commissioner and the brother of Prime Minister Trudeau of Canada appeared in an air-conditioned limousine. Apparently they deemed it worth the effort to hazard the treacherous 100 miles through Andhra's desert wilderness. The High Commissioner was well known for his friendship with the Dalai Lama.

They were given the octagonal building owned by Indian royalty for their stay. Kasturi, Kerry (the Canadian nephew of Marshall McLuhan), and I acted as liaison. The evening after their exclusive interview with Sai Baba, while we were serving them a five-course meal on silver plates driven up in the Land-Rover from Raja Reddy's private kitchen, they could do little more than fidget and sigh. Spellbound, it took them quite some time to keep the conversational ball rolling.

Baba had utterly disarmed them. They had encountered the brutal reality of the supernatural in the primitive regions of South India. If the Dalai Lama had been quaint, Sai Baba was an atomic bomb. The most spectacular gift, reluctantly taken out of Mrs. Trudeau's purse, amazed us. It was a large heavy rosary made out of 108 semiprecious stones. At the bottom was a large bloodstone crucifix, with her name, the date, and Baba's blessing written on the stone. They spent a long time describing how it could not have been prestidigitated. Out of Baba's quivering extended hand, the rosary exploded. As usual, the sleeve was pulled back. And there had been no forewarning that they were coming. How could Baba have carved in bloodstone her name and that day's date!

Baba did another remarkable thing. He simply touched the gem on an old college ring that the High Commissioner had worn for years. It changed right in front of their eyes, still well-mounted in the base of the ring—it went from something like ruby to sapphire while the metal changed somehow as well but still retained the identical scratches and inscriptions. Then Baba gazed into the private regions of their souls: How could he have known of their childhood dreams, or some of their well-guarded secrets that not even trusted family members knew? It was too much. Now they had to make the psychological adjustment that he might be God on earth after all. A little man in South India in a red robe. I sensed they were more afraid of losing their free-wheeling jet-set lifestyle, the prestige and pleasure, if they came to terms with the implications of who Baba might be. If people like Jai, who talked to Hindu gods as a child in Brooklyn, or Gill were weeded away, I doubted these people had the backbone for more than three days "on the path."

Kerry and I watched the dust trail rise in the distance as they left. We automatically started humming the same song then stopped, looked at one another, smiled, then sang the words, "There's somethin' happenin' in here, but you don' know what it is. Do you, Mr. Jones?" Kasturi was smiling, halfway with us. "Bob Dylan," Kerry smiled at him wryly.

Five months later, in March, the Canadian High Commissioner was back, in Whitefield, this time with a New York publisher. Baba, forever unpredictable, and swarmed with important people and projects, hardly noticed them. (He could see them the next day, but they were only in the area for that day.)

But by the latter half of November, Kerry and Janet were also having bouts with faith along with several others. They had been sticking with each other a lot, avoiding just about everybody except me, Ed, and Chris. They had gone on long walks, staring at cloud formations and sunsets, looking for a sign while they talked. Their spirit guide Red Hawk had been cut off since Whitefield, and they needed reference points fast. Who was Baba? What was his real secret, the final message? And who or what were they? The answer was tabulating slowly, they hinted with a note of defiance.

The first indication of their newfound freedom and boldness came soon. The long months of having to use the mountaintop as a commode had festered within them. It was an indignity, a degradation. Especially when they fancied that the wealthier cubical-owners looked on with a sense of satisfaction and superiority every time they had to stumble up the hillside with a tin can of water. What kind of dual standard Brahmin hypocrisy was that? Didn't they realize that the joke turned back on them? Intoxicated with a feeling of cultural superiority and bathing in an idealization of tradition, the fact eluded the Brahmins that had they not been backward, at times almost in the Stone Age, and instead, had been civilized and educated, such things as squatting like an animal in the bushes would have long been abolished. What the average giggling little Brahmin needed to see was the vast, spotless toilet facilities at Dulles Airport. But he already knows that. That's why he feels the need to giggle. He is ashamed that as much truth as his culture claims to harbor, it can't even put up the simplest outhouse. But Vivekananda had already said that back at the turn of the century. Things were still no different.

Sitting in a deck-chair outside his cubical, perhaps 20 feet down the long porch from where Kerry and Janet lay their bedding, was a well-to-do banker from one of the large cities, reading the equivalent of the *Financial Times*, perhaps with a few good Hindu slokas interspersed for good measure. Since the banker had arrived, he had made painstaking efforts not to acknowledge either Kerry or Janet. He scowled when grinned at, adjusted his glasses, and kept reading. Each succeeding confrontation soured worse between them. Kerry finally opened the floodgates of hell, turned on the burners of his intellect to full blast, and stood over the man's deck-chair giving him a well-versed multilevel character assassination that was a work of artistry if not genius. What the incoherent and stunned little provincial could not explain was how so bedraggled a hippie, as he had often labeled Kerry, was able to effortlessly command levels of fluency, multivac thought structures, that well surpassed him. Of course, he was too unsophisticated to understand the irony of the scene, or the connotative import of the name McLuhan.

Still as red as an ember, Kerry confessed to me that this particular character type was one of his worst stumbling blocks. The smug supercilious religious hypocrite. Was it an accident that this particular character had been so strategically placed near his porch? Kerry could tolerate almost anything. What strange timing for so repugnant an adversary to show up.

With the scoreboard grossly uneven, and with the battlefield of direct verbal confrontation out of the question, a more subterfuge approach was needed. Till then, the highborn banker would have to gnash his teeth in silence and summon up the full expertise of a genealogy of subtle and glib tongues, namely, rumormongering; getting the old ashram rumor mill going.

Tired of the hillside walk in the noonday heat, and perhaps in protest against so needless a tradition, Kerry quietly disappeared behind the long row of secondary cubicles whose backs faced the street with a barbed-wire fence. In the hidden shadow of the foliage, Kerry squatted down to defecate. Several of the Westerners had learned this expedient method from the Veda School boys.

Suddenly a battle cry was sounded. From out of the little barred window directly above Kerry, a shrill hysterical woman's voice addressed the Untouchable, "Pah, Pah, Pah," voice trembling with righteous indignation. This was a means of addressing the most scab-infested dogs.

Kerry was glued to the ground in the act, and couldn't move. "Pah, Pah, Pah," she wouldn't stop. She and her husband had him in the clutches of victory, and wouldn't relinquish an inch. They looked on and discussed him between them, as though unaware that even foreign Untouchables have a degree of human dignity. There was no honorable escape, and they knew it. For even the most imaginative, resourceful, and sublime of Indians would melt in humiliation, denuded of a means of counterattack or escape.

However not necessarily so with true yogis and mystics. The house of the banker failed to account for the fact that an adept, as well as having had experiences in the beatific, has had equal command of the cosmic sewage conduits of subterranean abominations and infernalities. Some of the most astounding all-time vulgarities, traumas, of ego-busting were performed by the most enlightened sages. The other half of humanity who could come out the victors in so awkard a situation were the rednecks of the deep South.

Anyone so savage as to look on such a scene ranked on par with something on a hog farm. A prolonged stare down the eyes of the Indians didn't register shame. So Kerry whistled and looked at cloud formations, holding the dignity of an Edwardian polo player. He washed his hands and anus with a quarter of a can of water, as was the Indian method, stood up, looked through the bars of the "hog shed," and blasted a column of water straight into the window while yelling, "SOOWEEE, SOOOWAAAY," and walked off as the two onlookers sank in stunned silence. This act clearly defied their universe of thought.

Kasturi later ambled over in the form of the disciplinarian, giving Kerry a lecture on ethnic traditions and local etiquette. He was giving a bad name to the Americans, according to Kasturi, already disastrous rumors were about. Kerry told Kasturi the other half of the story and he ambled off, later in the evening, toward the house of the banker.

An unforeseen source of contention for the old Western contingent, already in a malaise of testings and spiritual battles, was a sudden wave of 15 new arrivals from the States. They rolled in about four days before the birthday festival effervescing like bottled Californian sunshine. They had been sent up ahead from

Whitefield by Baba. Sky-high with enthusiasm they paled the older crowd. For one thing, they were brimming with health having just come from the West. They wondered what sort of undeserving crew the old contingent was to be around the spiritual magnetic pole of the world and yet look so somber? No, they were the chosen ones, high enough to handle who Baba really was, and set the standard. But the older crowd under me wasn't impressed.

Finally, the new contingent had to ask questions like where to go to the bathroom, and what was the word for water, and soon the old hierarchy was absorbing the new. One hard-to-get-around institution happened to be me. I was one of the "main men." If they were slow to learn it, Eddie told them in a language that stuck. A greater authority figure, who was not bowled over by the presence of the newcomers from the West, was Kasturi. It made me appreciate how much he had embraced me immediately. I was the only one who got his full open acceptance.

The most dramatic reaction to Baba's force in an interview was one newcomer who reminded me of a medieval village idiot. He had to be nursemaided around the ashram by his wife as he staggered and stumbled into buildings, swaying and falling from side to side, from about 6:00 in the evening until late into the night. I couldn't tell whether he had been attuned to a very acute state of receptivity by Baba, or whether his capacities were indeed so pea-sized that he was like a flea in a barrel of rum, confusing the thimble with the ocean. He ended up hyperoxygenating in huge exaggerated gasps, heaving his entire torso up and down, head rolling loosely on top.

Meanwhile Ed, myself, and a new fellow named Wendel took a cassette machine to the mountaintop with the latest music from the West. For me it had been over ten months. I was listening to another world on the other

end: James Taylor, "Fire and Rain," "Country Road";
The Band, "The Night They Drove Old Dixie Down";
Crosby, Stills and Nash, "Long Time Gone," "Wooden
Ships"; all songs I had never heard before. A strange
sentimental longing infected my innards with an al-
most haunting passion for release.

## A Strange Honor

On November 21, I was again called on to balance
delicately within the paradox of spiritual leadership. I
was to give another speech. This time before several
thousand in the second largest shed-auditorium completely closed off from the general public. None of the
new or old Western contingents would be present. The
audience was a composite of the All India Sathya Seva
Dal and the All India Sathya Seva Samithi, a signifcant
cross-section of India's superrich, intelligentsia, nobility, and political officialdom, including cabinet members,
ministers, governors, right up to the vice president. But
this honored moment had a strange twist.

Before I came up on the large stage to join Baba, the
famed yogess, Indra Devi, spoke. Baba looked bored
when he invited her up. She was an elderly Russian
countess who had come to India decades ago now resid-
ing in Tecate, New Mexico. She was also a bestselling
writer in the States on Hatha yoga. Wide-eyed, shock-
faced, and severe, she resembled a Victorian matron
passing a bawdy armed guard at a wayside tavern. Her
tale was full of revelation: She was on a Los Angeles six-
lane freeway. Her arms widened to communicate the
immensity. Her front tire blew out, the car careened,
she screamed "Sai Ram," the car spun around, went into
the median as about six other cars and several Mack
trucks barely missed her. Baba's supernatural covenant
of grace was summoned at the instant she pronounced
his name. Baba smiled patiently and she left the stage.

Then he looked right at me, and smiled gently. A son in whom he was well pleased. As I stood at the front microphone, he whispered to me and I came over. With patient kindness, "Talk ten minutes, *Bas.* You have a message? Good." As I spoke, he left his chair, sat against the front-stage wall, at times curling up in concentration, hand bracing his head.

I first dwelt on the astounding fact that Baba had never once had a teacher or guru of any kind. Rama had teachers; Krishna had teachers; I was sure Christ had teachers; Ramakrishna had a number of gurus, as did Buddha, Chaitanya, and Shankaracharya. But not Sai Baba. At the age of eight he discoursed Vedanta spontaneously with traveling pundits. They were always amazed, wondering where Baba learned these things. Truth seemed to be his essential nature, the meaning of his name "Sathya." So far the audience was with me.

Now it was time to syncretize the world religions. The whole war of good and evil was about the physiological transformations of enlightenment. "New Jerusalem" was simply that instant of enlightenment when the Kundalini Shakti reached the thousand petaled lotus, the ultimate chakra. I spoke on the Kali Yuga and Saint John's Revelation. I was synthesizing apocryphal revelations about a time of worldwide upheaval when the embodiment of truth was to appear in a blood red robe. Indeed, Baba had been predicted from various global revelations. I was formulating what more than a decade later would be known as the New Age Christ.

I ended the message with passion and urgency but did not feel the smooth flow of carrying the audience. There was a barrier in the air. I said urgently as my time was running out: "It was Truth that turned the world upside down after Christ had come, and it will be the same Spirit of Truth at work in this age. The zeal of the early Christian martyrs must also be ours. The wickedness of the Roman empire is here again today. This time it is the

Kali Yuga mentioned in the Agni Purana—the Bible calls it 'the Great Tribulation.' Now Kalki, the avatar, is here with the Sword of Truth." I looked at Baba sitting against the wall deep in concentration.

"For the Bible also says, 'He will wear blood red robes....He will ride a white horse.' Remember the picture of Baba on horseback at the doorway of the prayer hall? 'On his robes will be written King of Kings, Lord of Lords.' Truth, the very truth of God, is about to revolutionize the world. We are in an age of turbulence and sifting, and have to come to an individual, heartfelt decision whether we have fully made our choice to be with the Spirit of Truth."

It was over. Indra Devi stepped across the red dividing carpet into the men's section and threw her arms around me. "Thatt vas turrific."

Baba, whose movements can never be predicted, got up and left from a rear entrance.

A funny feeling came over me. Something was wrong. I somehow had to get feedback from Baba immediately.

As I ran out into the crowds, where Baba was now out giving darshan, a catastrophic feeling mounted. Baba hastily walked between lines of people, followed by several close attendants. He saw me. I sensed a heavy emotion in him. I forced my way inside the swaying mass of men shuffling around and making room for him. He almost walked right past me but stopped, looked to the side with a frown. He spoke in low rapid irritation. "Too long. Too fast speaking. Words too complicated. American accent not understanding. Not enough surrender, sir."

"My accent is the same as the last speech. Everybody understood that."

"Indra Devi just now tell me that she not understand, and Indian ladies not understand." My eyes fell to the ground. I looked back searchingly, and Baba walked on.

No self-defense would either justify my performance or get him to appreciate it any better.

Indra Devi could not have possibly talked to him. He went out from the back, leaving several minutes before either of us had left. Besides, she was with me, and not only that, told me to my face that she thought the talk was terrific. If she had been double-faced with me and Baba, then what kind of discernment did he have to choose an emissary like that? Besides, the only way she could have told him would be to have run up to him, panting, and marching right behind him spilling out her feelings as he moved quickly about the ashram. If Indra Devi had not in fact spoken to him... well... the implication forced a kind of vacuum inside me. My heart sank, I had to be alone and think. Somehow, I would have to extract the truth from Indra Devi. And I did.

"Say, did you run into Baba right after he left?"

"No."

"Well, Baba said..."

"He must be testing you. I've been tested many times. Don't let it get your goat. He only does that to his most favored disciples."

The heaviness of my mood lasted into the night. A rare thing for me. (Though a day later I was again invited onstage with Baba to sing before 40,000.)

During that time I ran right into the next trouble spot. The second serious showdown that Kerry was having with the authorities. This time as the divine standard-bearer of humane treatment to animals. Baba had ordered the dogs off premises again, and some of them had been stoned, indeed cinder-blocked, by a number of Veda School lads. None of the authorities protested. Kerry warned the kids himself. Fifteen minutes later, a number of them heaved a rock on "Talking Dog." Kerry went over, slapped two of the kids hard, and hammerlocked another one. This brought a Kasturi reprimand.

On the final day of the festival, after I had come to terms with my own precarious dilemma, Baba spoke in the open air before tens of thousands. He made an enormous and cosmic statement about his own Godhood. As India's greatest physicist had told me, he was the only one in India who could make these statements and get away with them.

Baba was backlit by the crimson light of the setting sun as he announced:

———————

"I am the embodiment of truth. This is the first time in history that mankind has had the chance of being with me in this number. In the Dwarka age and former ages, the rishis would meditate for years, and yet your chance is much greater than theirs. The moment you come into my presence, all your sins are forgiven. I can give you full self-realization, and take you back to the eternal limitless God-consciousness.

"Do not try to compare my power with those petty powers of magicians. My power is divine and has no limit. I have the power to change the earth into the sky and the sky into the earth. But I don't because there is no reason to do it. If all the 14 worlds and planes tried to join up against me, they could not make a dent in trying to thwart my mission. If all the 28 worlds and planes were to try to join up in opposition to me, they could not do a thing. I am beyond any obstacle, and there is no force, natural or supernatural, that can stop me or my mission. Do not lose this chance, it is more important than you will ever realize. Do not forfeit the chance to be in my presence."

———————

We left stunned and challenged, pondering these words into the night on the various hillsides.

The following day, November 25, Baba wisely and in loving kindness told the entire camp of Westerners to follow him back to Whitefield where we could live for several months with him in a different and cooler setting. The old contingent breathed sighs of relief, and left with various new members to find housing in the Whitefield area.

On departing Puttaparthi for Whitefield, my sights were now greedily set on a prize piece of property, a spacious Swiss-facade house in Whitefield itself that about ten of us, my most favorite of the lot, could rent together. After five months of the desert, I felt justified. So Ed, Jerry, and I soon rushed off with a new addition to our fold, Wendel, to land this prize. Wendel would be the only possible Westerner to eventually rival me in proximity to Baba in the inner circle. I sensed this the moment our eyes met. Perhaps of all the astounding backgrounds of many in our group, his was the most astounding. My love and admiration for Wendel was immediate as was his for me. He, I knew, had the true qualities of genius. Our rapport I found incredibly catalyzing. Wendel had been a top first-class honors student, a national AAU pitcher in university, but above it all, he was hailed as an artistic prodigy from childhood. In time, I would bring this to Baba's attention, as I would watch Wendel spend long days in intense concentration doing works of art rivaling Salvadore Dali in technical execution. And this is no exaggeration.

It was all a marvelous and costly destiny that propelled our lives into this mosaic of history. We knew it.

# Chapter 15

# *A Brief Respite*

*O*ur house colony of 12 was in Whitefield and was the most coveted locale of all with its generous land and European facade. The "Major's house" as the locals called it, faced a quiet center circle surrounded by other westernized houses. The other Western colonies were scattered. I loved being back in the Bangalore area no matter how pristine and exotic Puttaparthi had been. I craved the sensory input of a nearby metropolis with the very things I was supposed to be transcending: coffee shops, milk bars, bookstores, movie theaters and what not. We lived in the hub of what had once been a famed British farm community. Having lived much of my youth in England, I loved it. I also loved the fact that at 3,000 feet elevation, this region was touted as having one of the best climes in all of India.

I returned home one afternoon to tell the group that Baba had just told me that Jai was to be off-limits if anybody saw him about. I carried my rented bike into the large front hall as Ed's barking voice plied me with more questions. I took pride in censoring some of Baba's private comments which might have confounded some of them. This gave me a to-be-coveted solitude from the others at times. Baba as usual relayed messages to all the Westerners through me.

Wafting through the house was a peculiar fragrant intermingling of Himalayan incense, sandalwood, and kitchen odors of soojie, bananas, chapatis, fried eggplant, Kitchrie (rice and dal), and mango. Togetherness exuded from everyone. The cooks, Kerry, Janet, and Victoria, were heavily absorbed in a conversation about aura fields and the inner light. Jerry, pandabearish, sat in his little side room with an etheric smile pasted on his face, wrapped in a towel, and sitting on an air mattress. Dinners were a delight for we had access to a vast range of foods now that some of us had discovered where the British got produce, the old Russell's Market in Bangalore.

Our activities were a strange mix of East and West. At meals we sat in a circle on a flagstone floor, holding hands and facing the candles in the center. We chanted Asatoma sat Gamaya and ate to the music of Ravi Shankar from Arnie's tape recorder. By 10:30 the cassette player would be filling the hall with The Band or Neil Young. We turned on the front porch light, found an old board and nylon ball, used the front door as first base, and played baseball. Wendel and I were the opposing pitchers. By midnight we were all back on our floor mats, silently delving into the mysteries of India's highest mystics: The Ramayana, The Tripura Rahasya, The Srimad Bhagavata and the writings of Shankaracharya, Ramanah Maharshi, Sri Aurobindo, and others.

At the next day's darshan, I noticed Dr. Bhagavantam, back from his long tour halfway around the world which had begun soon after the Dashara festival. I had requested some favors of him, and was anxious to hear the reports. One request was that he see my father, a retired United States diplomat living in London. I figured that my father, a hardened skeptic and atheist, would listen to a world-renowned physicist, a Nobel candidate who was also diplomatic liaison to the United Nations as well as the chief scientific adviser to the government of India. I had cabled my father of the tight time schedule that the famous scientist had, narrowing down their meeting to a two-hour dinner in a London vegetarian restaurant. As far as I knew, I might never see my father again, and wanted him to at least know that I had not squandered my life away on some unhinged mystic, but was under the discipleship of the most universally recognized holy man in India.

But Bhagavantam, a brilliant distinguished-looking man, shook his head when I met him at darshan. The meeting was of little avail. My father had asked pointed and probing questions about my welfare, accepted the reports of the miraculous as untenable, short of a first-hand empirical look, and even then, there would remain plenty of room for doubt. What remained was a deep love between a father and a son, and a gulf of geography and belief in between, frustrating every channel for that love to pass like an interstellar vacuum. One of my deepest sources of inner torment and anguish that would periodically emerge from even the most dulled equanimity I might muster, was that the inhuman requirements of the path that I had chosen to walk could not help but cause deep grief and bewilderment in those whom I loved—above all my father. To annihilate the ego—this very cancer that kept me from God-consciousness—I had to cut every strand of worldly attachment, including those whom I loved, with the brute coldness of a fisherman cutting up an earthworm on a dock. My pain was the one-sided misunderstanding and deep hurt that would inevitably slam back on my father. That for every gasp of love that went out searching for me, it would meet a vacuum. And my father's love would bray like an abandoned sheep forlorn in an arid wilderness not knowing how or why. And still covered in a dense cloud of unknowing, he would pass out of life ignorant of the splendor of my fate, bereft of a sense of hope, and instead, anchored by a peculiar sense of injustice. While somewhere in India, his son would have vanished forever, becoming the non-son; the body still living on, yet a different look in the eyes, and a different voice speaking. Just a hollowed-out shell, filled with the soul of the universe. I returned from darshan deeply sad.

As dusk was setting in on the Whitefield house, the electric lights coming on and dinner procedures underway, I tried to enter the flow of our group togetherness. Yet, a lingering mystery remained. With all the positive things happening with us, why was Baba becoming more remote?

Despite a kind of group spirit and frontiersman's sense of purpose which our colony induced, things were not all well. A cold desolation still leaked through my mind in the silent hours.

As far as Baba was concerned, I feared that the togetherness of our colony was little more than a distracting illusion getting in the way of my relationship with him. It was like all the distractions of social life at a prestigious university filled with talented fascinating people. I could feel my mind arming me for a split-off, now realizing that these new and dear friends might be just as transient as the whole procession of faces that had floated by me in the past. And no group happening would change one's solitary accountability to ultimate truth.

## An Unplanned Encounter

I went out the back door to visit Kerry and Janet who had since appropriated the rear cottage in the backyard. Lights ablaze at twilight faintly patterning the lawn, and the smell of soojie and papaya melon issuing from the kitchen, both of them chattered while busily cooking, washing, and sweeping.

As I approached the cottage, it was obvious that something had distracted Kerry and Janet. They froze in midsentence, laid down their stuff, looked at each other, and put on their most spiritual, brotherhood-of-man, goodwill-to-all-beings smile. If Norman Rockwell could do an illustration of the good-hearted, neighborly, albeit slightly cosmic American-Hindu couple, this was it.

Standing facing them were two elderly figures smiling ear to ear with Christian goodwill and loving concern. They reminded me of two tall splendid oak trees with the fear and reverence of God etched deeply into the bark of their Midwestern faces. Other than as Walt Disney depictions, these two salts were an extinct species that I had not seen outside a storybook setting. The world that I knew had pushed them off the quiet simplicity of their farms and country churches, replaced them with the high-life of neon-linked boulevards. Liberated modern minds had transcended such bygone squareness.

I was divided right down the middle—with gladness on the one hand and rebellious contempt on the other. They struck me right off as the types of incredible people who would cry if they told a fib, were honest right down to the last rusty button, and would give you the shirts off their backs while still feeling repentant before God that they hadn't given you more. The light within us, it was evident from the start, was slightly different from the light that was within them.

The tall, hickory-thin man looked down at Kerry from six-feet-five, and cheerfully extended his hand, speaking with a grinning, soft-spokenness, "Hello. I'm Reverend Carroll and this is my wife, Winona. We just saw your lights from across the circle there and thought we'd come over and greet you. What brings you to these parts?"

His face dropped when he heard it was the holy man two miles down the road. We too were familiar with the

Bible verse concerning the prophet not honored in his hometown. Kerry, smiling back at the Reverend with a flicker of irony in his eyes, was yesteryear's face from All-America High, a rural handiwork of national pride but with red hair a foot-and-a-half long knotted back like a Sumo wrestler's, and a long patterned wrap-around, extending from waist to ankles in the Watusi ceremonial tradition.

The Carrolls obviously needed to be ushered into a more universal understanding of the great truths, to shake off provincial prejudices. I fancied it might be my private mission to show them where Christ and Krishna converged.

From out of the back door of the big house emerged a self-proclaimed "four-foot dwarf from Brooklyn" with a satyr's smile and a voice like Edward G. Robinson. It was Ed. Mrs. Carroll, a white-haired lady with glasses, alert as an owl and glinting with keen-humored good-will, looked probingly into Eddie's eyes while greeting him. His smile widened defiantly as he responded with "Sai Ram...Hare Krishna."

A sobering concern slightly eclipsed the smile of the Reverend's wife. Mrs. Carroll opened the doors of their home any time. For a chat, for a meal, for help, or medical aid. "And I want all of you to know you are invited to our house for carols on Christmas Eve. And there'll be treats too." She winked at Eddie who was somewhat pacified.

As the group spokesman, I responded, "And we'll share with you some of the songs we've learned." The rest of our colony had been filtering out of the back door with knowing grins. From out of the motley tribe of all manner of semiactualized "gods" and "goddesses" surrounding the Reverend and his wife came the assent of "Right on...tell it like it is." The Reverend and his wife politely waved and went back across the circle to their house on the other side.

But when I saw Baba at darshan the next morning, my carefree mood shattered under his gaze. He completely ignored us. I felt about as significant as a cigarette butt. Feeling my discipleship to him threatened, I forgot myself and stood by his side-door till he came out. He looked at me as if I had betrayed him. I grabbed his hand imploring to know what was wrong, and how I might right it.

At last Baba spoke, in disappointed tones: "Not good, all men and women living together. Now Indians think Americans bad devotees. Living like hippies." In grudging disappointment, "I never make an order, only give advice. *Bas*. It is always my advice that men and women separate."

"But Baba, most of them are married. Besides, we lived together in the first Kadugodi house, and there were no complaints. No impurity, Baba, strict Brahmacharya," I declared. It went without saying among all of us that rule one for serious disciples was abstinence. And as far as I knew the rule had been kept.

"This tall Canadian man and girl in Puttaparthi living together," Baba's voice rose in incredulity, "... under one mosquito net on the porch. Not good. Indians seeing and talk bad things. Now is bad reflection on Swami."

Realizing he meant Kerry and Janet, I rose to their defense. "But Baba, they are married, and have told me many times about their purity, Brahmacharya."

"No, sir, bad example. Now faith is spoiling." I felt fearful for them.

"And 'the doubter,' complete spoil. Now, no faith. Living in Bangalore hotel with Americans, running after worldly pleasure." Baba spoke in a wounded tone. "Complete finish. Mentally confused, bad thoughts, rotten apples all." Baba rotated his finger by his temple.

Fearing that judgment might fall on our entire group if Baba's list of grievances continued, I tried to plead for mercy, forgiveness, and another chance, assuring him we could make the required corrections and split the men and women up.

"Rotten apples will be cut off," I promised.

Baba's features softened as he granted my request for another chance. Then he slapped me on the back and ordered me to divide the flock.

I passed on the order that all were to split up and that those who declined should go off to live by themselves; they should in no way jeopardize the others. Two of the most indignant were Kerry and Janet.

By that afternoon the Whitefield colony was scattering. Kerry and Janet remained adamant in the rear cabin. Victoria moved in with them, dreading the prospect of the girls' house. Chris, Eddie's wife, in a leap of obedience, moved in with the other girls. And so on. In the end, that left Ed, Wendel and me in the large empty "Major's house."

The next day Baba suddenly left to go to Goa in a long caravan of cars. We remained in Whitefield until Ed came running to our house with *The Deccan Herald*. It announced that Baba had suddenly come down with appendicitis at the governor's palace in Goa. We departed immediately. And almost with supernatural help, rocketed into the central bus terminus in Bangalore in record time.

Our bus to the tropical beach state of Goa took an exhausting day and a night to reach the capital port of Panjim. Ed, Wendel, and I walked down to the beach and drew deep breaths of spray-filled air. We smiled in exuberant thanksgiving. For Ed and me, it was like a taste of heaven after those long months of wilderness still in our bones.

We managed to rent whitewashed cubicles on the beach. But as we put our stuff in the beach house, we were dominated by a gnawing concern for Baba's condition. We dressed, bolted the door, and made for the governor's palace.

When we reached the palace, the latest radio reports were that Baba had burst his appendix. Pink and turquoise clouds curdled in the sky of the setting sun, while amber reflections from the sea below gave a scarlet tinge to the balcony. As we rounded a formation of military guards to the side of the mall, coming into full visibility of the residence, I now understood the reason for the concentrated quiet of everybody. Baba's red robe blazed from the balcony as though the penumbra of a divided sun was bringing the orbit of our own journey into perfect timing. This was Baba's first public appearance since coming to Goa. I suspected he had got over his illness.

As we stepped into view, a welcoming wave from Baba confirmed our faith in making the trip—and left the assembly wondering who these visitors could be to warrant such exalted attention. Nearby was the governor, Nakul Sen, looking edgy and attentive as he held his hands prayerfully up to the true king of the palace. Baba withdrew, and news quickly circulated that as many as could fit were invited to an open gathering in the stately bhajan hall. Uniformed servants tried to regulate the flow at the bottleneck of people pushing around and up the wide burgundy-carpeted stairs. Heaps of shoes lay in the foyer.

As we reached the teak and mahogany landing, an exuberant Kasturi standing beneath a large crystal chandelier, reached out to greet us. "Well, Mr. Tal," he smiled eloquently, "I see Baba has brought you into his presence within the very hour of his healing. Go in, I think Swami will say a few things about his sankalpa." The governor stood at the door of the darshan hall. He put his hand on my shoulder and directed us toward the front row. Raja quietly sank down next to me at the harmonium, squeezed my leg and smiled as I looked over. The feeling of welcome couldn't have been more timely for me.

Then an extremely vibrant Baba spoke, lifting our hearts right into the air. His splendid condition belied the fact that he had just overcome, merely an hour ago, a condition that meant certain death for virtually any "mortal." The reason: "I had to go to the rescue of a person who had surrendered to me—even his judgment. I took over his illness and went through it. His continued good health is desirable for the task dear to me. Pouring grace on the devout is one of the functions of the avatar. The abcessed appendix could only be cured by doctors by removal. He could not have survived it. I have come with this body in order to save other bodies from pain. This body is ever free from pain. Disease cannot affect it."

# Chapter 16

# A Return to the Ocean

*I*n the temperate shadow gray of 5:00 in the morning, Wendel and I slipped out of our bedrolls on the rear terrace, and headed over several hundred feet of sand dunes and beach to the shore, passing a number of large sows running about.

Through the twilight mist we wandered, passing effervescent sheets of cool spray. Gulls glinted in the sky above, and danced along the shoreline as flecks of silver. The far peninsula vanished into the distant haze, passing out through a charged gray tide of breakers rippling into the horizon.

It broke upon my fatigue—the residue of Andhra's prolonged wilderness—like a beam of light entering through a cellar door as my thinning frame stretched to sponge the vitality around me. Forty-five pounds less than when I came to India, my body took root in this balmy clime like a stubborn weed, not unmindful of its former prowess. Already less sluggish, aches leaving, and kinks in bone joints gone, I gladdened at the prospect of regeneration.

Suddenly shafts of the golden dawn streamed from behind the tall palms lining the shore, dyeing the sea an emerald green. I began to smile within. Then it burst out all over my features. I could hardly contain myself.

My God, I was happy! I felt like running through the surf—so I did. I felt like jumping into the foam. I did, and so did Wendel. And then I rolled and tumbled, and dived through acres of foam as though it were the very doors of paradise: a place, a thing, or a state of being that my soul, sometimes in brokenhearted beseeching, other times with wrenching anguish, and yet, at other times, rejoicing in the very knowledge thereof, had been striving all my life to find.

But after about 15 minutes I began to wake out of my joy. A remote part of my soul was quietly shedding tears. It was only a mirage that I had been rejoicing in, lasting no more than the ocean foam which soon vanishes, far from the heaven of incorruptible perfection, bliss, and ineffable communion with God. The reality was only shadowed in the ocean; it remained the climax of demands far greater than a splash or two.

That evening, at the Cabo Raj Nivas Palace, we arrived as the crowd was dispersing from a rather brief darshan. Baba was to give special audience to the team of doctors who had diagnosed him, but whom he would not permit to perform any kind of operation.

On the veranda, sitting at a wrought iron table was an immaculately dressed man in vest and tie with his opulently adorned wife. He called over to me, "Do join us please and take the chair. We are just waiting for a call from Sai Baba." He was Dr. Varma, Surgeon-General of Goa.

"I just didn't think this sort of thing was possible," he confessed with a refined accent. "You know, I went to the Medical School at Cambridge University, and soon became infected with what they called a 'healthy Western skepticism.' Well, since that time, I have dismissed all these rumors of miraculous accounts among certain holy men as just superstition. In fact, I scorned them. Now, I'm just too amazed. I feel as though I have to start all over again in thinking through what is reality." I nodded slowly. Then asked him to relate the details of the whole episode.

Baba played cat and mouse with the doctors, bringing them to a crescendo of anxious medical certainty that he was going to die if he refused an operation once more. But suddenly Baba healed himself. Kasturi explained all the details later.

Within a day or two, Baba left Goa to continue his tour to Bombay. By then, we were so caught up in the drama of being with Baba on tour that we soon followed, taking the boat from Panjim to Bombay. I loved the healing air of the Arabian Sea. Meanwhile the newspapers were going wild.

On December 22, after a windswept night on deck with catnaps interspersing our talk, we pulled into the dark Bombay docks at about 5:00 A.M. Several hours later we rode to the Central Train Terminus, had breakfast, then took the commuter train to the Bombay suburb of Andheri out beyond the Santa Cruz airport, miles and miles of middle-class high rises, and the giant brackish marshlands of sewage conduits and tin-can and cardboard shanties which are bridged over by the Bombay freeways.

We arrived at Baba's massive Dharmakshetra complex as crews of workers labored round the clock to get the reception hall and stage ready for the coming event.

Not long afterward, as Wendel and I watched the Seva Dal crew working on the stage design of the superstage, Kasturi appeared, calling over the present chairman of the team, one of Bombay's industrial magnates. In a trice, I was elected head of organization and logistics and Wendel was the head artist and designer. Hearing about Wendel's ability, the former chairman stepped down graciously pledging us his full cooperation and support. And it so happened that such support was more abundant than either of us would have dreamed.

This man, who talked like "GI Joe," happened to be Umong Mathur, one of the largest contracting and building magnates in the land. His empire encompassed a total monopoly of construction equipment. "From Bombay to Delhi to Calcutta to Madras, all construction equipment has to come from one of my assemblies. When we get the parts from Germany, we put them together a few miles away. I have really big hangers to do it in. You name it and we've got it: bulldozers, caterpillars, cranes, jackhammers, steamrollers, steam shovels, cement-mixers, air-compressors, and the lot. See this huge auditorium, we cleared it out, leveled it, landscaped it, brought in the crushed rock, everything."

Umong waved his chauffeur to come up the drive. Almost pleading with us not to refuse, he handed us some crisp hundred-rupee notes to purchase any art materials Wendel might need, and asked what he might do while we were gone. It felt like we had walked right into the middle of one of Bombay's garish movies as we rode down the highways and suburbs into the city, lounging in the spacious car, leaning out of the window, and marveling how the tables of providence had flipped since we had left Whitefield.

Yet, if we had arrived as urchins only to be given the keys to the great city of Bombay, we had yet another battle, the lusts of the eye and the waywardness of the mind. A strange, ominous sense rippled my mood for a second, as I scanned a desolate garbage-strewn highway, bordered by blackened apartment buildings. Circling high in the air in wide arcs, wings six feet wide, dotting rooftops, and hopping around refuse and dog carcasses, were black, scaled, bony vultures. Wandering through this blighted region were two Shaivite sadhus with tridents, yard-long knotted hair, ochre rags, and a chalky powder covering their features. It was a passing vision of death. This mystical epiphany of the abyss tiptoed almost undetected on the horizon of my mind. By nightfall, we were back.

I strolled outside and passed several tea shanties while bhajans screamed over the loudspeakers. I finally stopped a few hundred feet away at the barbed-wire fence surrounding Dharmakshetra. Other than a large open field packed with cars, the area was quite barren except for another modern architectural wonder nearby, the Christian Mission Hospital. Conscious that it was Christmas Eve, I needed to be alone and dispassionately reflect for a while. I was fighting a general disgust with "outward appearances" in general. But there was more. The unthinkable thought: I wondered if the paradoxical fusion of beauty and gaudiness—or even bestiality—in Baba's features wasn't some higher riddle of sublimity.

At that moment, I was suddenly confronted with a scene that reminded me of the "Golden Cactus" in Reno, Nevada. Sitting on the elevated landscape with the monstrous full moon just above it, was a brightly lit object that fully resembled a flying saucer about to take off from a landing site. It was Baba's private quarters. Then from the pit of my stomach came the logical question to ask on a Christmas Eve. "If Christ were here in this century, would he live in something that looked like a flying saucer on a launch pad?" Because it looked exactly like that. It was pure architectural audacity.

I could not decide whether the object on the hill was awesome in some strange way or just another modern architectural fungoid affronting all good taste. The large double-storied elliptical cement saucer was alternately glowing green and red by hidden lighting, paling the full moon. With 1,008 separate facets, it represented the 1,008-petaled lotus of the gods.

In the saucer's forefront perched on the hillside beneath it stood a giant cement lotus which burned in dayglow colors. A plexiglass hemisphere above it glowed ultraviolet, like the eye of a colossal arachnid, transforming this platform into a "sci-fi" transporter tube, a Venusian fire-plant, and Vishnu's loft, all in one.

I suddenly saw this Being in a brilliant red robe step onto the platform of the flower. It was Sai Baba being adored by 20,000 onlookers in the massive auditorium who could see him on the hill. This little man, whose head of hair resembled an anther blossomed out of this cyclopean flower while radiating some phosphorescent otherworldly light. The crowd went dead silent. I studied the scene trying to reconcile it with Christmas.

Afterward, still bemused and not necessarily in the Christmas spirit nor particularly elated, I sat glassy-eyed in a wooden tea-shack sipping tea.

Wendel was working all night on a titanic work of art for the stage, a Christ nativity mural to celebrate the coming one-world religion. It was a work of genius, everybody felt. But my soul was trying to get at something beneath this riddle.

# Chapter 17

# *Ending the Bombay Jaunt*

*O*ne week later, the crowds in the large auditorium were amazed at Wendel's large circular nativity scene center-stage. It looked like the work of a modern Michaelangelo. Meanwhile, I took charge of leading the surging crowd in bhajans before a battery of microphones when Raja Reddy nodded in my direction.

Wendel and I were treated almost as celebrities. By now a few others from Whitefield had joined us. It was now three weeks in Bombay and we were glad to be with Baba on the road especially with the recent tragic news from Whitefield.

Ed had heard from his wife, Chris, in Whitefield. In plain language, the group in Whitefield was hurtling into confusion and schism, with a whole number suddenly going off by themselves. It sounded like chaos.

Their last moment of group togetherness was at Reverend Ivan Carroll's, of all places, on Christmas Eve. From all reports, it had actually been a brief interlude of relief and contentment, if not joy, for many of them. Forgetting themselves, they all sang Christmas carols and made themselves at home in a genuine American household with chairs, tables, dressers, a couch or two, bric-a-brac, a piano, and regular toilets. But what really gave it that down-home flavor, out in the middle of nowhere, was a midnight snack of gingerbread cookies, cakes, ice cream, hot cocoa, and pumpkin pie. But surely that shouldn't stumble them. Love was love regardless of divine form.

The sudden arrival in Bombay of a distraught and despairing Victoria, thin as a broomstick and wearing a dark blue sari, was a fearful omen that the seeds of light in our own community were not taking root properly. And if the seeds weren't growing properly right under the direct radiance of Baba then what chance did those myriads of seeds in America have who may never come closer to Baba than within a mile or two?

The same Vickie whom I met under the "tree of wisdom" at Puttaparthi a year back, the companion to the handsome young Englishman, Anthony, who was now exiled in Malta, was wearing her bravest chin-up expression, but it didn't last. When I escorted her past the sentry gate, the modern complex all completely new to her, up the flower-lined drive to the base of the ramp, she soon began to waver as Baba came out of the saucer, down the ramp, and stood with us at the base. But he was hurrying to his car. He did not acknowledge her and it almost killed her.

That night, Vickie stumbled through the story, frantically dropping cutlery and battling with her food as we had dinner in her modern hotel at Juhu Beach. Her flight to London was the next day. "The doubter," Peter, Benno, Martin, Kerry, Janet, and Vickie had held nightly get-togethers in Whitefield. Apparently, they had been having many similar perceptions and doubts about Baba. Then grievances were aired, along with feelings about India in general. The blight became an epidemic, one rotten apple had spoiled the barrel, and all of them became alienated not only from Baba but from one another. Each was proceeding along his own course. But just before complete ruination, Vicki, too weak to hold it on her own, repented. What the others had said about Baba just could not be true. She had to get away from the other backsliders as quickly as possible, leave India, and think things out again in the quiet of Dorest or Malta, or wherever she was driven.

How sad to have been with Baba for a year now, and leave by such ignoble means. Vickie could clutch at the diminishing microbe of her first love, faith in Baba. And like a marriage vow, she would faithfully hold on to this if nothing else endured. Vickie was English peerage, the daughter of Lady Hillingdon and Lord Mills. I had quite a love for her, this tall pretty stately blonde who was on her last legs in India. Accustomed to estates and manor-houses in Essex and London, nursemaids since childhood, and the English easy life of gentry such as her parents and other lords and ladies, Vickie now had her own trust fund from the family estate that would insure her from ever having to worry about the struggles and inconveniences of living. I wondered if this rather inviting door, always open to her, combined with the soft life of her past, had gotten the better of her. She emphatically denied it. She and I used to wonder, when my dad was on his first diplomatic assignment in London, whether we had bumped into each other as kids when our families were members of the exclusive Hurlingham Club.

Vickie left in a whirl and we stayed until Baba's tour had come to an end. By the time we were on our way back to Whitefield, we had been gone for a month and a half, four weeks in Bombay and two in Goa. We also had added another member, "Surya Dass" Herbert Grubb. I wondered how Baba would handle the Whitefield remnant. It didn't take too long to find out in the darshan line.

# Chapter 18

# *The Anvil of God*

*P*ah, cracks, all cracks," the hard face of God declared, a tone of wounded anger resembling a father disinheriting a recalcitrant son. Across the Brindavan darshan line, as we arrived, was a sad collection of faces. The unfaithful long-crippled Western remnant now deep in shame. Facing us on the girls' side was a motley of pale faces with quivering mouths, making it evident that they were slowly dying inside and now looking back pitifully at Baba.

Baba hurried up to me as I approached the darshan line and said in a whisper, "Faith of others now complete ruin. Your group, go to Puttaparthi now. Stay separate. Soon, I'm coming also. Huhhhh?"

"Yes, Baba." He abruptly left back toward the private gate, passing the others without a glimmer of recognition.

Now that exclusion from Baba's presence was imminent on them, the value of even a tolerant glance from Baba was beyond measure, say nothing of the original hope that Baba would chase them around with tears in his eyes so common with penitent parents who have ignored their children for too long.

After Baba's command, we were on our way to Puttaparthi in a rented car. I was not about to complain about returning to the wilderness. Besides, Bombay had filled my quota for high energy city life. The old hangers-on at Whitefield would be ignored by Baba while new arrivals from Hilda's group in New York would first reach Baba at Brindavan, be embraced as long-lost children, and then sent up to the main ashram where we would welcome them warily.

I carefully looked at the hard-line holdovers, who either never went to Whitefield in mid-November or returned soon after, for signs of change. India and Marsha conveyed that they had grown in grace. Others survived.

Sandy the Australian and Zolt the Hungarian had taken a fascinating turn. Sandy was the same, ever resembling a thinned, sparkling water-nymph, though perhaps sparkling less. Zolt, who before resembled a Bruegel medieval peasant, now vied for the dubious distinction of the Simple-Simon village idiot. He had a new emaciated, knock-kneed, watery-eyed look that spoke of an ostentatious self-denial bordering on torture. The prematurely wizened Zolt would now be escorted around the ashram with the same vacant stare as those in sanatoriums, while Sandy could take pride in holding up her own budding little rishi and Vedic ascetic, head wobbling on a chicken bone neck. He needed his rib cage a little bit bonier and a slightly larger walking stick to resemble Ramana Maharishi. It was sainthood through torture, one more path that a grinning perverse ego could hide behind, the ashram equivalent to a Porsche in a parking lot. Sandy just loved gliding her man around, or perhaps "non-man" around.

The hangers-on and "cracks" arrived like Bedouin wanderers congregating along the far end of the ashram.

When it was rumored that Baba's car was finally coming—a hotline phone call from Brindavan to the phone in the ashram postmaster's office to Kasturi—a wild plan of reconciliation was thought out by the "crack ringleaders" in the turbulent short hours following the call. The idea came through a channeled voice as many of them, now somewhat removed from the herd of the ashram, turned to signs and inward psychic channels to reaffirm their closeness to Baba. The surface rejection was to test the mettle of their faith in the ever constant love of Baba. This was because they were now test-worthy in their walk.

In the final hour a group of them skipped, walked, and ran out the side gate holding hands and beaming know-ingly with a newfound exuberance. They went down the barren road, running for a stretch, swaying a bit, skip-ping again, and marching with flowers in their hair, lapels, and bunched up in their hands, as children bear-ing forth their true playfulness. This enviable childish spontaneity was a hallmark of essential purity and innocence. It showed that their inward nature was with-out blemish. The fornications of the past were mere passing clouds over the clear moon of the eternal atma.

In the final lap of the journey, Baba's car edged around that one narrowing section of road clustered by trees on both sides. Meeting him head-on was a human road-block, daisy-chained across the road, smiling, singing and prancing, now jumping up and down in jubilation as the car strained to a dead stop. Inches in front of the bumper, the ringleader gazed through the windshield with a goofy grin plastered across his face. The gleeful girls, giggled, shrieked, and pranced, adorning the car with flower petals, while the human tentacle wrapped around the car. Now for Baba's forgiving delight.

The window rolled down, two black orbs radiating fury. Then came the judgment, tearing up the air with the force of thunder rippling out in waves of blackened light. "Pssssttt. Foreign cracks get out of the way. Go away from Puttparthi, acting like hippies, not my bhaktas. Go. Get out."

The car sped on. Exuberance turned to wrenching despair. The inner message had betrayed them, and now they stood doubled up, feeling like something in them had been torn out like a rotten onionskin.

On the roof, an infuriated Kasturi attempted to carry out Baba's command of eviction. The "cracks" lay back and moaned. If it came to it, they would have to be dragged away to the fence where they would lie out and die in the sun rather than leave.

A new wave of Americans had recently arrived, effervescing over their destiny. In their presence was a plump Indian girl named Tatu from a prominent Bombay family of film producers. She commanded sufficient charisma and eloquence to quickly take over the emotionally bankrupt rooftop community of outcasts. She was "the rooftop prophetess" claiming a psychic channel to the very heart of Baba. Her activities carried the fascination of a games room discovered by a wandering horde of bored tourists aboard an ocean liner. She had "guided" the group to meet Baba's returning car. They should not let outward rejections fool them she told them later. Now, instead of the wasteland of exiles that the roof was supposed to be, it hummed and crackled with messages from the "higher Baba," proving that theirs was the greatest access to the coveted master. Soon, a small group of girls was selected as sufficiently anointed to share Tatu's most cryptic confidences. All but one of them was from the new arrivals.

Even though Kasturi, by Baba's command, declared Tatu off-limits, the inner circle knew that it was merely a high test designated for the final unshacklings preceding enlightenment in so stupendous a soul as Tatu. In the dead of night, the spirit voices had hinted more than once that hers was to be a great mission, and none but the "three American sisters" knew it. And they weren't about to tell.

But just when the "cracks" seemed irreparably alienated, Baba suddenly called everyone in for an interview. Our group had grown so large that Baba directed me to assemble everyone in the prayer hall, closed off from the outside. Sitting before Baba was a crowd of vulnerable and broken people and any word of kindness, at this point, would endear these lost people to Baba forever. And those words of restoration came. Baba hit dead center when he began to outline what is now known as the dysfunctional American family. Family estrangement was a common trait among this bold group of seekers.

"Many of you coming on a long journey to India, taking many risks, going through many difficulties. For many years searching, searching for love. You did not get parents' love in American families. See, American family is divided. Selfish. Each person thinking of himself, not his duty. Not good, very bad. Parents in America give many material articles but no prema, no love. I am speaking of human love, not divine love. Human love far less, but still important. Without human love child is like a plant without water, withers. Growing up hurting, angry, even hating parents.

"Indian family different. In India, there are large families, growing together many generations, all members: father, grandfathers, sometimes great-grandfathers, uncles, mothers, grandmothers, many relatives. Not separating from home at 20 years like in America. Members in Indian families are loyal, very dependent. The child is molded better. He is obedient and takes pride in pleasing his family. Very afraid of displeasing parents with moral sin. Moral sin selfish. If he is bad, the whole family suffers. Yes, his mistake tarnishes the family name, and all suffer with his mistake. But all over America is complete immorality."

And then came the missile to the heart:

---

"You come here for love...the mother's love you missed. I love you more than a thousand mothers. And a thousand times more than your mother."

---

There was a long pause, the silence welling underneath with choked emotion. "This is also a privilege, because this is divine love. God's love."

Baba gave us a long, searching look. "I would give my blood for you." Many of the girls from the old contingent starting sniffling. I just squeezed Baba's foot, and looked up with contrite gratitude as his gaze seemed to envelope me in an oozing nectar. "Yes, I also need your love."

The interview ended with many people in tears. Baba's mercy seemed overwhelming. The Avatar with the sword of perfect timing had left his victims pierced to the heart and broken by his will. With such forgiveness, who could resist his command to worship him as God, as he proclaimed in the early days? And what more suitable sacrifice than a human soul should one offer upon his altar? Such was the fabric of divine timing.

# Chapter 19

# *A Different*
# *Light*

*T*o my utter joy, Baba bade us return to Whitefield after the recent festival—just like the year before. I was grateful that it was only three months in the Andhra Pradesh wilderness. His words of endearment in that last interview to the group I was certain would inoculate any and all of us from schisming and falling away.

On the night of February 27, the cab took us from the central Bangalore bus terminus out through the 12 miles of countryside to the quiet little town of Whitefield. We stopped on the large circular park in front of the "Major's house," where all ten of us had stayed before the Goa trip. My backup option was the Blake cabin out in the open fields over a mile away, an impossible target for an ordinary car, considering the riveted boulder-strewn approach road.

Then sure enough what I feared most happened. The light coming from the Major's house revealed that the once bare rooms had since been filled with furniture. I checked all the doors, running around the house in the nippy air. Ed soon found out from the Anglo-Indian student rabble next door, drinking and playing poker in their little cabin, that some "blokes" just started moving in the day before. I had my heart set on this large house, hoping a better era would follow. Now we had to let go of the cab, for we had nowhere to go.

From out of the chilly darkness, a slow inspiration dawned on me as I caught the yonder light emerging out of the Carrolls' frosted windows. Indeed, I had all but forgotten the two missionaries whom I had only seen once on that November day when they came over to invite us all over for Christmas carols. The breadth of their offer, should we ever have any needs, came to mind.

Ed and Surya Das noticed me caught up in thought as I tentatively moved in the direction of their house. "You all guard the luggage, I think I've got the answer," I yelled back.

What concerned me as I went through the gate was the delicateness of the moment. One spiritual block would be facing another: the broad and subtle path to God with its resilient brilliance facing that ever so faithful remnant of "straight and narrow wayers" whose relentless grip on the hem of that one avatar, Jesus Christ, was of such magnitude that for me to march in upon their own encampment and split that bond asunder—so that they might acquiesce to the Godhood of more than that one single Messiah—would be a spiritual victory of titanic proportions. Perhaps sensing the weight of this, my spirit welled up within as though nervous before battle, seeking every full breath of air available before the doorbell was answered. To be sure, we needed no help from them; if we had to, we could brave the chilly air in the little park, for Baba's abundance was with us always.

"Hi," I projected with stouthearted abandon as the door swung open revealing the two clear eyes of Mrs. Carroll beaming back warmly behind a plain pair of glasses. Then another face popped into view more or less through the crack along the top of the door, grinning down good-naturedly at me. "Well, hello. Come on in, we were just thinking about you." It was Reverend Ivan smiling like Jiminy Cricket.

Within a minute my plan was in effect. Soon after, Ed and Surya Das emerged out of the blackness into the porch-light after I called them, perhaps resembling two Mexican banditos in waiting. On up the path they smiled, Ed somewhat impishly and Surya Das as transcendentally as ever. Inside the house, the Carrolls' helper had all but reset the dining room table, having already put out three cups of hot steaming chocolate. We mutually nodded to shelve the debate on higher truth till the food, soon out on the table, was disposed of.

The table scene must have, at times, resembled the tenor of W.C. Fields as Dr. Quack, lodging in with the good old simple folk in *Pioneer Days Is Here Again*. A trickle of spiritual banter was maintained, no matter how overpowering the next bite of food was, putting in evidence our true ascetic willpower. This was a true Midwest farm feast, from home-style mashed potatoes to the roast beef which we religiously avoided, though I wanted to eat half the side off it being a carnivore by nature. We ate grilled cheese sandwiches instead. I had noticed recently that my hands trembled when I ate food this good, the deep perpetual hunger in me was so great. The fork in my hand shook noticeably as I tried to conceal it.

Playing in the background, I heard for the first time, in any depth, the first traces of classical music since coming to India.

After the sumptuous meal, I opted for an excerpt of Wagner, and sank into an armchair. Mrs. Carroll asked Eddie what sort of music he liked.

A wry smile disengaged an imaginary Havana; he looked over to her and responded, "Ya ever hear of 'Aqua Lung' by Jethro Tull?"

"No, can't say I have. I'm sure you all listen to brands of music that we don't even know exist," Mrs. Carroll responded diplomatically.

The tall Reverend finally broke his long stare off through the ceiling, and said, "Reckon it's time for us all to hit-the-hay. In this house we generally have a moment of prayer with the Lord before turning in. Are you folks averse to joining us?"

"Oh no, not at all," came our unified response.

As the two missionaries prayed, the light-key feeling of the evening went away, bringing in a quiet might of conviction, a power I found to be most baffling. Another finger than that of Baba pointed to the secrets of my heart, exposing thoughts and attitudes from the standpoint of a different light, indeed a holiness, that would have no yoking with what I called the negative polarity.

I could also feel a quality of love which the Carrolls seemed so familiar with, suggesting that unpleasant notion of my own unworthiness and how far short of perfection I was in terms of...well, some kind of godly standard. This was an experience that I found to be most radical, especially since coming to India where this sense of deep "goodness" was nowhere to be found (it was certainly absent from my atheistic upbringing). Ecstatic, exalted consciousness, yes I experienced that— but "goodness"? Not really. During the Reverend's heartfelt prayer it felt on the horizon of my mind as though some fiber of consciousness in me was on the fulcrum of oblivion.

As the Reverend and his wife escorted us down the hall to the main guest room, they urged all of us to unabashedly feel at home, that what was here was not theirs but the Lord's. In certain ways, we fellows reminded them of those times their son Dale was with them. A picture atop a dresser revealed a large athletic blond fellow in glasses with short hair and strong eyes, the ideal son of devotion, integrity, and thoroughbred moral character, what Eddie would call a "straight cat." But it seemed that it took a wholesome family to produce such an honest good guy. Parental modeling was not unimportant.

Eddie grabbed the adjacent laundry room which had a small cot. Surya Das and I got the main guest room with two handsome beds. Naturally, we insisted on sleeping on the floor while unrolling our mats over the rugs. Perhaps we thought we might convict them of their sin of sleeping on beds when other people slept on the floor. It might have even occurred to Eddie to drive the point home by curling up in the washing machine. Advanced adepts just didn't need beds. We knew that the only way of escape from the prison of maya was to divorce oneself from all comforts. Yet our explanation didn't put them to shame about their excesses. They were rather amused at high-sounding nonsense, and I felt like the infantile martyr who insists upon eating out of a dog's bowl, while the others sit at a table: the same food mind you, but rather in the corner, slurping, where one can look morosely around at those eating at a table; those who would dare feast at a table while you undergo such hardship.

Surya Das and I talked in the darkness after deciding it might be interesting to try out the beds since no one was using them. It had been over a year since I had slept on one. Surya Das' roots were in the deep South, but he had transcended them by being on the cutting edge of the sixties.

"Did I ever tell you about granddaddy?" butted in Surya Das. "He was hornier than a bull toad. Used to keep dirty pictures hidden around the house. Talked to me about girls sometimes. If grandma ever got wind of it I 'spect she woulda just about died. But no wonder. I doubt if they'd gone at it even once in 20 years. I tell you," Surya Das chortled, "he was hurtin. Sometimes when I used to lie awake late at night I'd hear him callin' down the hall, 'Thelma...Thelma.' And a weary voice would answer back, 'Aw what is it George?' And there'd be a long silence, and then granddaddy would think of somethin. 'Uhhh, what time did you say that picnic was tomorrow?' And she'd answer back, 'Come on George, 4:30. Now I was practically asleep.' Half an hour later it'd start up all over again. I'd hear, 'Thelma... Thelma.' Sour as a lemon, she'd ask, 'What is it this time George?' And he'd answer back 'Aw uhhh, never mind... uhhh.' It was pathetic. Sometimes, they'd do this back and forth five or six times. If that's what their religion does to 'em, it ain't right. Who'd ever want to marry an old prune like that anyway. I'd a kicked her out of the house years ago if I were him...why stand for it...he was just yeller. If she can't even put-out, what good is she? Certainly, there's no earth-changing magic in their company. I'd prefer a dog, at least they're cheerful."

"Yup, I know what you mean. Boondocks consciousness. She wants it just as bad, but maneuvers the poor dude into playing the dirty man who initiates the thing again and again till she approves, does a noble deed, and then comes out wearing white robes. Your grandma's whole concept of sin connected with marital sex is perverted. I don't even think it's Christian to be honest. It's a pride number. But she'll get burned for such hypocrisy in the long run."

"There's probably a special astral hell for all those who engage in sexual blackmail."

"Yeah, all that dammed-up desire of a lifetime consumes them, while they get stuck with some wet noodle who reads the cosmic *Wall Street Journal* all day and night and doesn't even want to talk."

Surya Das concluded, "The thing about celibacy over here in India is that it isn't vindictive. The Hindus do it more than we do, but they understand why they're doing it. They're abstaining out of a sense of higher love, that's why. They're transmuting that energy."

Meanwhile, my energy was transmuting into sleep as I sank into one of the most untroubled and refreshing sleeps I had had in a long time. The bed itself, for a body now adjusted to straw mats and cement floors, reminded me of a cloud. I hated the idea of leaving it.

At 7:00 A.M. I reluctantly awoke as the gentle dawn light fell on the curtains. I became conscious of sounds emerging out of the living room. First low mumbling, then a motley of Indian and American voices singing hymns, then both of the Carrolls speaking in subdued tones. Then a flowing music soon caught me in lazy reflection. I didn't have that edgy sense of alienation from the world or the confusion of thought I so often did at the ashram when I would awake to a music that would also flow and echo in mysterious twists, the unfailing melodious voice of Vijaya contorting and whining through the beautiful but sad scales of the *Suprabhattam*.

Mrs. Carroll's hand gently rapped on the door to alert us for breakfast. They would be off to perform church duties. And we would be going about our business of finding a place. The remnant of the Sunday school, Indians of all ages, gleamed when we appeared, only to suddenly look disappointed upon hearing of our discipleship under Baba. Some of them had been Baba devotees.

That morning we foreclosed the possibility of other disciples beating us to the Blake cabin. It was almost picturesque as it sat under a cluster of trees on what had once been productive farmland. We had tea with Mrs. Blake, an old Anglo-Indian woman, who liked us. Over the entrance of the little cabin were words that Gill had scrawled crudely with chalk, "Shanti Kutir," or abode of peace, which belied everything it became for Gill in tragic irony. We agreed to move in the next day.

After a sumptuous Sunday dinner that evening at the

Carrolls', conversation in the living room wasn't light-key for long. Evidently, the Carrolls had some kind of burden for us.

The living room oozed with power as the circle of faces looked at each successive speaker. Both blocks of belief could not be true at the same time: Either we could successively synthesize "A" with "Non-A" or "A" would be right in its stubborn affirmation that it was intellectual schizophrenia to link it with "Non-A." In other words, if it's all one, we could engulf them, Christian or not, but if they could keep us from engulfing them, then it is not all one. The gospel was uncompromisingly unique and exclusive.

First, I had to deal with the formidable task of the Bible as I looked at the rock-hard determination behind their eyes. After all I proposed, was not the "Logos" an eternal principle forever repeating itself in a multitude of contexts? And was not the entire written account of this Logos an allegory of truth too exalted to articulate by its overt examples? What about a yin-yang theme in the Garden of Eden? They disagreed to the very foundations of their personalities.

We had no trouble with either the supernatural or miracles, that was old hat to us, we saw them every day. We also knew that Christ was legitimate, so what were they getting at? We believed in him along with other avatars. Didn't they know that the *cosmic mind* could easily work out so complex a scheme (accurate to the very final atom), as Christ's advent? But they countered—it wasn't an impersonal cosmic mind, it was a transcendent God. And Christ's advent stood on hundreds of Old Testament prophecies, not the cosmic mind.

Then was Scripture infallible they asked me? "Oh sure, the God who can hold the North Star in the heavens can easily preserve all Scripture, be it the Bible or the Upanishads," I responded.

Indeed, He could provide that Scripture not be adulterated through the ages, but let us make sure exactly what that Scripture is, they recommended, pointing to one Christ and one incident of incarnation.

Agreed, I said, that Christ was a person in history as much in the flesh as Tiberius or Xerxes, and more historically substantiated than any single human being of antiquity by all legal-historical criteria. But he was also the cosmic Christ, having incarnated before as an absolute principle, and as such, he has touched all Scripture in all forms. I was pushing the Universal Logos theme.

Where does it say that? they asked.

Surya Das, smiling like the noble savage, interjected his wealth of Indian lore. Why the Yacqui Indians, the Aztecs, and, at least one other tribe had all seen appearances of the "Great White Master." Joseph Smith of the Mormons also said bluntly that Christ had appeared to the Indians in America. Besides, I now continued, Cayce in his readings from the Akashic records, the skeen of the cosmic mind, unearthed a long genealogy of Christ's past incarnations: for instance, his appearance as Melchizidek. Besides, Levi, who like Cayce went into the cosmic mind to write *The Aquarian Gospel*, a gospel more revealing for this age due to the higher evolution of souls, endorsed all of Cayce's observations, agreeing especially on the unknown years of Christ, from age 12 to 30, where Christ sojourned to the East as part of his training as a master. And where could there be a greater theme of unification than to have Christ share in the spiritual wealth of the East?

The Carrolls observed that it was a dubious wealth of which an army of saints could still spend forever picking up the pieces of wretched humanity, but go on.

Christ learned healing in Benares, transmutation under a master in the Himalayas, and in Tibet he went under the highest initiates only to transcend them.

The Carrolls observed that this was a myth equaling Von Daniken's *Chariot of the Gods*. It had no backing in historiography.

Besides, if it's all one, why didn't Christ just remain in India? He could have just as easily taught from there. Why even return to Israel? A greater syncretistic statement would have been for him to have taught from India and remained there. And if he had been to India, why did none of his disciples breathe a word about it or go with him? Why, out of hundreds of documented patristic documents and letters going back to the first century, does not one of them breathe a single word about any trips to India? Rather, Christ is viewed in the exclusive historical context of Palestine and never out of that region. No eyewitness ever saw him go beyond upper Galilee.

Likewise, does it not seem possible that rather than the wise men of the East coming to train Christ, they actually indicated Christ's uniqueness by bearing gifts to him. Indeed, did they not show that His redemptive plan was a sign of salvation to even the people on the far distant ends of the earth, as well as the children of Israel? Was it not God who promised Abraham that all the earth would be blessed through his seed? Their "wise men" were not sufficient in the East, otherwise these wise men would not have come to seek the promised One. And how interesting that not once throughout the New Testament does Christ make reference to any of the standard Eastern concepts of pantheism. The Carrolls had a point. You had to look between the lines to find hints of all-is-one and navigate around verses that were clearly dualistic, not monistic.

"But," one of the Carrolls continued, "if you're going to pick and choose what is, and what is not Scripture in the Bible you are making yourself the final authority for adjudicating truth. You are also viewing yourself as being on par with the ancient apostles and prophets of

Scripture, therefore qualified to write your own edition. And if each man can do that, there is nothing left. We may as well throw in the writings of Edgar Allan Poe and every science fiction writer that ever lived and say that each has invented a valid cosmology. And if you do that, needless to say, there will be a spaghetti of contradictions. Under the authority of such a web of deception, you will become irretrievably lost to wander into deeper delusion. The Bible has to stand as its own standard, otherwise you are on shifting sand." They also claimed the Bible was a grid to sift the false from the true in the objective outward world as well as the spiritual world.

While the Carrolls pressed home this theme of a trustworthy standard, their argument amplified in my mind. Mrs. Carroll observed that if our ultimate basis for judgment was a private inner experience of intuition, well, experiences and feelings contradicted and betrayed—the hallucinatory vision of the drunk talking to the purple elephant. To him it's real. We had enough examples of this in our own camp—the rooftop prophetess, Gill, and others. Besides, what standard could I, in turn, use to discern the false from the true, the counterfeit prophet from the genuine article? For did I not realize that the Bible repeatedly tells of coming counterfeit spokesmen of God, awesome in their subtle arguments? How could I, on my own, supporting myself by my own intellectual bootstraps summon the relentless standard to judge between the true and the false prophet? Was there some magic about me, as though given an impunity above deception by divine favor, that made it such that practically all other men could be prone to deception but me, Tal Brooke? No, no, I was too democratic in belief to do other than rank myself in the general family of man, when such questions emerged. But it's a fair universe isn't it? I countered in my most humble, family-of-man voice.

Behind the question, the Zen Master of my intellect was detached from the arena of conflict as it carefully watched the chessboard for openings. In a sense, each pawn was that precise persona within that would most persuasively manipulate things to edge them into the next square. Then at that acute unsuspecting moment, a potent mantra or Koan would be sprung to utterly disarm them. To bring this off, however, I needed more than ever to surrender to the Tao, the indwelling Baba, as a guide, always a step ahead of the rational thought.

I now answered why it was a fair universe. We can adjudicate Scripture, I proposed, because we have the perfect light of God within, and that becomes our touchstone of truth to test everything. As we evolve spiritually, we gain in intuitive wisdom to enable us further to see beyond the mazes of life. Thus, perfect inner intuition-wisdom is the standard, because the highest scripture is written in the skeen of the overself, deep within.

Meanwhile, my question still hung potently in the air. "It's a fair universe, isn't it?"

"Insofar that God would that none should perish, but have everlasting life through His Son, Jesus Christ," came the answer directly from the New Testament. "But this does not mean that we are free to adulterate God's Truth to suit us. Dictating reality just to suit our whims. That's like the child who refuses to get out of bed one morning because the world does not conform to his wish of being made out of candy-cane houses and streets. He can lie in bed forever, yet never change what is, nor blackmail the Creator into obediently dusting up creation to suit his fancies. As humbling as it sounds, we have no choice but to accept what is."

The mighty weight of Truth, they went on, is that man in his unredeemed state not only stands in eternal judgment, far from the holy presence of God, separated by a gulf of sin as wide as the universe, but because of this, is at enmity with God. This problem of sin is so great that man is numbered among the adversary. It is anything but an illusion. It is a massive dilemma. The stupendous thing about God's grace to fallen and imperfect man (merely a created creature and no more) is that it would yet be so broad and deep as to love man in his sins to the extent of formulating the perfect riddle of bailing him out of an impossible predicament. Not only that, at the same time, grace fully satisfies a perfect standard of justice and love. Fully a mystery so deep as to baffle all the hosts of the universe, cherubim and all. And what was that riddle of grace? It was the space-time incarnation of the Logos as the long predicted Messiah, Jesus Christ, fully in the flesh of whom even Thomas, the doubter among the apostles, had to finally say, in empirically testing the reality of the resurrection body, "My Lord and My God." Not a gnostic spiritualized resurrection abstracted into a principle of metaphysics, but the kind that left an empty tomb guarded by an alerted Roman guard who would undergo death by Roman law, if they failed.

This was the kind of resurrection that would change a small weakly band of men who denied their Master once on the cross, and once fearful of the drastic forces of the Sanhedrin and their nation, not to speak of the power of Rome, into changed men who were instrumental in turning the world upside down for a man who was what ... dead? Men so sure of this fact that each apostle, barring John, died a martyr's death. And the apostles were not the only witnesses of Christ's resurrection appearance. The Bible spoke of an assembly of 500 who saw it, and yet, lived to tell about it even during the apostolic ministry of Saint Paul. And even the lowbrows of the day knew that the easiest way for the Jewish opposition power to dispel the spreading rumor of the resurrection was to produce the body and drag it openly through the streets. That would immediately end the problem. But that was the problem, for some reason they couldn't. (Nor was "the body" seen wandering India!)

Now the Carrolls made the proclamation of utter exclusiveness that truly made Christianity unique. Part of the riddle was in Acts 4:12 as Reverend Carroll opened his Bible reading, "There is salvation in no one else, for there is no other name under heaven given among men by which we must be saved, save that of Jesus Christ." That narrow gate was to accept Jesus Christ exclusively as Lord and Savior. Not bow down to any other: Buddha, Krishna, Chaitanya, or yes, Sathya Sai Baba. Christ never said he would keep on coming. He came once and for all, that one specific purpose, and his predicted one and only return will be for the specific purpose of consummating all of human history as we know it.

I went deep into my mind to find the key in philology to deal with the "no other name" category. The synchretic key that I had found in the past was through the writings of Paul Tillich in his books *Dynamics of Faith and Biblical Religion*, and *The Search for Ultimate Reality*, among the first things exposed to me under the name of Christianity, following my huge LSD trip. Looking for "God" I took a course on religion at the University of Virginia. We also read Bultmann, and Buber, but for some reason we never looked at the Bible. In these open-ended theologies lay the groundwork for me to build a synchretistic matrix with the other world religions. But sitting in the Carrolls' living room, all I found was a haze, void of the raw facts: no linguistic key of ethnic word origins which might connote "Universal Logos," instead of that particular name, came to mind.

The Tao in me froze in a cross-current of static from an opposing force, jamming my dials seemingly with more power than a million kilowatt Russian jamming station. Going to the question of Baba, I had yet to deal with the incongruity of such good and wholesome people as the

Carrolls, who surprisingly, would show such an unpremeditated visceral repulsion of Baba, that the very idea of linking him to Christ was anathema.

I had for a while discoursed Baba's great love and the raw virtue and sincerety of people surrounding him such as Raja Reddy and Kasturi, models of excellence and patience. For surely, I gambled such credentials as goodness would break through to these missionaries. But this brought on a whole new line of thought.

"A man can appear good, and still be deceived. Our own seeming goodness is not sufficient to bring us into the full light of God. Scripture, in fact, tells us repeatedly, 'None is righteous, no, not one.' For there is no better salesman for counterfeit truth than a good man." This thought hadn't entered my universe.

We sought to quell the tide of 'bigoted fanaticism,' lest the Bible be misunderstood in a context less than the most spiritual. "These are universal axioms that speak to all men on their own level of consciousness. But to derive the highest meaning, you have to go above duality and all pairs of opposites, and realize that this is a road map guiding toward highest unity. But such understanding only comes with considerable spiritual evolution." Then as a second thought Surya Das observed, "I just can't see someone running around with little horns and a tail."

"I don't believe the Bible asks you to do that, believe that Satan has little horns. I would not be a bit surprised, in fact, if that wasn't his own idea in the first place, to camouflage his true picture by an act of demythologizing. To the contrary, I am not at all convinced that this popular imp in any way resembles what Saint Paul was talking about when he says in Ephesians 6, 'Ye wrestle not against flesh and blood but against principalities, against powers, against the rulers of darkness of this world, against spiritual wickedness in high places.'" Satan indeed was cosmic. Even Lucas' eventual Star Wars imagery did not approach this being.

In the same vein, the Carrolls opposed Surya Das' idea that the Bible was most of all directed to a tiny fraction of high spiritual initiates. Rather, the plain statements of Scripture stated the opposite. Far from just communicating to Oxford Ph.D.'s, or at the time, Pharisaic scholars, Christ was reaching out to those poor, unsightly, and abandoned orphans of the earth whose only credentials were a humble sincere hunger for God's love and forgiveness. Turning to chapter one of First Corinthians, the Reverend emphasized this: "'You don't see among you many of the wise (according to this world's standards) nor many of the ruling class, nor many from the noblest families. But God has chosen what the world calls foolish to shame the wise.'"

Well we the disciples of Baba often prided ourselves on this identical clownish aspect, where our true exaltation appeared ridiculous to the world. Yes, there was a parallel.

As for an esoteric standard for interpreting the Bible, "Why is it also," the Reverend pursued, "that Paul states emphatically—and here he went to the Phillips translation of the Bible—"'Our letters to you have no double meaning, they mean just what you understand them to mean when you read them.'" That kind of provision allows your farmers and simple ordinary folk like us through the door if you see what I mean," Ivan emphasized. The gospel was not elitist.

The three of us sympathized with their plight, but we also knew that the Bible in its great multilevel complexity spoke a different form of angelic language, beyond even symbol, to those who were ready. And the true quantum leap occurred for true initiates where the Bible speaks of an absolute division in the universe between good and evil. The "simple" reading portrayed a God of holiness who cannot look upon iniquity with his unadulterated eye without burning it to a cinder, forever apart from the fallen segment of his creation till some are reconciled and others consumed in the fire of judgment. After the old creation passed away with its elements disappearing in fervent heat, came a fully new perfect order of creation, even deeper in its goodness than the first (and only previous universe) and now immune, as it were, from further adulteration by the hypothetical entrance of sin, now no longer possible, no matter how subtle it be.

But we knew there was something deeper than this simple reading: The leap here, upon transcending the realm of biblical literalness, came with the realization that this epic was a cyclical cosmic paradigm, a portrayal of the dual function of maya, beyond which was the oneness of all existence. It was the idea of this unity which was so difficult to drive home to the two missionaries. Especially since they knew the Bible almost verbatim, at least on the literal level, and we had to constantly stall for time to find verses to support what we knew intuitively to be true, finding verses that we could barely recite whose location was more obscure to us than a needle in a haystack. Therefore, we sought to find the overview, and again look at the general allegory of Genesis. We did know about that story. Paul on the other hand, we were quite frankly rusty on. But we knew that our dogged zeal and faith would make the difference, the Tao would show us.

Perhaps by the resonations of the right utterance, the barrier in communication might be broken. Surya Das, a Cherokee half-blood, now appearing more oriental than usual, his Mongolian features enhanced, awaited the right moment of silence and then uttered, "But it's all one," looking around calmly with an ethereal smile. His accent suggested the turbaned wonder boy, Mahendranath Gopal, riding an elephant through a curtain of Bengali foliage only to announce upon passing a tribe of monkeys, "Butt eet'zzz aul wan." The Carrolls, contrary to our hopes, were not bowled over with this proclamation. They had been in India for over 30 years!

To put it in understatement, the Carrolls were somewhat familiar with pantheism, and were thus not vulnerable to a surprise attack. I called them to admit that they may not have complete and total understanding of all the truths of Scripture, to which they agreed with predictable humility. They had no problem accepting personal shortcomings with gracious honesty. Here, the argument of individual capacity and "gifts" did make some dent. A brilliant mind could glean more than a dull or ordinary mind. For example, Paul and Augustine were geniuses, and the Carrolls would consider them great saints. Christians seemed to take pride in the fact that the more mediocre their capacities were, ergo, the more spiritual they were. They trumpeted their natural deficiencies and inferiority almost as a sign of trustworthiness. My father used to caricature with disdain the prejudices of the Bible Belt rednecks of the deep South. And the fact that usually the most ignorant and dull minded were the most dishonest like the tent evangelist hucksters. Of course, they were suspicious of him too, he was an intellectual (a Rhodes scholar finalist, etc.).

With a partial foot in the door, and speaking with rare glibness and force, I spent the next half-hour summing up the detailed highlights of my "mountaintop" LSD experience, the 3000 microgram "tree experience," as I used to call it. They stood their ground, and wouldn't budge as to its divine authority and nirvanic revelation. Being regarded as somewhat unsavory was a little unsettling for me, especially since the Carrolls were reaching across to me through this narrow door with the only love they could faithfully show without betraying their faith. Far from casting me off, they invited me in, yet with some fear and trembling, as though being cautious about the garments I was wearing. This was a little more difficult. I had to be as merciful and patient toward them as they were toward me.

The more I pressed the account of my own mystical experience, the more energy I tried to summon to validate not only my beliefs but my own identity which was inextricably bound to them. It became more and more evident to me that these two old Elms felt absolutely no need to defend their stance in themselves. Rather, they seemed to obscure their own meek prowess under the cloak of the mighty robe of another, choosing instead to point to the inestimable power of Him. And this "other" was another Logos, a different Christ, from the one that I had formulated. I was the one who had to prove my transcendent consciousness. They were immovably secure in their Redeemer. They were like granite. There was no doubt, fear, hesitation, or insecurity.

Back and forth the controversy over truth went, neither side seeming to win and neither block conceding any ground. There were times we pushed hard into the hallowed territory of the Carrolls as they held their ground with sober concern. At such times, I would begin to feel like the wolf in *Little Red Riding Hood*. And other times, with a gentle calm spirit yet speaking strongly, the Carrolls would counter us as always with just the right Scripture on their lips as though written for the sole sake of countering us. In turn, at such times, my fire was quelled down to the marrow. During several Scripture responses the Carrolls gave, a shock went through my system as though I had been slammed into a cinderblock wall at 100 miles an hour. I did not show it, but it was obliterating.

By about 1:30 in the morning, it was finally time to call it a night and turn in. But only after the most burdened and heartfelt prayer by the Reverend and

Mrs. Carroll that Christ would be the one to speak directly to our hearts and convict us all of the truth through the Holy Spirit. Little did they know the ramifications of their prayer as we the visitors nodded among ourselves.

The following morning, March 1, the gentle forbearance by the two missionaries suggested that they were "loving the sinner but hating the sin." After loading us up with a delicious breakfast, they graciously agreed to drive us and our belongings to the Blake cabin in their jeep where Surya Das and I would go on ahead, and move in. Ed, now a little ill, would stay on a few days with Jerry who had suddenly become quite ill, and join him in the guest-room. Mrs. Carroll, having also served for many years as a medical helper and midwife in the most primitive of south Indian villages, where they too had lived in the squalor of adobe village huts, applied her medical skills to Jerry, gasping when the thermometer registered 103.8° Fahrenheit. Off to the local physician he would go for some sort of cloudy booster shot.

Eddie that night, Mrs. Carroll would record dutifully in her diary, would quiz her privately if God ever spoke directly to her. "Yes," would come the sincere and inevitable answer. Finally, being pinned down directly as to what God had told her concerning who Baba was, she would respond to Eddie with Second Corinthians 11:13-15, "a false messenger of God." In a profound sense, we wondered whether these two people transplanted here in South India, were the greatest materialization of maya given by Baba to test our faith.

Even after the other two moved to the Blake cabin within two days, throughout the week the four of us would pay the Carrolls friendly visits, forever extending Baba's grace into their home. We challenged them continually to go and see Baba themselves at darshan, always in exchange for a warm meal.

But soon, they would retreat from the picture but for occasional visits, as Baba's domain would close in on us with more and more intensity. The yonder Blake cabin along the countryside between Whitefield and Baba's Brindavan Academy was another world, and our main truck would be between that and Brindavan on bicycles, and occasionally on the local bus into the modern city of Bangalore.

# Chapter 20

# *Telegrams from the Abyss*

*F*or a while I received extraordinary attention from Baba, but something inside me was slowly crumbling.

After an evening session, Wendel came home with me to the Blake cabin. In the main room, he moved in next to me, I assumed to stay. But Baba had other plans, and reticently, Wendel allowed it to leak out that he was involved in a staggering project out in Ananthapur. It was in the main entrance hall of the multimillion-rupee college which was being built on the land that Baba surveyed when I first met him. Wendel was to do two giant murals, perhaps in fresco, perhaps tempera, or perhaps in acrylic, he wasn't sure. But each mural would be about 10 feet by 20 feet, facing each other along opposing stairways. Baba had shown him what needed to be done, showering him with grace constantly.

In the candlelight in the Blake cabin, hunched against the wall, Wendel sketched secretively, guarding the product as we talked, catching up on events, the sandbox interview, Baba's nature, and Aurobindo's concept of creativity as a means of escaping maya. In the early hours of the morning, Wendel was still dissatisfied with his various attempts, still straining for something original and showing me some of the results. I was impressed.

The morning of March 11, a Thursday, Wendel left and I woke up after having had one of a series of terrible nightmares, now in my deepest throes of doubt and depression. I had shared none of it with Wendel. I chose to go into town alone, missing darshan, in order to think, to find some clue to patch my cracking monument of belief. Whatever secret momentum was at work within my mind, I could not locate its source.

Maybe a part of the oppression had been the Blake cabin itself. A damp, dark little mortar hut without a strip of furniture, and nothing but a crusty cement floor to sit on, its bare walls were fully like a jail. The latrine adjacent to Ed and Jerry's room smelled, and rats scampered throughout the place at night: huge blue-nosed rats that were common carriers of bubonic plague and rabies.

One night we finally resorted to a 3:00 A.M. exorcism using every mantra we knew. As we encircled a flickering candle, the four of us joined hands and screamed, "Om, raksha, raksha, Hum, Hum, Hum, Phhhattt, Swahaaaa," again and again to drive out whatever demonic presence had filled the place, our yells echoing out into the lonely black wilderness. The rats had been noisy that night, knocking over cutlery and tins in the kitchen area while scampering between that and the latrine. But that wasn't unusual enough to bring on the exorcism.

What had done it was a rather grim battle I had undergone reminiscent of Gill's discorporated battle with the Chinese familiar spirit in this very same cabin: indeed, the same familiar that had followed Gill to Ananthapur to battle it under the stars that January, over a year ago, when I had first met Baba and Gill. Such spiritual attacks were not utterly foreign to me.

I had been lying stretched out along my mat at 2 A.M. Then I experienced the same semiparalysis and borderline dream state that inevitably accompanied those rare times when I had apparently astral projected in years past. Just the effort to get a single digit on the little finger to move would require huge will. In and out of this state any number of times, I let go and tried to drift into sleep. It would start up again: first the utter paralysis as though held down by 10 G-forces, then my mind would begin to hurtle as a loud siren would start up in my head.

It was during this prone state that I felt a certain baleful presence in the room. I was momentarily pinned down and unable to move. As I drifted deeper into the "buzz region," as I used to call it, a large rat tore through the room, scampering right up the length of my body. When it hit my head, seemingly carrying an explosive static force, I saw a configuration of blue energy crackle around me, first in an electrical pattern, then materializing into the hideous shape of some demonic aerial creature. I broke out of the paralysis, and tried to chase it through the wall, slamming into a thick block of mortar and pelting back on the floor mat. The others awoke. Angry and slightly shaken with fear, I instigated the idea of an immediate exorcism, to which they concurred, having all awakened in the midst of nightmares.

But my inner struggle a week later, that Thursday morning of March 11 when I went into Bangalore, though much less spectacular, was more far-reaching in its ultimate philosophic pervasiveness. A root problem remained as to how I might dispose of the reality of supernatural evil: either as an illusory stratum within the godhead, merely a cloudy phantom within the region of polarities inconsequential when in the face of ultimacy, or...as a shuddering in my gut sometimes told me (and it was this unpleasant "primitive" response which I was really seeking to unburden myself of), a non-unifiable wing of absolute reality at utter enmity with God, whose infinitely greater holiness, power, and just resolve was such, that this evil had no other final destination than what Saint John's Revelation termed "The Lake of Fire." In terms of the total span of eternity, it was a relatively short-lived phenomena, and the emphasis was neither to identify with it nor have any dealings with it if one wanted to know God. This was why the Bible warned the sons of Israel not to play with the idols and sorceries of Babylon.

With an ice-cream cone in one hand from Nilgiri Dairy, to relieve the angst, I ran into something that far from resolved my inner battle. In a long row of imported paperbacks at Higginbotham's Bookstore on Mahatma Gandhi Road, I felt a speedy urge to play a chance numbers game with the long row of paperbacks, and pull out just that one which would seek to answer my grief. I plunged one out, barely noticing the cover, flipped it open halfway, and facing me on the open page was a visionary account of "The Coming Anti-Christ." What was unnerving were the standard biblical references of prophecy. Here was a concept, one of a false Messiah purposefully out to deceive the world, that had been far from my mind. One that I was not sure I had ever in my life really considered.

The portion of this vision which did not contradict Scripture, showed an Antichrist with numerous counterfeit attributes of the real Christ, supernaturally energized. It had succeeded in seducing almost all the inhabitants of the world. The world followed. Along the way, it paused, looked back to assess its flock, then ever so slightly veered just noticeably to the left.

Soon after, another fragment was hammered out of place in my cracking monument of belief.

At a modern paperback store farther down the main street, I repeated the random selection routine, this time drawing a book that curiously amended the other book. Its basis was what it claimed to be that self-same infallible external standard of truth that I had just been puzzling about. I had wondered when you really knew that you had arrived at 100 percent certain intuitive knowledge. The paperback made some claims about the Holy Bible: that it was God's written word to mankind by direct revelation to men of God's choosing, faithful servants of integrity who would rather die a martyr's death and undergo persecution than alter or take back one written letter of that revelation. The book was entitled *Twentieth Century Prophecy*, by some biblical scholar named Bjornstad. What was interesting here is that the book sought to weigh individuals with regard to their self-claims of divine revelation by the Bible's standards.

I scrambled through the pages of the book amazed that within ten minutes I should find another book that would at least endorse my caution regarding the "vision" of the first book. Yet, it retracted not a jot of the prophetic content of the Bible. Soon enough I began to dislike its tone, too narrow in its acceptance of belief and divisive with its sword of truth rather than unitive and universal. Edgar Cayce, by strict biblical standards, failed the test as a legitimate prophet. Then I discovered what the Bible's standards were, as the author quoted from Deuteronomy 18:21 with the question brought to Moses, "How may we know the word which the Lord has not spoken?" The answer from the great prophet followed in the next verse: "When a prophet speaks in the name of the Lord, if the word does not come to pass or come true, that is a word which the Lord has not spoken" (18:22). Such false prophets, who spoke prophecy that was any less than 100 percent accurate, by Mosaic law in Deuteronomy 13:1-11, were subject to death. Edgar Cayce and many others failed this perfect standard repeatedly. They were false prophets.

Once back in the Blake cabin, I received a third shock as I was glancing through a stack of photographs that I had just picked up in Bangalore. It was a shot of me in the wilds of Puttaparthi approaching the well, half a mile from the ashram near one of the rice paddies and a small cluster of woods. Ed had snapped it. I recalled the conscious effort of surrendering to a spiritual umbrella surrounding me. There was no mistaking its identity, it was Baba. I was to surrender so that it would eclipse my own identity. Upon a hasty glance, my expression in the photograph looked fairly typical.

But with a magnifying glass what had seemed shadowy in substance now took on a diabolical reality, similar to an enlarged microphotograph of the harmless looking mole that turns out to be a raging carcinoma. It came out even more clearly when I had the photograph enlarged. My face was grossly distorted. It was monstrous beyond normal limits. One eye—huge, globular, baleful, four times the normal size. The other eye—thin, Mandarin, a slit, resembling the eye of death. The composite picture of both eyes was an ancient occult enemy staring up from the photograph. But for the horns missing, it was a perfect likeness to the Goat of Mendes, the Satanhead. I felt that this was no accident, whatever the cause of it. A deep chill went through me.

There was no doubt, I was caught in an inner war of faith. Now what I longed for more than ever was some kind of intermission. Some kind of distracting drama to turn my mind from this relentless eye of the hurricane. As single-minded as my will was in persevering through to enlightenment, in not losing faith in Baba, something stronger seemed to be overcoming me.

# Chapter 21

# *The Cosmic Road Show*

*E*xactly 24 hours later, Friday, March 12, "central casting" sent in the sort of "intermission" to my nightmare of cracking belief that a team of Hollywood screenwriters would be hard pressed to beat. The most effective and zany movie script would not quite do justice to what actually happened. A car engine purred down the drive of the Blake cabin as Eddie ran in with the announcement, "Tal, you're not going to believe this."

Hurrying barefooted to meet the envoy, I ran head-on into Ram Dass as he hopped out of a paisley Volkswagon bus! It was one of those once-in-a-lifetime super cosmic *déjà vus*. My inner battles of late vanished as I faced the famous New Age teacher and author of the soaring bestseller, *Remember, Be Here Now*, which lay open on the floor of our front room. Someone had just brought it from the States and I was turning to it for inner validation during those dark moments of doubt.

Eddie, who often kept Ram Dass in New York at his apartment when the famous "Upa-Guru" was passing through town on one of his lecture tours, announced, "Ram Dass, meet the chief. This is Tal, he's probably closer to Baba than just about anyone except a few Indians."

The six-foot-one, bare-crowned long-haired ex-Harvard Professor who had so upturned the consciousness of America over the past decade (beginning with the psychedelic movement with Timothy Leary), smiled with a nod. His traveling band of admirers—fellow disciples—emerged out of the van forming a semicircle around him. As the film of history was being made they stretched in the country air, marveling, while others smiled with a mellow knowingness. Their world tour was winding up in India. It had been a long time coming.

Ram Dass' luminous eyes, now taking it all in, searched me. It was the psychic connoisseur appreciating another very high soul, another beacon of the coming transformation that would rock the West. The surrounding onlookers were quiet. His hands rested on my shoulders as he remarked quietly while his eyes sparkled with recognition, "I know I've seen you somewhere before."

"Yes, you have," came the deliberate response.

Ram Dass gave me the embrace of the long departed now in reunion. It could have been the Kiev railroad station at the end of the Russian Revolution. The only other master of the embrace I knew of from the West was Gill, the difference being, however, that with the latter, there was a narrow line where fierce zeal took on the attributes of a death struggle. At the perfect moment, the hug ended as the merry chuckles of the various extras on the set signaled that gold had been struck after all. We all went into the Blake cabin as Ram Dass and I pinpointed who had been where and when.

"Remember the Millbrook Castalia Foundation years when you and Tim Leary and Ralph Metzner came through D.C. and then to Charlottesville?"

"Yes."

"Well, that was one time we got together. Do you remember J.D. Kuch, Boo-Hoo of the Neo-American Church off McArthur Boulevard...yeah , that's right, she and her husband were also in Mensa. Okay, that's it."

"Wow. It's all coming back. I remember you. As I said, you look very familiar, and it must go back very far.

"It does," I responded again, thinking of Baba's proclamation eight months back that my "brother is coming. Spiritual brother, not physical brother, of many lifetimes." Baba nodded when I asked if it was Ram Dass.

Ram Dass caught a knowing grin radiating from Surya Das, "It looks like you're really finding yourself."

"I am," Surya Das smiled, "and when you meet the avatar, you'll appreciate why." Then Ed joined in.

Ram Dass spoke of Maharajji in Nainital, their recent stay in Bodhgaya near Benares under a Buddhist master, and the big tour with Muktananda of which this current stopover was near the end. It started in New York where Ram Dass met Muktananda through a disciple named Rudi and Hilda Charlton (who had studied under Nityananda, the guru of Muktananda). Overnight it blossomed into growing happenings featuring the two, Ram Dass and Muktananda. Large spreads appeared in the *Village Voice* and other underground papers. The caravan ended up in San Francisco and L.A. with darshans running well into the thousands in large well-known coliseums and halls, such as the Cow Palace in San Francisco, before it left for Australia and India.

Ram Dass asked me about Baba. Specifics were what his well-trained academic mind was searching for out of the reams of data with so little time. I brought out photos of the recent Mahasivaratri festival, narrated, editorialized, and everybody seemed inspired.

We left the Blake cabin with Ram Dass driving and me in the front seat and headed to Brindavan in time for darshan. The Volkswagon bus resembled a mini Benares with every conceivable variety of amulet, incense, tanka, and Hindu deity sitting about. Maybe the VW would end up in a museum of consciousness evolution in some future era, the psychic equivalent of a Model-T.

Ram Dass and his troop formed a line along the drive, most of them in the half-lotus yoga posture now suddenly quiet to tune into the flow of things. In Ram Dass' jargon they were "getting centered."

I quietly mounted the tiered steps to head toward Baba's residence by an obscure garden path. My movement went about as unnoticed as the British Air Corps marching through Sumatra, as I detected that even Ram Dass' luminous eyes had floated off center for a moment. Perhaps with good reason too as this was a liberty that he was not in the habit of taking with his own Himalayan guru, Maharajji, who by no means gave him any sort of preferential treatment above the local Nainital devotees.

For a moment I hesitated at Baba's door, slightly ajar, then plunged through the icy waters of doubt by pushing it open. Raja Reddy stood alone quietly at attention in the hall. With an unfaltering cordiality he welcomed me in with a polite handshake. I told him about the drama taking place, the surprise visit by the world famous Ram Dass. He listened attentively mirroring back my own sense of importance of the moment. He and I, in our earlier talks about what was taking place in America, had discussed Ram Dass' influence.

The sound of Baba's footsteps suddenly filled me with a reluctance to see him as Raja went to intercept him. I might have trespassed beyond my present measure of faith into hallowed ground. Baba rounded the bend from the back darshan-hall and met me with an indifferent look hued by slight irritation. By all appearances, the effect of my visitation was what happens when a reporter drops in on a famous film comedian who is scintillating at prearranged press conferences but is morose at unannounced doorbell interviews.

---

The unlit reception room was stone quiet as Baba sat on the arm of a nearby chair. Raja gave him his after-dinner betel leaf box. Musingly, Baba rolled a leaf up after painting it with lime paste. He slowly chewed it. The irritation in his voice continued mounting as he discussed something with Raja in Telugu.

Baba rolled the betel leaf around in his mouth chewing loudly and grimacing in the manner of a tobacco-chewer ready to spit. Grudgingly, he looked up to me and slurred the question, "What is this Ram Dass, Haaa?"

I reminded Baba of his prediction of my coming brother and Ram Dass' dynamic mission in firing up spiritual interest in America. Baba responded with a number of asides of which I knew it would be my test of fidelity not to pass on to Ram Dass or the others.

Scathingly Baba revealed, "Who is Ram Dass? Very impure. Now collecting devotees and himself does not know the way, seeking fame before he is ready. Ram Dass is not as pure as my American devotees, that's right, he should learn from you. Not as pure as you. Seeking fame is playacting, guru playacting, ego." After an ironic laugh, Baba asked, "Ram Dass is married?"

"No, Baba, strict Brahmacharya."

I assumed this would be an endorsement. Baba made some sort of cryptic pun about Ram Dass' past exploitations. I responded saying that in America it is very difficult growing up, that most of us come from confused backgrounds. I reminded Baba of his proclamation about me that my "mine shaft of experience was the deepest of the American bhaktas." Baba had told the others that the mountain of displaced terrain from my mine shaft was the highest of all. Baba conceded this. I appealed to Baba's great compassion to consider Ram Dass as misdirected as he might be.

"I am coming to darshan, don't worry."

In minutes I was again sitting right next to Ram Dass in darshan line as though nothing had happened. Baba soon emerged and quietly drifted tangentially away from us toward the school offices. He drifted back oblivious of the new envoy till he was right over us. Then all of a sudden Baba beamed at Ram Dass, "Ram Dass." And for now, that would be the extent of their communication. On the way up the drive, Baba informed me that afternoon bhajans would be as usual and that he would be coming. The others were invited.

After their brief brush, Ram Dass searched for words to describe his immediate impressions. "He's so light... he's almost not even here."

That afternoon, all of us surrounding Baba's seat would suddenly be treated to a surprise interview. Baba's chair suddenly turned away from the girls' half and faced directly head-on toward Ram Dass and me who were sitting side by side. Baba materialized a very large pendant with a pentagram in the center and gave it to a stunned Ram Dass. Then Baba agreed to meet the famed guru Muktananda the next day. For a while it was a three-way talk between Baba, Ram Dass, and me. Ram Dass left stunned, and later we had our picture shot together with the materialized pentagram around Ram Dass' neck.

Meanwhile, the next day's meeting between Baba and Muktananda resembled a bizarre scorpion dance between the two as Muktananda forced Baba into a hug, then Baba stalled for an hour as Ram Dass and I tried to get Baba to come out again. The final meeting was like a Mafia birthday party, or "The Gunfight at OK Coral" as Ram Dass and I were held out as beacons, and the gurus exchanged cryptic puns.

That night Ram Dass and I and several others drove into Bangalore for a Chinese dinner. He and Muktananda would head toward Bombay the next day.

After Ram Dass and Muktananda left, weeks went by as I laboriously wrote up these and other events to be a part of a book about Baba to be released in Calcutta in the fall. The high court magistrate of Bengal was financing its publication after he challenged me to write the book after one of my talks. Baba had blessed it and often enquired about how my writing was going. Wendel was painting while I was writing.

Midway through April, Baba departed for Bombay and I used the opportunity to go off alone to the coastal region of Malabar where Gill had once stayed. I needed a holiday desperately. I discovered how frayed my nerves were and how little peace I had. India was getting to me. I felt like someone who has held back endless irritations only to find a cauldron of fury within as various distractions are finally removed.

A self-critical inner witness would not leave me alone.

# Chapter 22

# *Strange Return of a Bent Disciple*

*I* stumbled through the dark approach path to the Blake cabin having just stopped by the Carrolls' house for dinner after returning from the Malabar trip. It was late evening. I crashed through the front porch walking right into a pile of milk pails and bottles in the cabin entrance. A howl came out of the front room. I hit the light switch prepared to swing at someone's head. I saw the one human form that was the least likely to be there sitting right next to my mat. The Lion-man Gill stared up intensely. He was sitting in a full yoga posture, his lion's mane of hair now straggled and knotted. Typical of a sadhu, his body was thin and sinuous in contrast to his large head. Gill wore a loincloth. A new light was on his features. What now inhabited him seemed wholly other than the transitioning personality I had known before. In a way it was as though I was meeting this person for the first time.

A peaceful power carried in his voice as he greeted me. Feeling raw-nerved from both the trip and having just come from the Carrolls, I could already feel my stomach tighten as though to combat a great foe. I asked this now classical embodiment of the master yogi how he had been faring.

"Well, brother, well. And yourself? Let's see. Step into the light and let's have a good look," the rugged voice proclaimed ever resembling Gregory Peck as Captain Ahab. Intoning he went on, "Ohhh you've softened a little, you're gentler not quite so hard and testy as before." Cautiously, I let a most ambiguous smile faintly trace across my features, my eyes still looking firm but not hard.

The presence before me was the last one I wanted to deal with. I did not want to create any openings by letting my natural antipathy and distrust for him emerge. At stake was the very real possibility that what was before me was not the exalted image of "egoless love" in that unknowable fraction of realized supermen but rather the unusual force of will of an unusually bent spirit. I could not decide whether Gill had been sent by God or Satan or both. I had already come to realize that the others would open up to him and lap up his words of power, and perhaps cunning.

The others pulled up on their bikes. Gill was in the process of telling me how Baba, just the other day, for no apparent motive, had him thrown out of Brindavan. He had sat quietly in the Brindavan darshan line, his dhoti now soiled, his hair matted and hanging like frayed ropes. When Baba appeared, he turned on Gill shouting, "Go. You go. Get out and not coming back again." Finally, "Psst. Unclean, what is this?" Baba looked around, drumming up local crowd support. Immediately, the weather-beaten American yogi, keeping even the tiniest self-doubt from escaping, lest it tear him apart upon surfacing, held down his private storms as hands seized him from all sides. The ushers quickly wrestled him up and forcefully walked him out of the front gate, permitting him less dignity than a common criminal or a madman. Baba's orders were that Gill was never to come back again, declared persona non grata.

The others quickly assured Gill that the difficult incident was sheerly a most unfathomable test in the final lap of *tapasya*, a straightening by fire for a near perfect adept which none less in stature could withstand. Gill differed. Not "advanced," but having now already attained perfection. A few eyebrows raised.

The deep reverberating voice seemed to flow at us from all sides announcing, "I am as sinless as Christ." The others looked on stunned, I was not too taken aback. I decided to remain a detached observer till things really got out of hand, then I would step in and throw Gill out.

The only thing I knew was that Gill now claimed to have finally attained "that state" and I saw no festive announcement coming from Baba. I saw the opposite.

"Why do you think Baba did it, Gill?" I probed.

"I don't know."

I theorized a dangerous alternative: that perhaps the higher you get the more unshakable your self-confidence becomes till even the mightiest sledgehammer blow from the guru will not break one's surety. If one does break, how great the fall. Untested and unbreakable, there still remains the even more dreaded possibility that one has hardened, in utter and total confidence, without the normal turning back, into a state that is not "enlightenment," and will continue until some final infinite barrier sends him back to the elemental beginning of time. Here is where the feedback of the guru is essential as a preventive, that is, if the guru himself is right. He was sure of his state, was anybody else?

For almost a week Gill taught and shared what he had learned in the wilderness and on the mountaintop. Sometimes he could "even hear the trees growing" as he had in the California Redwoods. His eyes shone with an elfin light as he told us this. Such had been the beginnings of "total sensitivity" in him (except to others).

We asked him where he had gone for the last nine months.

Gill had been all over India and Pakistan. For so touchy a crab, as I always envisioned him, it was a wonder he hadn't gone berserk from the ravings and pandemonium of one train station after another, to the crowded streets, and every manner of hellish fruit stand and ramshackle tea stall where the natives just wait to swarm anything the least bit out of the ordinary. And Gill's appearance, well, it was a most rare and remarkable thing, impressively commanding and intense, ever verging on volcanic unpredictability. The crowds following him must have been unbearable.

Gill agreed, the crowds were huge. But he assumed so for a different reason. The crowds followed him much as those rowdy and testy peasants in the Judean hills two millenia back must have, by their very contrasting worldliness and impurity, in a sense, been pulled by the divine purity of Christ. Gill too, by being in the world, suffered indignities. He traveled across India and went to Pakistan. Why?

"My brother is an aeronautical engineer living in Karachi."

It sounded so prosaic. "What sort of rapport have you all had?"

"Never very much, we are as unlike as any two people can be."

For his brother, I surmised, it must have been traumatic when they were small children. Like baby Snooks waking up to find an alien in the adjacent crib—you know, one of these weird things pulled out of the wreckage of a flying saucer, tentacles and psychic mind projections floating across the ceiling, bookcases passing through walls. And all hell breaks loose as a microwave tube enters baby Snook's ear, eyeballs cooked to a frazzle. . . . Somehow, I could never imagine Gill growing up in anything like a family of humans, but never mind.

"What happened in Karachi?"

"Well, when I arrived at my brother's apartment," he continued solemnly, "there was a party going on." Gill was no fan of frivolity or small talk.

"I came in the door as I am dressed now and what had been rather lighthearted, superficial, and perhaps frivolous chatter died as though someone pressed a button and switched them off. They felt immediately threatened by my presence. Some gawked in amazement, some made disparaging remarks, and those few men who had any guts at all, mustered the courage to make outright attacks. But as I looked them directly in the eyes they would falter. Then the only way they could keep their little thing going was to gang up. But I still looked at them searchingly. That really frightened them because they had no ready response to that. This is what happens to people's ego games when truth enters their presence. Everything they know begins to shake loose. And soon the energy level becomes too much for them to cope with, and they really become exposed."

Resembling a great sphinx purring as he narrowed his eyes and gently rolled his head, as though to loosen his neck, he continued.

"It is remarkable what some people will do to hold on to their egos. They look for some niche or weakness to try to control you with, or they try to be very articulate and abstract, and analyze the situation, not realizing that this is like prostitution. It keeps them from ever directly involving themselves in what's happening by always holding it at arm's length. And in their fear of looking uptight, they try to seize the conversation, playing one meaningless word game after another." A trace of irony crept across Gill's features. "I just stare back with love, searching into them. They lose the thought in midsentence or what they pursue becomes even more ridiculous."

One birdlike woman came up as he was sitting down. "Oh, you're so savage. None of these others," she looked around confidentially, "would venture out into this wild region in bare feet and a loincloth, hey?" The cool in-crowd of mockers looked on from their tiny circle on the side, joking, whistling, and shaking their drinks.

A deep resonant voice perhaps caught some people off guard as it cut through all the extraneous jabber in sober gravity, "I love you...you...more than you can ever possibly know. You see...I am you." Gill's eyes were stronger than the Rocky Mountains. There were some loud coughs at this point.

"Uhhh." She was caught for a moment. Then she found a way to one-up him. She sat in Gill's lap as some of the guests continued looking on in the awkward silence, while she felt his beard to see if it was real. She tugged it a little.

She got about as much of an emotional rise from Gill, as much passion, to further extend the analogy, as the stone face of a mountain. For a while, he let her questions peter out. First, about his tough, calloused feet, his bony ribs, his vegetarian diet, his bare-chesting the icy winds of northern Punjab, Kashmir, and Simla, his eter-nities of meditation, and the long, ropy, matted locks that hung down his back in frayed cords, bound by mud and cow dung, no different in outward mortification than a well-seasoned Shaivite sadhu, or naga.

Her little world just couldn't take it all in. She had her own ground rules for life: Practical people kept things in nice safe boxes. It just wasn't safe to stray from the popular mainstream of thought. For one thing, there was always the threat of losing social acceptance and being looked down upon as, well, different. And who could withstand ostracism? So everything out of the ordinary became a source of laughs. If some fanatic came along with strong convictions, then he might be humored but...really now.

Issues that make life meaningful are things like cars, a fine home, and steady income, and knowing fun people who are always there for a good time. Ultimate questions are off-limits.

And the unknown? Well everyone knows they've proven the origin of the universe (Fred Hoyle's "big bang theory"). Even grade school textbooks have pretty much thrown it all in, in explaining the origin of things (teleology). Modern man has triumphed by his own intelligence in answering "the question." Mysterious and superstitious fears just come from an animal vestigial remnant of the cortex carried over from some Stone-Age brain; it's all electrochemical.

Her inebriated party brain ticked away to find new ways to get a response out of this oddball (you know, all guys are alike and after the same thing). She poked her tongue in his ear. Not because she sincerely wanted to get things going, but to see if, just for laughs now, she might be able to get his defenses to break down.

Gill was what they called a "heavy." It was just the reverse of the lights, like Ram Dass and Surya Das, who could just radiate a gentle love. That was the usual Western stereotype of "the evolved soul." India, which had been in the mysticism business much longer, by millennia, gave the "heavies" much more stature. Gill could take your head off with a stare if he wanted to. People told me that at times I had the same effect, but I had to let go and surrender to another force outside myself, or perhaps within, to do it. Shiva, the destroyer, showed "divine love" by first annihilating the biographical ego which is unable to stand the force. What remains has been transformed like silver in a crucible. Baba, when he exposed his wrath, was supreme in doing this with his Indian followers of longstanding. I had seen them literally fall apart before his eyes and buckle at his feet, pleading, as though for another chance at life.

Back at the cocktail party, the gal sitting on Gill's lap moved back to look at him after nibbling his ear.

What confronted her were two immense black pupils through which she could almost see another universe. Then the voice wired up to that other universe spoke in terrible power, prying open her innards like a hand scooping out the mush in an old pumpkin. The voice announced inner secrets and cherished vulnerabilities deep in her psyche. It put terror in her eyes. She was a microbe on a slide before a vast alien intelligence. In minutes a quiet frenzy swept the apartment and people left with nervous excuses. She totally came apart. Frivolity among the yuppies had been totally dismembered. It was Shiva in the living room.

The Blake cabin crew were impressed. Now Surya Das had his own brave accounts: He had been present when Leary and Alpert (alias Ram Dass) had their marathon stone-in on STP in the bowling alley at Millbrook, not to speak of his similar closeness and access to Yogi Bhajan (whom he aided at the Colorado festival of light), Swami Satchidananda, Kirpal Singh, and Steve Gaskin, to name a few. He'd "been there" almost every time. But the encounter with Gill was unique.

Gill completed the details of his ventures. The rugged months alone in the thatched hut on the shores of Udipi Taluk: spiritual attacks, astral battles, monkeys raiding the hut, villagers peering in, and finally police raids. Repeatedly the police hammered away on his door while he was meditating, and barged in wanting all the legal certificates of an alien. They continued to torment him heedless of his wish. He'd haggle, roar, and try to blow their minds. In the end, he vowed that he would just let go, no matter what happened, and stop trying to deal with it by aggression or cunning—the ego.

Then Gill went to a cave ashram in Gudjerat to sit for weeks on end, alone in the darkness as yogi-servants brought food and water, pushing it through a crack.

Gill told tales of the stormy seas of meditation in the cave, when hours stretched into eternities. The only way he knew day from night was by the food-tray slipped through a rock crevice. He added, "While you are in silence, if there is a voice within, with a pause before and a pause after, it is probably the teacher." This had come as a trembling announcement. "Heed the voice of the teacher."

A prophecy then followed as the others leaned forward to share in this nighttime revelation, one to come on Gill's final night with us in our particular valley of existence. It concerned me.

His eyes opened with dark mountainous power, "Fairly soon, your heart center will open completely, and you will come to know all the truths that you know but don't know." He had just spoken of the classic meditative phases of working through the chakras where smells emerge that have never existed, then the region of bells, and then the yogi begins to see around corners at things that are happening from afar.

I wondered if this flattering prophecy was not a partial concession to reopen a door of trust that had closed the previous night after Gill and I had had a conflict concerning my writing the book on Baba. It was tense. I got up and sat right next to him staring an inch from his eyes. It scared everybody but Gill and me (who were loaded with energy but not really afraid) as they sensed that a fight might start from my controlled fury and the sheet of power I faced off. After Gill was satisfied that I was not playing a game by writing, he gave a light warning of the pitfalls of confusing outer activities with really important matters. Gill breathed like a gladiator who had become a pacifist (years ago he was a sergeant in the Marines teaching martial arts). He let out a sigh of long-suffering patience; I should write but not become attached. "Your greatest strength is your greatest weakness." I pretended I knew what he was referring to. I didn't. Then he answered it.

"Do you know what it is?" Before I could answer him, he responded, "Your intellect." Again I felt manipulated and let the moment pass.

Eddie asked if Gill had met Ram Dass. Yes, and Gill was not particularly impressed.

In Gill's judgment Ram Dass had a long way to go. He was soft like the mayor's pudgy son who thinks he's clever enough to bluff his way into the local hoodlum gang, and thinks he has fooled them. Until a crunch reveals that he is a coward and he goes plodding home to mama's doorstep.

Gill also implied that Ram Dass was being "taken" for all he was worth by the chain of spiritual command who was giving him more leverage than his level of maturity deserved. His flamboyant joyride and shoulder rubbing would eventually end in the humiliating brunt of a cosmic joke (Which did happen in New York some years later when Ram Dass followed a divorcee named Joya as the incarnation of the divine mother. It ended in a scandal lampooned by *New Age Journal*.) Ram Dass was not made of that tough fiber required to scale the slopes of Himavat, but was an opportunist, a loquacious, slightly theatrical dilettante in the tradition of the moaners in the Ouija Board brigade who howl at the nuances of a full moon, read tea-leaves, ever reminiscing over their Atlantean lives and kitchen cupboard visions. Though devastating Ram Dass, Gill was also violating his own rule about not judging. He then told us about the time he reached full enlightenment which we then judged privately among ourselves.

Little did we know then that within a few years Gill would be the famous Central Park Guru of New York City and leader of the *Yea God Ashram* in upstate New York. (His group toured America on buses, an engaging story that the media wrote up. By then Gill wrote me an absolutely astounding letter—he had listened to a Christian radio program and given his life to Christ—for a time. The Yea God Commune converted en masse, burning all its guru pictures. Then this mercurial creature changed courses once again. Gill reclaimed his Hasidic roots, went to Israel, dressed like a Hasidic rabbi, and spent long days praying at the wailing wall. He married the niece of a famous Princeton physicist I had met through a fellow student and close friend, Gregg Hammett, who was getting a doctorate under the famed Dr. Styx. And there was more.)

The following day, Friday, April 30, we took the bearded mystic to the Bangalore train terminus. Gill reached over and grabbed my shoulder, "Someday, brother, we will both be hitchhiking down a superhighway in Nebraska, each on the other side of the divider without a penny in our pockets. We won't need to run across, we'll just look at each other and continue hitchhiking." Gill mounted the old steam train. Crouching like a beggar and holding a walking stick, Gill sat in the boxcar as it slowly moved out of the station. His eyes stared right into ours, never averting, never blinking. When he was gone, I felt relief.

# Chapter 23

# *Edging Upon the*
# *Eternal Choice*

Surya Das crouched in the entrance hall of the Blake cabin, resembling a prehistoric monster in a horror movie as he stalked forward.

"Ya ever see a pterodactyl about to take off? Like one of those museum models all perched up on a cliff, 15-foot wingspan and all. That's what she looked like, I'm serious." We laughed. Surya Das had his arms out like a bat creature, head hunched forward, and back bent. He slowly stalked into the room. He was imitating the darshan of "The Mother" of the Aurobindo ashram at Pondicherry, near the tip of Southern India, where he had recently gone before Gill's arrival.

Once or twice a year the 96-year-old "Mother" appeared on a third story rooftop balcony in her Franco-Indian mansion, the headquarters of Auroville International. She would look down silently on the crowd below, then, resembling the Pope, give her blessings with a signal or a wave. Silhouetted against the stark Madras sky, she indeed resembled that ancient reptilian bird, the pterodactyl. She claimed to be immortalizing her body, this French Jewess who was once the "shakti" of the great Indian sage and God-man, Sri Aurobindo.

Aurobindo, the most cerebral of all the twentieth century "enlightened" visionaries had written thousands of pages of complex metaphysics and poetry before he died in the 1950s. He was the Sage who had looked up into the night sky November 23, 1926, and seen the great light descending at the moment Sai Baba was born in Southern India.

Surya Das had stopped on his way home to tell the Carrolls of the wealth of modern India. Consequently, in her diary, Winona Carroll would record that Surya Das' visit was "oppressive as he raved on about Auroville, Teresa Neumann, and other stigmatists." Upon this tricky subject, the Carrolls would hold fast, stating only in the words of Martin Luther, that Scripture alone was all-sufficient as God's revelation to man in providing the guiding light. We did not need other human intercessors to get us to Christ, but the "God-breathed" Word alone was trustworthy. The Carrolls were not too receptive to Suray Das' argument that the peaceful vibrations validated the various shrines Catholic and Hindu.

Meanwhile, a newcomer named Barbara was due to have her baby at a clinic down the road. Laughing, poised, and assured, Baba celebrated the moment of birth during an interview, resembling a midwife who has just aided the easiest delivery of all time. At the instant of the birth itself, recorded by the clinic, Baba shut his eyes and rolled back his head gently. A gleeful babyish smile greeted us a moment later, as Baba mopped his brow. "All is well. Now baby is born, and Barbara very, very happy." He named the sex as the entire group went giddy. Later I would use this as evidence to the Carrolls of Baba's goodness.

Then Baba's giddiness pursued other matters. Baba's asides resembled a nun telling a most mild joke, and flushing as she did it. Though with a slight change in expression, the mode would have become sardonic. "Too much LSD, you go crazy." The group knew well the story of Ram Dass consecrating a piece of hashish, and giving it to Muktananda to chew. A comment followed suit about Ram Dass. "Too much LSD had made his mind unstable like an old woman. Now he is out collecting devotees when he himself is only a devotee. He is a bhakta, that is all, not a guru. When he comes here, complete change. Not name and fame, but same. Like all my other devotees."

Then Baba turned to the subject of Gill who had recently been there. "And Mr. Freedom, now complete finish. Also going around like a guru. Outer show, not inner love, delusion." Baba smiled at me as he imitated Gill's standard Hatha yoga tapasya, the grimly set jaw, breathing slowly. Some of the girls giggled nervously. I felt remorse for Gill.

Baba's rasping voice chuckled the question at us. "Is this Divine?" And Baba tilted his head back like an Arab drinking arak out of a spouted urn in a steady stream, thumb pointing to his mouth. "No, deep wine!" And he laughed.

The final brunt of his humor was Sri V.V. Giri, the President of India, whom Baba had seen within the last few days. Giri, like many renowned mortals, was obnoxiously arrogant, and blinded by this. Giri appealed to his fellow statesmen, in a formal address, to press on with the urgency of population control. Perhaps somewhat mutedly Baba challenged the President as being an unworthy example of the population philosophy he espoused by having "11 children himself."

But the President backed down from what might be a challenge from Baba, and by the end of the festivity, spent considerable time talking with Baba, becoming more and more humbled by the superhuman powers of this most bold and omniscient creature in the red robe. Giri would soon be coming to see Baba. And on this awesome note, the interview ended.

In six days, on May 10, the Blake crew took a bus toward town, disembarking outside the Bangalore airport, a modest airstrip with an almost cosmopolitan veneer to it. Baba was about to fly to Bombay for a tour. And to our surprise, so was a whole squadron of the American bhaktas. In saris and make-up the select sisters were chattering exuberantly about the plane ride with Baba. They would be in for an interesting drama. We found out later that they actually believed that Baba was going to marry Tatu, the off-limits rooftop prophetess. I grinned sadistically as the plane took off.

With Baba gone, I needed another change of pace. It was perfect justification for a trip across Mysore to Srirangapatnam, an ancient town sitting in a subtropical jungle on a river. I needed to work on the book. It was another pristine setting that we had heard about. On the bus trip, I read Norman Mailer's *Fire on the Moon*, serialized in *Life* magazine. This would give me access to the "global mind" and its most recent frontier. I also read *The Immense Journey* by Loren Eisley, a pantheistic epiphany by a scientist seeing new paradigms of monistic reality.

I soon discovered the purported "guest house" in an idylic setting. A stunning residence was elegantly tucked away in the jungle. The mansion was off the main road on the outskirts of Srirangapatnam, right in the jungle and away from the ancient village. When I had passed down the richly foliated long palatial drive with a well-cut median, it almost took my breath away to see a large white mansion with pillars and wide stairs, now virtually empty but for a handful of servants. It had been a summer guest house of the great Maharaj of Mysore, now taken over by the Indian government. It was a prize exhibit for foreigners, and surprisingly cheap. Enhancing my writing would be the coming monsoon season, reminiscent, I commented to myself, of some nineteenth century scene of British colonial Bengal out of a film by Satyajit Ray.

I was able to rent a suite immediately. My suite was stupendous, with two huge rooms, high-ceiling fans, a rug, canopy bed, British dining-room table, chairs, sitting area, and marble-tiled bathroom and shower. A side porch opened out to face the riverbank. The setting was like a call to past glory, of aristocracy and nobility, the genealogy-conscious traditions of men: that very mentality from which I had once come, that in actual fact made me an heir to "The Society of the Cincinnati," an ultra elitist "Wasp" circle that no *nouveau riche* could buy his way into, for admission was by direct descendence. I couldn't really take it seriously but what had stuck in my mind were the trembling bedside whispers of relatives and family about former greatness and nobility of heritage, indeed British peerage, though the degree of trembling would usually vary according to my daytime acts, often construed perhaps as a spurning of my ancestry.

Mysore, . . . I would finally breathe to myself, alas, so good to be tucked away in the private enchantments of your verdant forests and tropical foliage, full of aromatic mists and enigmas of sound. Finally I was alone in Srirangapatnam for a 17-day stretch of absolutely grueling concentration, reflection, and writing. But I was also in an escalating spiritual battle.

I had written numerous chapters. But I had yet to complete the heaves and birth pangs of some internal process before I could quite embark on that final chapter of the book on Baba. That constant quiet-room of sadness and mourning within me had to be resolved, the nagging doubts, the wondering where all the bliss was, and the pinpricks of conscience from passages of biblical Scripture once uttered by the Carrolls, searching through my soul. I had to face up to the full implications that "I am truly God" after all. Said wrongly, the voice of self-assertion might be somewhat imperious, like an impatient British lord asked for his passport one too many times by the Malaysian customs office.

To Be God—that was the ultimate quest. The very heirdom I now sought to conquer was no less than the very dominion and eternity of Deity Itself. This was the final slope that has made the greatest men in history stagger in blindness and stumble in the intoxicating headiness of the final proposition, "Do you prefer to be related to kings and princes, or would you rather it be God Himself?"

What was this final leap into Godhood? It was a hero's journey infinitely more hazardous than all the epics of Indiana Jones put together! The stakes were colossal because one's very soul was the gambling chip in the ante.

The final ante required nothing less than all I had and was. One literally jumped into the pot clutching his soul as the final ante to await the verdict. If he has won, then truly he has been God all along and he has inherited, rightly speaking, the entire universe as his due. If not, then what is to follow is now no more reversible than a tiny speck of a figure plunging off the New York Trade Center seconds away from impalement on a guardrail. The wind whistles as the body plummets, while the full thrust of one's entire act causes the mind to race with feelings it never dreamed it could contain. Repentance during the descent into the void will gain no more than a sardonic chuckle from the dark hosts who egged on the jump, if you subscribe to the "opposition view." But either way, after the jump one's fate and ultimate destiny is sealed: either the loss is merely the transient ego sacrificed in exchange for Godhood and all that there is. Or the soul itself has been lost in exchange for something worse than obliteration. Even in my "advanced state" I could not escape the demonic implications of this risk from the Carrolls' perspective. Yet intellectually I knew it as "the pull of dualism," which the mystic must in the end transcend or never ever become enlightened. I was on the razor's edge.

I wrote eight to ten hours a day, thousands of words a day, thinking until my head was about to split open. I would cook one meal a day of rice and dal on a kerosene stove on the back porch. Two or three times a day I would need a break. Often I would go down to the Cauvery River and swim, eyeing the foliated banks of palms, papaya, mango, and eucalyptus trees, pink storks, and roaming tribes of monkeys. If my head was really thick, I would take a cold shower then walk to the ancient temple on the outskirts of the village. My soul felt like it was in the balance no matter what I did.

The ancient temple was a strange teacher. It had been built in the far past, before Columbus discovered America. I would often stand in the large empty temple courtyard at twilight, as dark thunderheads shifted across the firmament like chariots. And crimson streaks from the horizon gave an orange cast to the thousands of inter-twined deities enjoined, dancing and beckoning, from the rising stuka gate, tier after tier, 50 or 60 feet into the air. Then I might find myself reflecting and soul-searching.

I would walk the temple lawn between the tremendous granite outer walls, dotted with black crows, and the immense granite center temple, a gray, plain-faced fortress in the tradition of those forbidding temples at Karnak and Thebes. After a bit, I might stroll within, past wizened old Brahmins in the gusty central corridor, musty with ancience, down into the subterranean acres of candlelit corridors. I would pass 50 shrines of shining metal gods, through wisps of sandalwood incense, to some central god, the temple deity, a reclining granite idol of Vishnu 50 feet long surrounded by robed priests chanting away. There was always a small cluster of pilgrims bowing down offering coconut and alms. I might lean against the wall, unfocus my eyes and take it all in. Or I might lean on the railing and study the god. Either way, I was fully accepted by the priestcraft as a pigrim and mystic. Someone told me that they had turned away hundreds of Westerners from the ancient holy of holies. But the Brahmin priests let me in "due to the look in my eyes and level of consciousness." I might buy a coconut and break it at the feet of the god. Then I would stroll through the cavernous cool corridors, stopping at each strange god to quietly stare at it through the bars.

I was sensing a dead dark spirit of India. These temple gods seemed so far from the real level of enlightenment, so dreamlike, so astral, so full of imaginations, and phantasmic planes. Indeed, so sadly lost, I would wonder why they ever built such forbidding shrines, as imprisoned celibates with shaved heads babbled away strange Sanskrit mantras to stone monsters, their lives a continual mechanical prayer, eyes ever more glazed, the spirit, by all appearances, frighteningly devoid of life, exuberance and spontaneity. More akin, I might morbidly observe, to the product of a Russian underground brainwashing camp. Not ecstasy, certainly not that. And that's why, I would say to myself, my writing was such an urgent breakthrough, not into these dead yogas of epochs past but a new handwriting of God for this century. Something contemporary, yet timeless, vital, and routed in the never-ending principles of Vedanta. But God forbid that America fall into this, well, idolatry?

So ancient India spoke to me through her gods about the sacred mission of my writing, and its age-shattering significance, along with other human channels of the age. The spontaneous formation of words, like a mantra, would flow out to all the world due to the very potency of the words. But only that leap, I knew, and nothing else would make me the acceptable vehicle. Yet these very temple-gods themselves were a stumbling block, and I assumed that the "illusion" only became progressively more offensive to drive the aspirant more desperately to find the answer. And right now one of the stumbling blocks that I would have to break through before I could defend the ancient gods before a modern world were the very gods of India themselves.

The truth was, when I walked away from one of these black monoliths, the voice of one of the Carrolls would run through my head with the ancient words, "You shall not make for yourselves idols, nor shall you set up for yourselves an image or a sacred pillar, nor shall you place a figured stone in your land to bow down to it; for I am the Lord your God" (Leviticus 26:1). Modern India to this very day was still practicing what the Old Testament described as accursed. It was the same idolatry of the Canaanites. I was on the dividing line between fleeing it or reinterpreting it and finding the lost meanings behind the idolatry.

Then one morning before dawn several days later I sat at the large oak dining-room table in my suite. My typewriter sat before me while I stared out of the main window to the monsoon rain pitter-pattering on the freshly mowed mall where the jungle stopped. Then I had, in a flash, a direct inspiration from some stupendous source. The final chapter would be guided by a five-stage visionary poem, which was the first factor out of the ordinary, since I never wrote poetry. Automatically, at the typewriter, I started the first poetic vision entitled "Chaos."

The ancient goddess of destruction, Kali, appeared to me not in the frozen antiquities of a temple image, but in a new vision, popping out of her disguise like an optical illusion. She now appeared as the destructive force behind civilization. I was receiving the new metaphor of the ancient goddess. The freestyle verse emerged:

## Kali: Vision One

Kali, come in a formidable guise, is a country, specifically America. A dancing shimmering Gemini, her pullulations of high electric form the schizophrene creatrix that she uses to give birth to innovations that are awesome, terrible, grotesque, and upon occasion, very, very beautiful.

The parameters of her being progenerate and expel out from the formless and into the form, and then form is ingested, like Chronos devouring his children. These forms are wild and heretic. They are as audacious as the tinkery-toy neons of Las Vegas and the bacteriophage housing plazas of polysterene wafers and concrete doughnuts.

Kali, bedecked in a galaxy of Chevrolet lights and chrome strips, perfumed with phenil hydrazine and ionized smog, laced with threads of superhighways and excruciating boulevards, speeds up the high tension cables of her nerves with new isotopes. In the murky din and fanfare of jack hammers, bulldozers, sirens, and traffic cacophonies, she exudes from her million uteri the playthings of her children, in the maternity wards of Detroit, Chicago, Minneapolis, Milwaukee, and Pittsburgh. She peers back at her children through laser crystals, cathode ray tubes, sonar, and radar, and listens to them in the air waves and through the circuits and wires, as they communicate in code.

Kali is burying her children in technology, devouring and beheading them in Vietnam, and resurrecting some of them through the sun disc of disillusionment. She is offering them a strange mystical vision and is uniting them in tribal communities on the precipice of rebirth.

Many of these children might well see through the veil, as her costumes approach utter unbearability.

———

Then, over the days, the rest surged forth as quickly as I could write. It was a mystic tome on the West. The theme of this was that the postwar children of America were brought up in a sterile white world where society was determined to dominate the mysteries of nature and control all and everything. Pragmatism and logical positivism sought to anodize and vinyl spray-paint the grand eerie old cathedrals, it sought to put sodium vapor lights in every nook and cranny that contained hints of intrigue and signs of wonder....

———

## Kali: Vision Two

Through the sun disc of disillusionments, Kali hints at unlimited possibilities as she scours her children and purifies them in the intolerable radiations of her endless thermonuclear laboratories of civilization.

Burying them in a garish cornucopia of opulent showpieces and toys that crumble, she dismembers their greed with the anomie of perpetual dissatisfaction.

She invades the fumigating stench of camphor flake design, tortures the suburban complex until the cubicles of false identity and roles collapse, and then she disintegrates the machineries of shyness in her children till they lunge out of the icy wasteland into the company of shivering tribes of the heart. In slam bang concussions, in electrocutions, to the nerve endings, and in shock to the senses, she drives them to detest the surface contours of her form. Intoxicated from the poisons that flouresce in her vats of deceit, verily in paralyzed isolation will they lie and scream for dear God.

---

## Kali: Vision Three

### The Tantric Vision

Kali, with unforeseeable capriciousness, discloses to her children the revelation of a partial glimpse behind the mysteries of her topology. She presses out into the skies the entire panorama and paradoxical end-points of her most exquisite and appealing sensate delights, as they quiver in clever design concealing an abyss of misery.

Through the projection lenses on the other side of atoms, Kali displaces the movie film of externalized phenomena, before the eyes of her dearest children, and reveals dazzling unadulterated pure light. She silences her children in a moment of awe as the groaning celluloid beasts of the outer world finally lose their magical potency.

Such children of Kali sit perched on the eve of a final rebirth, through the causal nexus, to beyond the beyond.

---

Whether I was writing, walking, reflecting or going to sleep, a requiem seemed to play quietly in my soul. It spoke of the very cessation of my life with such certainty that living memories were already being eulogized and stored away in some vault of the dead. I was getting ready to say, "Goodbye green hills of earth." I knew I was appoaching some kind of death. The muffled drum, the passing bell approached, not to announce the death of my body but rather an eternal slipping away of that mutable awareness that I had always taken to be who I was, the individuality and personality of Tal Brooke. What would come in its place, and how the me "in office" could benefit from this, was a mystery behind a closed door. For now, with a certain remorse, I would wave goodbye at the parting gate to all that had ever seemed to matter, the pith and core of sentimental longings embodied, to borrow a certain phrase, in the remembrance of things past. To be killed on the altar of Kali were memories that had once been life and joy in my life: Me on my BMW motorcycle exulting through the Blue Ridge Mountains and Albemarle County with my beautiful blonde girlfriend riding on the back. Going to Sweetbriar then off to a field to picnic with some beauty and other University of Virginia classmates and their dates. Memories of crossing the Atlantic on the SS *United States* to England. Paris, Athens, Rome and so on. In ways it had been a charmed life.

Should I be strolling through the ancient town of Srirangapatna, after an afternoon's writing, the knell of anthems past reviewed events in my life associated with them, comprising a sort of grand finale.

Usually some visual obscenity would evoke the really bad musical scores. At one point, I stopped to see a bony, hairless, sore-infested dog kneading its way over cow dung on two thin front legs, balancing and dragging its rear half. As it struggled along painfully, it would pass ferocious local strays, growling and nipping at it from one area to another along the road—a living vision of Breugel. I would run to kick the tormentors out of its way. By then the song playing in my head would be "It's Bunty the Bouncing Bassoon" or "Old MacDonald Had a Farm." My fall from grace would be from the sublime to the ridiculous, but always some distraction to hold back the impending void.

Nothing stopped the raging fire deep within me. I knew that I had to be able to finally say, "I am God." And there was no avoiding this leap. It involved my saying something that most of my life I swore was unthinkable. There were deep barriers in my way, I assumed, of enculturation. Nondualist mysticism helped me cross many of these natural barriers, as had my mystical LSD experience. And certainly Baba's power and presence had taken me the farthest. But in the end, I had a solitary choice ahead of me. My impasse needed supernatural intervention, and I got it.

During the predawn hours of June 5, a Sunday morning, an occult dream invaded my mind with a powerful message. Indeed, so soul-rending was this, one of only a handful of such dreams of this intensity in my life, that my quiet shedding of tears lasted through the duration of that gray rainy morning. No small thing, since I was never one to cry, and most of those few times had to do with private loves.

During the dream my mind and soul were peeled back, and my eyes were held open as I stood on a high ledge and watched the events flow helplessly by. In some inner chamber I could almost sense a gigantic spirit with a censer, for the first time, fully beaming down on me during these hours of decision, like some early hours rite in Brindavan just for "Talie."

The clincher was that the evidences within the dream fell down to the last atom on both sides of the balance. And rather than my terrible choice being resolved, it was heightened in its frightening magnitude. For a part of me would feel the love of Baba all the more and repent of those doubts, realizing that it was through the divine focus of Baba that I was able to take this walk into the night. But another part of me would detect something going on beneath the machinery of the dream that was from a familiar source—like visiting the land of childhood nightmares and feeling the dreaded monster around the next corner. An amnesia clouded my mind. But like an amnesiac seeing the source of his trauma and not identifying it beyond a general mood of fear, so too I would feel a warning chill. One might liken it to smelling a thick pungence of cinnamon in the air but detecting a hint of chloroform underneath. The dream felt like a propaganda communique bearing an SOS message underneath.

## The Dream

It is in the future, at some multiple location: in London at the Savoy or Regency on the Thames, in Washington D.C. at some huge Sheraton or Hilton on the Potomac, and yet also on the Nile River in Cairo, all places that I have been to before. It is in the evening.

I pull off a ramp into a large Holiday Inn-type parking lot filled with cars. I am late for something or other. Along with me are Kerry and Janet and a few other Baba devotees from the early days. As we rush through the crowded lot, the entire panoramic building complex is absolutely teeming with activity. In one wing, a huge buffet dinner, in another, several dining rooms are serving dinner for hundreds, all Baba devotees, at various levels of closeness to Baba. Through a huge plate-glass window, as I approach the electric doors, I am able to glimpse Baba's form, hurriedly passing along a banquet table. People stop chewing and hold up their hands in prayerful salutation. Baba is in the impersonal mode, and apparently very busy. Only the most urgent matters will engage his attention. With him are Raja Reddy and a few others whom I don't recognize. I have absolutely no idea what color badge I will be given, nor how long it has been since I have seen Baba, nor where I stand in the "inner circle" if at all.

The size of the function brings to mind political conventions at the Chicago Hilton, or corporate conventions at the really big hotels in New York. And these are the elect. Lesser devotees throughout the land are celebrating together variously.

I enter, and am separated from Kerry and Janet, being ushered through lobbies, corridors, vast dining halls, through more plush, smaller, and more exclusive dining rooms, to the very elite area where a gold-black badge is pinned on me. It is obviously among the most precious and esteemed badges. Clearly, Baba has gone global.

Baba enters the dining room among swirling valets and messenger boys. Trembling American dignitaries, of all aspects of fame, are at bay just to get a word in with Baba. He passes them by. My boldness of approach is no different from that of the India days. I mask all uncertainty, pressing to the limits that I have a special sonlike relationship.

Baba busily acknowledges me saying a few hasty words, but his manner is more remote. He quickly moves on. But Baba in a fraction of time has transferred an impulse to me. It may have been a command. I am to go through something very important like the final chance to pass some sort of ultimate exam. I am no longer under my own control.

My body automatically begins moving hurriedly out to the parking lot. My soul and mind look helplessly on as some other force guides the machinery of my arms and legs. I get into the car and speed out into a temperate drizzle, through nighttime boulevards and a maze of ramps and flashing lights. Along the river's edge, it becomes more like the Nile and less like the Potomac, Thames, or Seine rivers. In an industrial dockside area, down cobblestone alleys, there are a number of huge granite buildings that, though appearing to blend in with the rest, evidently have been camouflaged. In fact, they are thousands of years old, remnants, as it were, of the monumental cryptic chambers of ancient Egypt, huge vaults of stone. I enter one dingy doorway of a vast gray building composed of ten-ton seamless blocks that without windows climbs five stories high. The only ornamentation is a half-moon roof that looms against the brownish fog.

Inside the very warehouse walls themselves are hidden stairs to the upper vaults. I enter upon the landing of ancient stone and am ushered by a single guide to a doorway 20 feet high. It is directly from Thebes or Karnak. A supernatural power swings the door open as I enter. Then the power swings it almost shut behind me. This room seems to be the focus of every mystery initiation in history, right up to modern Masonic rites in Paris and London. It is the room of ancient mysteries, spanning the earth, from ancient Babylon on.

I join a chanting line of initiates in the dark shadows. They appear stupefied. We are all facing a high priest. The flickering light is from two black sulphur candles at the altar, revealing the chamber to be quite large. The priest has a distinctly Fu Manchu appearance. His companion priest is now quite familiar. I recognize him as the principal of the Veda School in Puttaparthi, the same little gnome-man with burning eyes. The butterflies in my stomach are in a nauseous terror, sensing the anvil of choice.

Standing above us at least 20 feet high against the front walls are two stone giants that can be found at the British Museum, the Cairo Museum, or the tomb of Ramses the Second. They are Seth and Anubis, the Egyptian god of evil, and the jackal god of the necropolis of death. The priest holds a burning censer as something tells me that it is tanus leaves burning. The hypnotic chanting becomes more intense.

I now see that to our left, behind thick curtains, are circular stairs that lead to an upper chamber. A priest has pulled them back to beckon us on with a lit candle.

The initiates that I am standing in line with slowly turn around and face the stairway.

With helpless terror I am close to losing my mind. For suddenly, both granite giants, perhaps 50 tons each, have unglued themselves from the wall, and have now started to slowly edge forward with hideous strength. The gigantic feet sound like hydraulic hammers each time they hit the rock floor. A wind has entered the room from nowhere. These stone giants are now scanning the room with eyes of fire.

Then as the others move beyond me I try to stall in such a way as to escape detection while I desperately calculate an escape. I know my soul is on the anvil of choice. The priests move up the stairs as the two living statues slowly follow. One stops and searches through the crowd with burning red eyes.

My spirit fights with my body not to proceed. My choice rests on a particle of time. I must escape in the vanishing seconds of dim hope much the same way that a field mouse instinctively dodges the beak and talons of a hawk. A question is ringing out in my guts—"Why is it that everytime I reach this same gate, this narrow choice of initiation, that no matter how light, airy, loving, and innocent the pathway has been, the doorway, the rite, cannot be made in any other fashion than that which is unbelievably sinister to my deepest feelings, bearing a total resemblance to the very horrors that I most instinctively feared as a small child, the deepest things of Satan? Why does the final doorway always have to be evil rather than good? Or can't it be somewhere in between? Why never the bells of bliss? For, at the final moment, the carpet is pulled from under you, and you still have to pass through the fire and kiss the feet of some demon god. And only then can you pass through some dark tunnel—one that you can never see the other side."

In the final possible moment I gained back the control of my arms and legs. To do this I had to follow my most heartfelt leading, something that I knew deeper than anything. I called the name of Jesus, of all things. Then the door opened and my legs sped through the front door. Instinctively I ran down the inner stairs with such nimble quickness that the somnambulistic procession could not stop me. Perhaps, miles or hours later, I stopped running. I knew I had escaped with my life. I also sensed this deep well of hope.

But before I can wake up or collect myself, a second dream immediately follows like a new video cassette punched in to replace the old one. This dream is a direct sequel to the last one. In it, I now realize that I have blown that final test by letting instinctive fears keep me from the gate of Godhood. I am not advanced enough.

In this dream, the dial of my emotions shifts. And I am lost in a lost world, back in the West without roots, estranged from Baba. Then in a grand act of cosmic forgiveness, Baba descends from his float in a grand parade in Washington, D.C., as the World Avatar, to reclaim his lost disciple. In a blur of heavy emotion the dream ends, leaving me overwhelmed as I wake up.

The next day I packed and took the bus back to Bangalore. My spiritual crisis was mounting to a vast inner war—as though a contest between God and Satan. Checkmate on the board of eternity felt to be only moves away. The inescapable choice remained on the horizon, a final initiatory rite. And like the occult dream, my response was crucial. Would I or would I not bow before this force and enter the unknown tunnel? And was the end of the tunnel blissful Godhood or some demonic abyss? I could not deny the SOS message underneath it all.

# Chapter 24

# *The Terrible Revelation*

*T*he Blake cabin provided immediate diversion from my profound inner stuggle. Though I was looking, "The Clue" had not yet appeared. So I looked for lesser clues for the time being. As I said, among us there was a pool of many talents. I didn't need to go to any fortune tellers, I was surrounded by them, the creme de la creme of the Age of Aquarius.

Wendel and Phil had been amazed at the position of my stars (triple Aquarius) and a consequent tarot reading that was almost identical. The result had been a growing fame among the Westerners. Now a new addition to our group, whose peculiar talent involved going into mediumistic trance channeling, shook and sweated as the readings came through the "Masters" about my grand destiny on the Western scene. As he stared at my planet signs and worked through the "houses," he was in awe between his seizures of rapid speech and Brooklyn exclamations. Psychological half-truths gave the channeling a hue of credibility. But in the end, though I wanted it to be true, it felt like cosmic flattery and did not feel real. He said, "You will be the beacon of future change in the world. John the Baptist of America, a voice crying in the wilderness. Siva comes through you and dances upon the head of the average man. You are Siva."

The channeling ended like the ultimate fortune cookie: "Heroic life, heroic proportions. If you could control your temper, you could have the whole world. Then you will have so many siddhis (powers) you won't know what to do with them. I look at you and have to say that you are not a human being, you are a great being, and must have come here out of great compassion." This sort of grandiosity always felt dry in the end, like past-life seminars where participants reminisce about their lives as Plato and Mahavira.

By mid-June all the others but Surya Das began moving back to Puttaparthi by Baba's orders. Surya Das wanted solitude to get his head together, and I wanted solitude to finish that last chapter. Baba himself would be well-nigh unreachable throughout the month, traveling intermittently between Whitefield, Puttaparthi, but spending most of his time at the women's college in Ananthapur which was now rapidly being completed. Thus I had even less impetus to suffer the heat and hardship in Puttaparthi when I had the cooler cabin with Surya Das with its greater sense of freedom and privacy.

Then "The Clue" appeared and it utterly changed my life. I would never be the same. You can forgive and forget at times, but you cannot go back and undo what has taken place in history.

## "The Clue"

A cloak of darkness was beginning to cover the desolate wilderness around the empty Blake cabin. It was the evening of June 18. I could hear Surya Das' steps near the front porch. I had had a fruitless day sitting alone in the cabin struggling for inspiration, while Surya Das had spent the whole afternoon, presumably, out wandering. I was hungry and I figured we would try to get supper together on the little kerosene stove. But when his form slowly lumbered through the dark porch into the living-room light, I knew instantly upon seeing his face as he flung back his shawl headdress that there was a surprise but it had nothing to do with food. The awesome burden of whatever revelation he had flooded his face and I knew it might be unbearable. He stood in the doorway, hand on hip, sighing, slightly shaking his head, the anxious depth in his black eyes carrying a look of silent tormented abandon. The kind of look I expect he had when he was a 12-year-old lad living near Chattanooga, and heard that his parents had decided to divorce. The only word that he could get out of his mouth was a ponderous "Well..." and I second-guessed the rest with a tone of total certainty, "... I'm not going to believe what you're about to tell me."

"Right."

"It's going to totally blow my mind."

"Yup."

"It's about Sai Baba."

"You guessed it."

My heart was beating furiously, my mind somehow in tune enough to be already arming itself for something fully as obliterating as my mountaintop LSD experience. I literally tried to get into the most optimal physical position to receive the shocking news, in the center of the room in familiar conference fashion. Then I told him, "Okay, let's hear the whole thing from beginning to end, every detail, don't rush to the crux of the thing without leading up to it."

"You know the teahouse in Whitefield, the one where a lot of the Anglo-Indian guys hang out?"

"Never been in there, but go ahead."

"Well, I went in there for some tea and ran into some of the guys whom I've talked to a number of times. I joined them, and we soon got on the subject of spiritual things. Well, they were sort of half-interested. Then I got on the subject of Baba. They wouldn't say anything. I kept pressing it and they kept quiet. Finally a guy named Raymond and I went for a walk near the Carrolls' house. I kept pressing him. He was very quiet. I knew he had something to say, so I got his complete confidence. He asked me to tell nobody, to swear to keep this a secret, that what he was about to tell me only two other guys knew, that not even his friends in the teahouse knew it. Furthermore, he was under an oath to his best friend, Patrick, not to tell a soul. He said he had a sudden feeling of responsibility for my soul, and that was why he was taking the chance, despite his legitimate fear of Baba's supernatural powers. That unprotected, he or his family might get destroyed, that there have been instances before of local people really being under a curse."

"Right, I know what you mean. Phil once dug up some unpleasant stuff among the local villagers of Puttaparthi regarding the original source of Baba's occult power. Something about an ancient lingam on a hill. But I didn't want to hear about it because there was no way to substantiate it."

"Anyway, Raymond described to me how about two years ago, a few months before you met Baba, Patrick... you know the one, the real good-looking Anglo-Indian with long hair and the sensual look. Yea, the really good-looking, well-built guy who hangs around Whitefield.... Okay, well Patrick went to Brindavan one day, and sat among a whole crew of Americans who were just passing through town for a few weeks. Well, Baba thought that Patrick was one of the freaks from the States you know, because of his long hair and light skin. So he invited Patrick in with all the others for the interviews he gave to the Americans."

"Uh-huh," I responded with a slow deliberate sigh.

"Well, one day after one of those interviews, Baba kept him over for a private interview."

I was going to keep silent for now for the only two people who knew about my own private interviews with Baba were Wendel and Phil, Prema's husband, because they had confided their similar experiences to me.

"Well...," Surya Das said slowly shaking his head. "...Aw man you're not going to believe this. But I'm gonna have to tell you anyway. At any rate, Baba treated him like he does you, you know, all the special attention beside the chair, addressing things only to him, smiling a lot. When all the others left and Baba got him alone, he did his usual number of materializing things and telling him his inner secrets, though I don't know why the devil he didn't know that Patrick just lived down the road. Well, the next thing that happened was that in one smooth motion, Baba reached down and unzipped Patrick's fly, and pulled his tool out." Surya Das stopped for a long pause to let this one fully drop on me. Then he looked up as though to say, "Okay, are you ready for this next one?"

"Well, when he worked Patrick up.... Man I don't know why the guy just stood there and put up with this crap. In fact when I asked Raymond, all he said was that Patrick was only about 17, horny, perhaps a little naive, and I guess didn't give a blue jay what the other partner was. Maybe he was curious or just wanted to see that whole weird thing through, or maybe the kid's a bisexual. Though Raymond told me that Patrick is only interested in girls, and just may have had some what-ya-call liberal curiosity. But at any rate he had an erection all right, and the next thing that happened is really gonna blow your mind. Baba lifted his robe and inserted the thing. That's right. Maybe he's got a woman's organ and a man's organ down there. Yeah, a hermaphrodite. But he honestly inserted it. Patrick said it felt just like a woman, though it may have just been between his legs."

I was chilled to the marrow, and really did not want to believe what I was hearing. The problem was that till then, I knew at least some of this stuff from firsthand experience. Now finally it had gone too far. "Listen, if Baba had been a hermaphrodite it would have gotten out all over the neighborhood. All Indian kids run around naked till they're five."

"I know, but maybe Baba's mom protected him or hid him, or 'it,' yeah, that's right, 'it.' Maybe she was really careful with it. Or some of those people, what ya call neuters, can be latent for years, and only develop a labia after puberty. I don't know all the physiology. Besides, with all his supernatural powers, he's got a sort of weird body anyway. Maybe the guy just transmutes, you know, shifts his protoplasm around at will. At any rate, Raymond told me that just at the moment before Patrick was through, Baba pulled him out and collected his semen in a little white handkerchief."

"This is really too much," I remarked grimly. "Do you think it's some kind of a lie or hoax?"

"I wish it was, but I get a total feeling that it's true. The guy just was not lying. It was not a come-on. He was dead serious and scared. He was sticking his neck out. I know people and this guy was telling the truth. At any rate, let me continue. Baba collected the stuff, and then told him that the whole world lay in the palm of his hand, and that anything Patrick wanted, he could have. That Baba was planning a special position for him, like Raja Reddy. That Patrick could move in and live there, and be with Baba to spread his mission throughout the world. Suddenly Patrick didn't give a hoot. He may have even laughed and told Baba that he was from just down the road, and that he wasn't even an American. At any rate he stopped going and that was it."

"Okay," I announced despondently, "are you ready for this one?"

"I guess I'm as ready as I'll ever be. After this I could hear just about anything and it couldn't be any more shocking."

"By the way, before I go into this, I should tell you that among the guys whom Baba has already 'purified' by pulling out the lingam, are Wendel, Phil.... Yeah, I know he's married but one day Phil confided this to me. And that's not all. There was the disciple of Yogi Bhajan, there was also 'Alpine Schwartz,' the tall dude with the blue ski cap. Yeah, he told Wendel one day at the Whitefield ice-cream stand how Baba materialized a japamala for him in a private interview, and how it had a white bug crawling around on it. Then Baba pulled his drawers down, handled it for a minute presumably to cleanse it of 'heat.' That's not all. There was also a guy who only passed through for a few days, and by the way, that's why. One day Wendel and I were at the Chinese restaurant off Brigade Road, and right at the table next to us were Gordon, the jewel-cutter from Los Angeles, and this guy from U.C.L.A. who I thought was blaspheming Baba. He was talking at full pitch, describing to them how Baba was a 'homo,' how Baba got him in for one of those private interviews and pulled his fly down, and started to go to town. He said it scared the hell out of him, and he practically ran out from the place with his fly down. Baba chased him to the door calling him panic-stricken as the kid just left. Wendel and I at the time just thought the guy wasn't mature enough to handle or transcend his own negative projections and cultural hang-ups.

"But then you've got to ask yourself, if Baba's omniscient, why does he pick people who're going to misinterpret it and blow the whistle on him?" I let this data sink in on him and continued, "But that's not all, there's one little card that I've been holding back on you till now. I, myself, am the main one of all of them. That's right, Surya Das, Baba has done it to me, though I never responded. And up till now I have pretty much sworn the whole thing to secrecy, believing fully that it was a form of *tantric* purification, or if nothing else, a test of allegiance."

I described my final gruesome encounter with Baba during that fateful private interview in Whitefield which has been alluded to but which the reader does not know about in detail. We will let the matter rest here, with my only statement being that unlike Patrick, I did *not* respond. In fact, I tried to keep my mind on the "clear light" assuming that I was being schooled on the unimportance and ephemeral irrelevance of the physical aspect. Baba never again approached me after that.

Surya Das, like me, was in shock. He got up and started making tea while wandering around in a daze.

"But there's another extra side of this," I added. "There is also an occult aspect about the semen. Check this out. One day I heard Phil's confession as we were returning to Whitefield on a bus. How Baba did to him what he had done to me. At least none of us even thought about getting it up. But what Phil told me, and you know he used to teach astrology at the Six Day School in Frisco, having been into it for over 10 years, is the fact that semen is one of the most potent things used in really heavy occult stuff. The vital essence of life or whatever. Perhaps even Alistair Crowley used it. No doubt that's why there's such a heavy emphasis on sex in covens. But one thing Phil mentioned was that when he and Prema were going to have their second child they both vowed to stay celibate for a year and store up their seeds for what they call a "solar year." It is said that if you do this, you will pull into this world the highest soul imaginable to incarnate into the body of your child, something on the level of a rishi or a master. You can also control their astrological chart somewhat by timing the conception. I think Phil's kid might be a solar year one, maybe that's why Baba has always taken him in ... well,

I'm not sure, we can even think that way anymore. But if semen is invaluable, sperm stored up for a solar year must be about the most precious thing that someone who is into sorcery can use."

A chilly silence filled the air. "Think what kind of unsuspecting gold mine Baba might have in the Veda School lads. Several hundred kids disciplined severely into celibacy whom Baba uses as a kind of sperm-bank. Even then, Phil told me that he quite frankly suspected that such was the source of Baba's powers." I went on to mention a dream I had a year before in Puttaparthi in which Baba went on an inspection tour of the Veda School urinals.

We sipped our tea numbly, while I felt my soul disintegrating. I would be under a dark cloud of unknowing for weeks, the constant pressure of despair pressing me to the outer limits of my endurance. If it cracked this time I knew the battle would be fully lost, for there would not be the slightest chance of navigating out of the abyss that I had gone so deeply into, particularly now that the invisible domain that I had allied myself to for so long was turning against me. I just did not want to believe the facts if I didn't absolutely have to. Within a day we would try to get Patrick himself to agree to come by and tell us his account. The issues were too important not to. Many lives might eventually be involved, even millions of them.

I also knew I could not make a patchwork of lies and truths self-servingly and call it reality. If I intentionally unknew or ignored what I now knew, verily, I would be like the Laotian monk immolating himself in the fiery corona of red, who at the irredeemable moment past the point of no return, begins to twitch a little before the newsreel ends and before the public eye vanishes. And it tells us that the emaciated figure twitching in flames is paralyzed into an agony that might just last forever. The willful monk just keeps a poker face till the body drops away, then when all the onlookers are out of view, he can scream forever. What a scream that's gonna be. Just himself and the void, endlessly black, forever and forever. The monk just has to look enlightened and keep composure while aflame. He can't embarrass his religion with bad theater! It is a covenant of the will. How terrible to learn that your trance is not enlightenment after all as 1,000-degree flames bubble and fry your skin in escalating agony that no force on earth can stop!

Almost as an afterthought I said, as the "Good Book" says, "And I saw the dead, small and great, stand before God: And the books were opened; and another book was opened; which is the book of life. And the dead were judged out of those things which were written in the books, according to their works.... And whosoever was not found written in the book of life was cast into the lake of fire" (Revelation 20:12-15).

We sat stunned, talking into the early hours of the morning. Sleep would not come before certain points were settled in our minds. We gaped at one another in shock, when we weren't reminding ourselves of such things as "The bottom just dropped out of my entire life. Can you believe it, would you ever have believed it, Baba is a queer? Twenty-five years of being guided to this incredible peak, backed up by all kinds of complex life patterns, intuitions, omens and signs, an absolutely astounding philosophy, and so convincing is it, so positive are you that it is the truth, all culminating in Baba, that you invest all that you have and are into it. Then one day, just in a second, it is all ripped away! Where do you go next, Las Palmas, the Caribbean? Do you just pack your bags and forget it ever happened? Stop thinking, like most people, and live the thoughtless hedonistic life waiting for the next floor to cave in? Never."

The consequences of our act would soon be felt by the others, and we knew that we had to deal with this immediately. The main obstacle in reaching the others was the impermeable blind-faith closed system of belief, fundamental to the whole path. Even those dearest to us would predictably launch a counterattack on our own validity. It had always worked this way before. I should know, I had done the same with others who fell away.

"We will have failed like so many other bright stars of promise who gave in to 'sensuality, ego, doubts, and weakness.' If it's our word against Baba's, you know whose word they're going to believe and it won't be ours."

But even if the group invalidated us, there was still a sore spot that they had yet to explain. And that was Baba's blunder in bestowing so much "grace" upon those who would turn away disillusioned from him and embarrassing him by even broadcasting their grievances, real or imaginary, to the entire world. Tal known for his zeal and faith, never known for an outward show of doubt, who would suddenly turn on Baba as an enemy. Tal who had written pamphlets circulating through Assam and northern India about Baba who now had a huge project coming out of the presses of Calcutta in the form of a book. The problem the American contingent had to deal with was explaining how the avatar, who sees perfectly above time, who knows everything that is going to happen, for he says so adamantly, could allow for so adverse an outcome. Why even my book would have to be scrapped as a bitter memory as it came out and those reading it learned that the once great Tal Brooke, who spoke to crowds of thousands and sang to them was suddenly persona non grata.

The next afternoon Patrick and Raymond did come. Very sobered, less flippant than usual, Patrick's account followed virtually word-for-word what Surya Das had told me the fateful night before. Then when I told them all my story, they weren't surprised. I aired my thoughts. "Your account can't be contrived because if there's nothing else I know, one thing I do know, and that is that I have personally stood alone before Sai Baba with my pants down to my knees." All of us would depart, sworn to mutual secrecy till more data came in. Patrick would urge me to remain quiet, perhaps to protect his family, at least from disgrace, at the same time understanding my relentless quest for the truth.

The gloomy days of June would stretch on, desolation wherever I was. This state of occult desolation really cannot be communicated. The difficulty in trying to portray this terrible state is total. It is not like a death in the family or seeing friends die in an auto wreck where grief enfolds. The terrible power of my occult desolation, let me suggest, comes through a spiritual doorway, and most people have no idea where it is and how far back there it is.

Should Surya Das and I, virtually oblivious of our surroundings, make our way along the same road, slowly lumbering to deep sighs of indignation, a circular prison of thought would go on. "I feel like I'm dying inside. I just can't believe I've been with this guy for so long, trusting him completely, a guy who is worshiped by millions who don't even know that he's a...," and there would be a brief pathetic laugh, "closet queen. He's up there on stage working miracles before their very eyes, claiming to be God Almighty, and behind closed doors he's toyed with any number of guys."

Another gruesome tidbit would roll in from Surya Das, "In fact on Mahasivaratri, all he's really doing is upchucking a stone phallus, that's all a Siva lingam is, what a joke. It's his big stunt of the year." Then we would remember the Jean Harlow effect on the swinging silver couch, the Jhula, adored by all the people at festivals. All things that smacked of some grandiose narcissism.

Then I recalled the dream in Srirangapatnam. That after having left Baba out of doubt, I would blow it. Yet I was dogged that I would not give the dream the dignity of being prophetic truth if the very hub of its message was to seduce me into Baba's dominion—the second dream that is! The first dream did highlight the demonic behind the initiation that I ran from in terror.

In my gut-wrenching depression I had to remind myself why I should not give up on all truth in disillusioned bitterness. Just because I had believed in some false light did not repudiate the existence of the true light. For counterfeits, whatever they be, were parasitically dependent on the existence of the real thing. Perhaps the victory of hell over me was the possibility that after such a bitter aftertaste from this last experience I would give up on all truth. I would turn away prematurely when the very light of God's compassion awaited at the door. One might see why an adversary to the true God might have such a lethal weapon in deception. I and others could ask, "If I can be so totally blinded and deceived, then when can I ever really know the truth and not question whether it too is not another lie? Will I ever be able to tell the true man of God from the false?" I could not answer that question. Though the issue of a reliable and trustworthy standard of truth that was objective had come up before.

By June 27, a week before the huge college opening festival in Ananthapur, Surya Das and I knew we still had some scores to settle. For one thing, much of my luggage was at the main ashram.

We locked the Blake cabin and, like refugees in flight, hastened with our terrible revelation into Bangalore. At the Regent snackbar we were most secretive with the friends of the "rooftop prophetess." Like a disagreeable older brother, I leaned on their table, masking my despair with that same armor of lonely control I used in Srirangapatnam, and in so many ways intimated, "Oh, yeah. Is that all?" in a kind of belch, and walked away. Their faith was sky high. Baba had psychically been preparing them for the drama of the age, tee-hee. They were so sure of this that they were staying in the fanciest hotel in town, buying silk saris, jewelry and otherwise preparing themselves for the great event— the wedding that was to never happen. Maybe if they hit bottom I could talk to them but now was not the time.

## The Painful Journey

With a guarded dignity, Surya Das and I left them to take the evening train to Ananthapur where Wendel was working on the mural at the almost completed college.

The school was stupendous. We found Wendel resembling Michelangelo standing atop a jerry-built platform working on one of his 20-foot murals. With a pang of brotherly love I would say, "You genius." He smiled back, and in my heart I would ask, "Why is it all for naught? This much talent and he's being squeezed for all he is worth. True beauty being grafted to an abomination." Immediately Wendel would catch something upon our faces and falter. Then he would hear something in the tone of my voice, "Wendel, we've got to talk."

We went up to the windy bleak four-story rooftop of the huge circular monolith overlooking miles of barren wilderness. It was a structure which was more giant and bizarre than anything either Antonioni or Felini had incorporated in their grotesque surrealistic cinematic obsessions with architecture. Wendel, thinner than ever, moving about like Joe Cocker on stage and wearing these ragged white pajama bottoms, painstakingly drew patterns in the cement dust as he listened. It was getting to him. This was the first time I had ever seen anything get to him quite like this. I could see his faith beginning to stretch and falter, stress lines of doubt briefly surfacing on his face. After five intermittent months of titanic effort out here in the wasteland, he has to hear this horror story, I thought. What a sense of loss, what a misappropriation of brilliance. The potent wave of thought we brought now threatened to extinguish his great effort.

Wendel sensed a most terrible compelling potency about Patrick's story. For a second he reviewed what happened to him with Baba. He was sure there was nothing erotic about it. No, of course not, it was purely purificatory. "But how do you explain what happened to Patrick? What if you had gone all the way?" He squirmed. Now it was just too unreal. And if it happened, well let truth win out in the end.

A sobering element in this for Wendel, who wrote me a very encouraging letter about my own mission when I was writing alone in Srirangapatnam, was the very real fact that I was suddenly leaving. Doubtless this reinforced his sense of loneliness inherent in the path.

After a while he returned to the mural. Wendel would continue working 18 hours a day in the hot wind, as perpetual crowds of helpers and visitors stood around gaping in silence when he didn't direct them to either clear off or bring him some supply.

When we left the central building that day, a limousine pulled up as its occupants gibbered away self-importantly in high-pitched irritation. Ratan Lall, the Bombay millionaire, made a token gesture of greeting as he climbed out. Surya Das and I took the afternoon bus to Puttaparthi. By evening we arrived in Puttaparthi unnoticed. Baba had headed to Ananthapur by another route, missing us by hours. This was exactly as I had hoped. I could not stomach seeing Baba at the moment.

On a hilltop that evening we told Ed and Phil the news. They received it with cautious alarm. Ed especially became disheartened, knowing that his choice would be to cut us off and remain with Baba or end up in the same hell of uncertainty. This sudden spanner in the works would end for them a perfect little story out here in India.

With Baba's unnerving presence out of the way I now had several final days to spend on the ashram alone, much of the time to reflect on the hills and otherwise remind myself of the sudden abandonment of such a great part of me.

Some of us would huddle together in the foothills to decide what to do next. Eddie would just listen on, at times helping us grope for alternatives as though part of the schisming group. Other times Surya Das and I would be alone. If Kasturi and I "walked down memory lane" together within the ashram, smiling and talking like old times, it took everything I had to keep him from knowing that the bottom had fallen out of my life. One, there was the possibility that I was under testing still. Two, there was that lifelong caution that he didn't need to hear the whole story and that the less Kasturi knew, the better for my livelihood. I was a fugitive, a hidden agent in the nest, a fallen chief disciple, and quite possibly, in the long run, the most internecine enemy of Baba if there were a true God that existed apart from Sai Baba. I felt utterly alone among friends whom I had virtually adopted as family.

In the late afternoon of my final day in Puttaparthi, I chose to go off alone to the hillside overlooking the entire ashram. I settled among the huge smooth boulders in the warm breeze, where the din of village and ashram sounds blended faintly. I brought my wrinkled Bible, retrieved from the belongings I had come to get. As scrambled as I was, I still dared to search for truth, this time in the Scriptures. I was utterly desperate and confused.

I was thinking, "Okay God you'd better prove yourself if you are real. This is your last chance because I've been looking for truth all my life." I was almost testy. "Because if you don't, and life is just a joke, I am going to live like someone driving a Ferari with his foot flattened to the floor. I will go for the good life ruthlessly, taking people with me. My innocence and idealism will be long dead. I will curse God and die."

Then I looked down at Baba's domain and asked God, "And how do you explain the apparent love of this self-proclaimed incarnation of God and his miracles... tell me that."

Quietly I laid the book open on a large flat rock while lying on my side where the panoramic view lay before me. Soon my concentration became rapt. For truly it spoke as no other book. There was no mistaking, its spirit and searching honesty was unlike any other book. Its stand on the way things were was utterly exclusive, forceful, unbending, and totally authoritative. Neither did it mince words nor speak in long drawn-out esotericisms. I prayed, "If there is a God, speak to me now!" Then I just threw the Bible wide open on a boulder, playing Russian roulette with its pages.

It opened up to Matthew 24:24:

> And there shall come False prophets and False Christs working great signs and wonders to deceive, if it were possible, even God's very elect.

This passage hit my eyes merely seconds after I had looked away from Baba's prayer hall asking how a creature like Sai Baba could be explained. The Bible said that he was a false miracle worker, an antichrist, out to deceive. The Bible had contained this message all along, down these long centuries. The words were those of Christ himself, warning his followers across time of what was to pass before He returned to earth. I then read the words surrounding this passage.

> And as he was sitting on the Mount of Olives, the disciples came to Him privately, saying, "Tell us,

when these things will be, and what will be the
sign of Your coming and of the end of the age?"

And Jesus answered and said to them, "See to it
that no one misleads you. For many will come in
My name, saying, 'I am the Christ,' and will mislead many. And you will be hearing of wars and
rumors of wars; see that you are not frightened, for
those things must take place, but that is not yet the
end. For nation will rise against nation, and kingdom against kingdom, and in various places there
will be famines and earthquakes. But all these
things are merely the beginning of birthpangs.
Then they will deliver you up to tribulation and will
kill you, and you will be hated by all nations on
account of My name. And at that time many will
fall away and will betray one another and hate one
another. And many false prophets will arise and
will mislead many. And because lawlessness is
increased, most people's love will grow cold. But
the one who endures to the end, it is he who shall be
saved.

"And this gospel of the kingdom shall be preached
in the whole world for a witness to all the nations,
and then the end shall come. Therefore when you
see the Abomination of Desolation which was spoken of through Daniel the prophet, standing in the
holy place, then let those who are in Judea flee to
the mountains, let him who is on the housetop not
go down to get the things out that are in his house;
and let him, who is in the field, not turn back to get
his cloak. But woe to those who are with child and
to those who nurse babes in those days. But pray
that your flight may not be in the winter, or on a
Sabbath; for then there will be a great tribulation,
such as has not occurred since the beginning of the
world until now, nor ever shall. And unless those
days had been cut short, no life would have been

saved, but for the sake of the elect, those days shall be cut short."

And then on the next verse, after looking up from my Bible to take it all in, I felt a fiery conviction as I again read:

Then if any one says to you, "Behold, here is the Christ," or "There He is," do not believe him. *For false Christs and false prophets will arise and will show great signs and wonders, so as to mislead, if possible even the elect.*
Behold, I have told you in advance. If therefore they say to you, "Behold, he is in the wilderness," do not go forth or, "Behold, he is in the inner rooms," do not believe them.
For just as the lightning comes from the east, and flashes even to the west, so shall the coming of the Son of Man be (Matthew 24:3-27 NASB).

There was so much in this passage that I had to close the book for a long time before I opened it again. In my caution, I just filed it away as evidence of an alternate explanation as to what Baba was, through a different lens, the lens of the Holy Bible.

Then as red veins stretched across the sunset sky, another fact began to sink in. That Christ would return like "lightning." I believed all these years that He would reincarnate, assuming that He was the same part of Brahman we all were. But no such thing was even vaguely implied. Rather, the long-promised Messiah had entered the world by birth, but only upon one occasion, through direct supernatural intervention. The Old Testament had predicted this long before the time of Christ.

The Old Testament predicted His appearance in an obscure town, "But thou, Bethlehem, Ephratah, though thou be little among the thousands of Judah, yet out of thee shall He come forth unto Me that is to be ruler in Israel: Whose goings forth have been from of old, from everlasting" (Micah 5:2).

But with this and other scriptures the Carrolls had once made a point that I was only now considering. There would be one and only one birth of the Messiah. Never again would he come through the human vehicle of a mother. Never would it be the Divine purpose for the Messiah to repeat the covenant of again growing up from childhood. That sacrifice of a perfect man to atone for the fall of a once-perfect man (and his seed) had been satisfied once and for all. This fact nullified the claims of every guru in the world who claimed to be Christ come again. Christ would be born into the world only once. He would return exactly as he had ascended: not born but in a glorified adult body.

When the ascended Son of God returns from deep heaven in power, in the very manner in which he departed, history as we know it, will stop forever. Perhaps it will be as sudden and as total as this Logos, through whom the warp and woof of the universe was made (as the Gospel of John declares) suddenly stopping everything in creation in midsentence, in mid-electron orbit to celebrate the precise instant of the advent. Every creature in the earth and beneath the earth will know simultaneously. "Every eye shall see." But that "Alpha and Omega," far from being a helpless infant born to yet again toddle and grow up, can only be that once-crucified Nazarene appearing in blinding and exalted glory, even so that those who are not His shall tremble in deepest terror. And only then will every knee bow and every tongue confess Jesus Christ as Lord, God the Son, whom Isaiah described with the words, "And his name shall be called *Pele* (Wonderful), *Yoetz* (Counselor), *El Gibbor* (The Mighty God), *Avi Ad* (The Everlasting Father), *Sar Shalom* (The Prince of Peace)" (Isaiah 6:1).

(*El Gibbor* may be translated literally from the Hebrew as God-man, whom Isaiah identifies with the prophecy, "Unto us a child is born, unto us a Son is given.")

The long green and white prayer hall in the valley below me looked far too diminutive and gaudy to harbor the returning Christ of the Bible. I could close the book before me having at least settled that forever. Later that night I returned. Under the starlight I was still very much broken and confused as I brought my despair before God, whoever and whatever He was. I uttered the Lord's Prayer then petitioned with heavy heart that I be shown by God Himself His true nature without the need to fear deception.

After two long years of frightful bondage to a god I was beginning to learn was not God, it was a most relieving thing to board the bus in the dark morning hours and rumble away through the wilderness shadows. Much weight upon my soul was yet to be resolved. I was not sure how yet, but an emboldened rage was slowly mounting within me about Baba, gathering in my soul, as armies before battle, for the needed confrontation to get at the truth.

As the bus rumbled into the night I knew that slowly shrinking to my rear was a community of now-distant spiritual relatives. Ironically, they were caught in a growing epidemic of infectious hepatitis. Strained to the limits these American and European brethren would wilt in the sun and answer their bodies' acute hunger for protein with overspiced starch, all the while thinking proudly to themselves that they were becoming purified and spiritually exalted. Baba's fruit on the desert, his languishing children.

# Chapter 25

# *Entering the Crucible*

*T*here was a rumor spreading that Hilda would arrive at the Bangalore airport in a few days to attend the massive event in Ananthapur. In my state of mind, I was hardly in the mood to go through the token effort. But Surya Das wanted to greet her and ask some probing questions.

Our waiting at the airport was little more than a formality. It was July 5, and the big school opening festival in Ananthapur was only days away. The minute the old gal got out of the plane, Surya Das and I would probably hit her with the whole thing. In the meantime, I was in anything but a receptive mood for hearing her predictable conciliatory pearls of wisdom in response to this recent scandalous "test." Indeed I had never held her in awe or reverence as the others had, never having met her for one thing, and having my own personal barriers and suspicions about women gurus. It just wasn't my style. As far as telling her the story, we would try to feel how receptive she was on the spot; Surya Das, who knew her, trusted her. I didn't.

Entrusting her with the information we now knew might be the most naive thing we could do, similar to the old movie formula of informing the friendly confidante who happens to be the enemy's number one undercover agent. Doubtless she would sympathize with us, but it would be a stalling tactic as the news got to the commander.

Baba's powers themselves expelled the possibility that he was merely an innocent bystander, an ordinary deluded man. His metaphysics was too complex and knowing, his ability to manipulate people far too devastating. And his powers topped it off.

My mood at the airport was mixed. There was the absurd dark-humor side to the whole episode that my mind wanted to conveniently use in order to flee from the incredible weeks of despondence, anguish, disgust, and bitterness. My mood of sardonic abandon might also lash out at Hilda, as she descended the ramp to view her illustrious reception party with one of Baba's former prime disciples. And my imagination went rampant with defiant mind-shockers to greet this saccharine "guru" from Manhattan.

*Fantasies:* defiant blue-denim mockouts. Surya Das and I chewing tobacco. He has his lemur on his shoulder, a little being with saucer-shaped eyes that looks as if it's from outer space. Our mouths hanging dumbly open as the old hag with the silver hair floats down the ramp. She walks up to the two big lugs chewing tobacco, mouths still hanging open in mock obscene shock, when not chewing, eyebrows knit together in hostility.

"Sai Ram seekers, oh dear, where is our master in this turbulent plane of existence... that dear sweet...."

A long pause, double takes at the sky, obnoxious chewing movements, hand on hips still looking around. She's definitely uncool. "Uh...I dunno," I look at the lemur, "Ya see where he went? He was here a minute ago...." The animal looks positively weird. "Aw yeah... some dude dressed up like Jiggoletto in chiffon, weird, walks in the French court manner with the ruffled silk...uh, I think he was walking by, let's say mincing toward the men's room. Seems to me that Baba took off right after him looking really excited about something. Followed him right in there, Lady.... See the men's room over there. Yeah, that's right. Ought'a be through in a sec."

In my next abusive fantasy, we are wearing Stetson hats, cowboy boots, leather jackets, and smoking hand-rolled weeds, looking really mean. Instantly my fantasy would die in disgust. I had just been reading William Burroughs' *Nova Express* near the runway. It was a treatise on transgalactic mobsterism, bleeping with paranoia and insights into the nature of the demonic and grand-scale con games. It had sickened my heart and soul. And I could not help but apply the tenor of the message to the entire Baba scandal, and the reality, to once again start up that perennial debate of the nature of supernatural evil as a force divorced from God. Burroughs' disjointed, heavy-powered phrases still ripped through my mind as I recalled that he had written it in Cairo, ankle-deep in morphine ampule boxes. The inspiration seemed to be demons blowing the whistle on one another's stratagems. Yet the setting was without hope, a Godless universe.

On some agonizing line about the hell-world Minruad, I would look up from the book and see the silver needle circle overhead.

Fifteen minutes later the plane unloaded, and each head that came out that wasn't Hilda's further confirmed our suspicions that it was just a rumor. Instead, like the messenger boy that gets the brunt of criticism for bringing the bad news, every face that wasn't the one received a sneer of disgust from us. By the last passenger, my fantasy about the hostile reception party was beginning to look true of Surya Das and me, we were starting to really sneer. We didn't even notice that the plump girl coming down the ramp was wildly waving at us until Surya Das came and said, "It's Lila, she must have come in Hilda's stead. Looks like she finally got her visa."

I looked over unable to mask my feelings, "Aw crap, she's not even pretty. You mean we've gotta go through this ordeal. Why it'll blow her mind...." Now I started to consider the factual ramifications of our less-than-perfect zeal for Baba. "She'll see right away that we're ready to float a lemon on the dude." Truly it would take a superhuman effort of will to chaperone her to the Regent Guest House and contain the inner hell we were going through. The last thing we needed was a bubbly turned-on bhakta, especially an old standby like Lila. And I was reminded by Surya Das that Hilda had almost made me a legend among her group in New York.

There was another surprise. Herman's daughter from San Diego was on the plane. After we got to Regent Guest House, Lila was in tears as I stood at the head of the table making the very cautious statement, "Again I would urge you not to overly adore the physical mani-festation of Baba...." Behind my black eyes was an ocean of anguish. She'd break again, practically bawl-ing. We left the next morning in a rented taxi, deciding if nothing else, to make our final ride to Baba one of physical comfort with the girls sharing in our expenses. I hated going through what I knew lay ahead.

By early afternoon, July 7, our dust-covered taxi went by the wire fence of the college compound to the gate. The building, four stories high and donut shaped, looked like a modern bauhaus imitation of the great Colosseum of Rome. The sort of bleached white architectural anom-aly that Felini used in his movies. Around the central building were other large buildings which sat in a huge compound closed in by a high wire fence. A policeman in a sentry box signaled us through. "Well, there it is," I announced, not exactly trying to disguise my lack of enthusiasm. The three girls in the back missed it, jumping up and down in their seats with glee. Soon we entered the large rotund monolith as crowds of devotees moved like excited ants.

The girls were mere grains of sand in the avatar's world mission. What had once been Lila's vaunted personal intimacy with Baba, when fewer foreigners flocked Brindavan, had vanished, and in place, Baba's eyes fell upon Lila with no more recognition than if she were a stranger in the crowd just arriving from some meaningless American city. She would try to press up to him with an insecure self-fueled joy on the landing of the second floor as Baba passed. Baba would hiss at the crowd to stand back not showing the least trace of recognition for Lila, whom he would order the others to restrain. She froze as he walked on, buckling at the knees with tears in her eyes. Herman's daughter also would be crying, though probably for a different reason—the price of faith in this stubby frog-king walking around chewing betel leaves as people in magnetic storms moved at his beck and call. Where was the love that her tender little soul was starving for?

Other Westerners with more talent and "spirituality" had replaced Lila. And like an old faithful, her role would be to just hang on hoping for that rare nod from Baba, that piece of bread thrown at the dogs in the outer court. Dead was Lila's dream of returning glory.

The grand entrance-hall was bordered by two gigantic murals, each by wide elegant stairs. They were crystal reproductions in the Wyeth tradition, one of Puttaparthi with miles of mountains, rice paddies, bullocks, arid fields and the main ashram, the other of a verdant pristine forest in the wilds of North America, a bird hovering in frozen flight in the gap of a narrow canyon between two luscious banks, dew drops glistening on leaves, every twig, every leaf in miraculous focus, a sublime rainbow in the background. And up on a platform would be this very high spiritual being in white, not even aware of the shifting swarms of awed admirers, and almost casual about Baba's frequent stops to survey his work, invariably to chat with and encourage him. Most humbling for Lila.

It was late afternoon. Wendel caught my eye and hopped down from the platform immediately, while onlookers puzzled like hungry groupies, pressing to get the inside word. Guards perpetually kept Wendel's working area clear, standing back respectfully as I joined him in the clearing. "Like old times," I told myself ironically. Wendel rested his hand on my shoulder saying in a confidential voice, "We've got to talk. Haven't got much time. This thing has to be done by the inauguration tomorrow. Probably I'll have to pull an all-nighter." The President of India was arriving with a constellation of VIPs. Wendel and I went up the stairs toward the roof as arm-banded volunteers in the Seva Dal stepped aside.

In the gray light on the roof, Wendel asked if I had resolved anything with Baba. Not yet, I said, still having found no occasions to confront Baba. I told Wendel that it would take a supreme miracle for Baba to convince me that he was who he claimed to be. Wendel then shared a great confidence with me, perhaps in doing so, hunting for clues as I had and exposing his doubts.

Wendel confided, "You know a few hours after you and Surya Das left, Baba arrived and the first thing he did was come up to me and bring me into his quarters down there." Wendel was bothered, his tone conveying bewilderment over the cloak and dagger mysteries under Baba when things could so easily be up-front. Perhaps Baba had let his guard down with Wendel. And for that reason Wendel would have to answer with richer faith as fully deserving of the confidence that his master bestowed upon him.

In the privacy of his suite, Baba looked into Wendel's eyes questioningly. "What is wrong? Have you seen Tal? What does he say? Doubts? Bad faith?" Baba even sounded hurt and jealous. At that point Wendel had told

Baba nothing about his knowledge of the terrible incident and our mission to him, evidently quite stunned by Baba's question. No human being could have told Baba a thing. Yet Wendel asked himself why Baba need question him. Wendel, attempting perhaps to protect me, gave Baba a vague answer. Tal was going through something, a test of doubt, but would come through.

Then out of the blue, Baba mentioned to Wendel a certain person, a rather pretty lad from Whitefield whom Wendel had perhaps seen a few times and knew of through Surya Das and me. Baba's words came in rapid, urgent, and even panicky whispers, informing and warning Wendel. Sequences jumped around like a fragmented dream. "Some two years ago, one coming, a Whitefield hippie. Long hair, muscles, American shirt saying 'love.' Not love, lust. Only interest is girls, not God. Sitting in darshan line, pretending to be an American. Swami knows." The rest was garbled until the teenager, Patrick, was accused by Baba of spreading damaging rumors. "False lies. Blind jealous reaction after I tell him to go. Now others believing lies. His word over Swami's!" Perhaps Baba gave Wendel a hug as a reminder of the purity of his love, and then Wendel was dismissed to paint.

After Wendel's account, I was chilled as well as infuriated into a more steely-minded resolve to combat Baba, now that he had broken, supernaturally, into my protective camouflage, smelling out through some kind of spiritual surveillance system that the "gasoline crack in history" of his blunders was growing wider and leaked out, as more evidence was beginning to collect like beads of oil on water. Exactly what he knew and exactly what he would do about it was another thing. One thing was sure, Baba had already partially blown his defense by giving Patrick's story enough dignity to talk about it, in a tone far from detached, even defensive as though in fear of being found out. To me it further implicated

Baba. But I could see the beginning of a widening gulf between Wendel and ourselves. I wondered if he had not already made his choice in his heart to go ahead and override the impediment to his faith. The scandal would be maya. Wendel would take the leap. I had leapt too many times already.

People turned in around 9:00 P.M. in the immense building. Women's dorms and men's dorms of the elect in giant classrooms now carpeted with sleeping bags and mats. 6:00 A.M. reveille would be bhaktis outdoing each other, in zest, zeal, and energy. People whistling loudly while shaving, doing calisthenics, looking self-important, slapping their chests like a German trailer park of hard-core campers. Wendel was on the eleventh plane of consciousness, oblivious to the frenetic insect movements around him, just a Neil Young sneer at all the obvious games and come-ons. As he smiled at me, for a second it would be like old times, but something had already started to change forever, and the twinge of sentimentality was almost a part of the past.

It would be a big day, July 8. Thousands upon thousands would come to see the massive opening of the multimillion-rupee complex as little sideshows would be going on. The kings and queens of this state and that, coming to see Baba, demanding special audience. They would have to wait in a long waiting line. Baba might even be chastising them. Once great diadems of devotion, such as the overly loquacious Dr. Gokkak, would now have to walk a little more carefully. Indra Devi, in all of this, would hardly be noticed. Perhaps that was why she too would feel the need to march around as though a part of some great secret mission. Peripheral curiosity-seekers would look up. Baba would hardly give her a glance.

Early that morning I resolved in my heart that I would break through to Baba. My time was running out as the crowd grew by the hour before the afternoon's inauguration ceremony.

I felt a new reaction and discernment to Baba growing in my heart. I had noticed it the night before, as he passed me on the staircase leading to his suite, ushers in the distance, others looking on. They may have assumed that I was the old Tal Brooke, but now I was an alien in the nest. Baba would float right by me, neither looking at me nor acknowledging my presence. I felt nausea, revulsion, a deep indignation of the spirit. It felt as though the spirit that inhabited the bright-robed body was so putrid, so foul, so horrifying that if the crowds could just see it for a second denuded, they would scream and run in terror. This tame-looking magnetic being, able to go in and out of people's force fields, would suddenly—with all his disguises removed—change character and pursue the screaming crowd like some giant man-sized scorpion with blazing red eyes and a thousand stinging tails.

Now the appointed hour of contact was drawing close. My revulsion of him was so great that I knew that "plan B" was out of the question.

What was "plan B"? To go through the deep indignation of the soul of remaining in the nest as a camouflaged enemy, falling back into grace through perfect obedience. Using flattery to blind Baba. Seeming to be the even stronger disciple, repentant of my brief apostasy. Only he and a few would know (I was satisfied that Baba did not have full access to anybody's thoughts. He had a patched access, the rest he bluffed) of the Patrick episode. Then during some festival speech, as I would dedicate my book to Baba, in one horrifying public gesture, I would grab the bottom of his robe, and tear it off his entire body. It would probably lead to my death, even immediately. But what it would reveal would be either two neuter genitals, or the naked fact that this self-proclaiming God come in flesh had been utterly deceived about his closest American disciple. His omniscience, telepathy, control of history, would be revealed as lies. There would be no conceivable good that could come from such a humiliation. Even more, all of a sudden before 10,000 shocked onlookers the web of energized control surrounding his spirit would be broken, letting out its ferocious native evil, the scorpion nature, before it could be held in check. It would suddenly go berserk in demonic blasphemies and rage in the heat of blind passion, now oblivious to the pinheads looking on. It would be a public display of spiritual abomination. The truth was I had to bring this thing to a head immediately. I was much too revulsed to even think of plan B.

By 10:00 A.M., the entire college complex was teaming with activities: Barnum and Bailey-sized awnings and tents being pitched, a Styrofoam and plywood stage in the front, the school bands practicing, acres of ground being roped off into sections, streamers and flags going up, loudspeakers being put everywhere.

But the main activities of the morning were in the large central four-story circular building with the courtyard inside. The four entrance ways to the building were suggestive of the Colosseum in Rome.

Raja Reddy emerged from a limousine like Rudolph Valentino in white, and briskly approached Baba in the inner courtyard, at first bowing down to touch his forehead to Baba's feet.

Then there was a token feeding of the poor as a few hundred wretched and maimed, a meager fraction of those in the ocean of bodies outside, were squeezed through the mesh gates by several guards and directed toward the circular park. They sat in neat, reverent rows within the monolith of the elect as the privileged caste of India looked on in a spirit of noble generosity. Baba dutifully ladled out food on banana leaves. When the peasants were finished, with an almost bored wave of the hand, Baba motioned them to leave, turning a deaf ear to their quiet pleas and raised hands as they hobbled back out of the gate. Most likely they would all be shooed away before the president's motorcade arrived. Because of who I was, I was able to stand just about nearer to Baba than anyone there.

The unreadable expression on my features belied the ferocity of emotions within me. Baba was on a routine inspection of the rooms and offices as a small train of attendants and dignitaries followed him ten feet behind. People appeared more awed and afraid of him than usual. The Western girls were 100 feet away from the front area. Most of the males were scattered about. Many devotees filled the courtyard, standing frozen. Others assembled at different points of the circular ground-floor veranda, while still others looked down quietly from above from the outdoor circular halls on one floor or another.

Wendel stood part way up the wide marble staircase beside his mural of Puttaparthi. On the mezzanine above and behind him was the polished black door to Baba's suite, carpeted and elegant within and looking out to the entire front compound from a wide balcony; it was most suggestive of the Papal apartments from where the Pontiff emerged seasonally to bless the Vatican square.

I was planted near a wide pillar where the circular ground-level veranda crossed the front lobby. Briskly Baba led a train of people toward me, heading for one of the main reception-rooms on the other side of the front lobby.

Calculatingly yet unobtrusively I stood fairly far out, counting on the fact that Baba rarely veered course but usually swept by the closer disciples. To onlookers this graceful act gave his disciples a special sense of privileged intimacy. I was gambling. Indeed it would be hard to describe my mental state.

I felt like a high-echelon assassin on a mission of doom, hidden in the ranks yet quietly on the verge of oblivion, seconds away from some act that would result in overwhelming deathly retribution. What made the risk even more electrifying was that I would not know exactly what I was to do until the last moment, and there would be no turning back. I just sensed that my soul already knew what to do. One possible outcome made it a virtual suicide mission.

Several of Baba's closer new Indian disciples, being brave, edged up slightly behind me.

In seconds the bushy red figure with a radiant face and burning eyes was upon us, quickly brushing by with great command. As his robe swept by, my hand, hanging harmlessly by my side, suddenly jolted with life, becoming tense and strong. My hand grasped a sizable fold of the robe, waist level on Baba, held it as he continued walking on till the tension caught him. Then I yanked it back. It happened so fast and my own movements were so disguised that the alarmed onlookers had not figured out yet what had happened.

Baba went three steps beyond me to fully realize what had happened, then he whirled around rapidly in a state of fury, spewing out words. He had pinpointed who it was. His black eyes boiled as he tried to contain the curses leveled at me. This was the predictable highly fissionable scorpion nature, the dreaded source of power, usually held in check. With an unexpected boldness and calm, again ready to pay the price, I looked right down his black orbs with a total conviction of knowledge regarding who he really was. I saw a despicable blotch, a mere cinder compared to the true Living God.

Suddenly Baba really did remind me of a wrangling hag who had lost all authority and now had to bluff. "Rowdie, complete spoil. Go, get out here...." I had seen this sort of thing crush people, denunciations far milder.

Perhaps he thought it would crush me, but I began to smile sneeringly just enough for him to know.

A voice was trying to tell my soul that it had just forfeited some undreamed-of chance. Yet already there was a golden trumpet of triumph blaring heavenward. Still I looked Baba in the eyes and nothing earthshaking happened, I had not perished. My cool and poised response persuaded the onlookers that this was merely a rather esoteric test between Baba and a highest disciple, thus rendering his authority even more impotent, for I knew he wanted a train of ushers to pitch me out. He wanted to break me. I now looked at this imposter with an implacable conviction that he had been found out, that his authority over me was gone, and that what resided within the shell was neither divine nor entirely human.

I looked at Baba a moment longer as he sputtered. Then I blanked him out and turned my head suddenly upward toward a very large gateway above him where the clear blue sky shone through. The act itself was freeing, bond breaking. The creature would boil. But I would be looking off as a feeling of hope, for the first time in an eternity of anguish, would break in upon my soul like a heavenly choral work or the sudden joy of a Purcell brass triumphal. And what splendor did that vast blue firmament hold when compared to the shadows of this coliseum. The still quiet voice of the Comforter had appeared. A sovereign hand and a restraining power seemed to gently cloak me from Baba's venomous crossfire. I got a very real feeling that an ancient battle was going on about me that I was only dimly aware of, a great controversy between the creature in red and an unnameable infinitely vaster might. This was a very direct feeling. In fact I felt protected all of a sudden.

Then I sensed a towering presence of almost limitless spiritual power standing like a column of light close by. It may have been through the portal, 200 feet high, standing where I was looking, invisible almost but present. I am not being metaphorical. I am being quite literal. All I could think of was that mighty biblical messenger of God, the archangel, forever present in invisible humility at what seemed crisis points in the world by God's perspective, when the glory of the very Creator demanded to be honored, not only before men, but among the heavenly hosts and powers of the air.

The closest image I would later summon to comprehend this towering presence, this noble warrior of the light, was the Eldila of Perelandra described by C.S. Lewis. And this presence had appeared for reasons that were far beyond my comprehension, dealing with a warfare that had spanned since before the foundations of the world, as a sign of judgment to this adversary in the red robe and as a banner of coming salvation to me, just when certain defeat had seemed imminent; in retrospect it would be the sudden overthrow of Mordar, the victory of Calvary, the angel putting the Roman guard asleep and freeing the apostle Peter in the final hour of need. This I did not articulate. It happened too fast. All I knew is that somehow I had been rescued in the face of overwhelming odds. The beast would be held at bay, like Daniel in the lion's den.

Impotently Baba spun around and marched off in a huff. I was still looking up at the sky. A few onlookers came to the area curiously studying me. Then Wendel hastened over to question me about the incident. Beaming radiantly I was hard put to explain my great sense of release and freedom. Some of the other Westerners overheard my comments and saw me smiling in relieved joy. Yet soon I would be removed from among them.

During the afternoon's festival I used the remaining hours to study the enemy in red. He knew that I knew, but nobody else did. The band would be playing, the limousines arriving, the great arena bubbling with tens of thousands, while hundreds of ministers of state, governors, politicians from Delhi, and men from all walks of renown, filled the reserved seating under an awning beside the stage.

Baba led a dramatic procession to the stage among the wailing of karnatic horns and band tunes. An honor guard followed. I walked over the front ropes to head past the men's bhajan area with a line of empty microphones. Quietly Baba hissed at me. "Pahh. Stay away from singing. Go out." I ignored it, knowing that for now I could still exhibit the special freedom of an inner-ring disciple that a large chunk of the assembly would still assume that I had.

Holding my revulsion I watched the event in the burning sun deep within the recesses of the crowd under the main awning. I had a new perspective. Baba's eyes occasionally sought me out. A procession of notables spoke before the lumbering pedantic address by the President of India, Baba's most impressive pawn who would become his own fool, not even needing to be mimicked or ridiculed by Baba. Baba would roll back his head and laugh again and again. This putrid spectacle appeared several weeks later in India's largest national magazine.

Then toward the end a noteworthy thing happened. Thousands of angry local citizens of the region started to riot, pressing through the outer fence and into the huge mass under the main awning. The crowd started to ripple. Then it began to look as though things might get out of control, something that according to Baba, was impossible in his "august" presence. Apparently the president's arrival had not persuaded the mob in Baba's favor, this rumor-worn and incident-filled stock that for two decades might have learned something about Baba to goad them into this. It seemed to suggest local scandals and unsettled scores, feuds, and grievances. For they yelled and chanted against Baba. Police with long sticks broke into the area slowly, staving back the threat. But the blotch was already there. Things were by no means going smoothly for this self-proclaimed God of the universe.

Nor had things gone according to plan for the American friends of Tatu, the "three sisters" in saris whom Surya Das and I had seen at the airport then later at a fancy hotel. By now, after hours of baking in the rays, they looked as though they were near heatstroke. They weren't even trying to smile or put on a good show now. True their arrival had been most theatrical. In a cab driven to the very border of the crowd, the three elect girls, disembarking like Bombay film stars, waved at everybody and spread a blanket in the front row of the privileged women's area. They had looked on knowingly for hours, slowly wilting, but determined not to show it. Their heads must still be held high in greater expectation and faith. By the end of the entire gaudy event, when their silk saris were drenched and their make-up was running, they didn't even try to smile. That is until Baba walked by, and they perked up for the last hope of a final sign. What would issue forth from the avatar was a vindictive rasping tone, chiding and demeaning them. It also flattened them.

Soon the crowds scattered in the crimson late afternoon light, and I strolled up to the three dumbfounded girls still gaping and standing in shock by the side of the stage. Near tears, they blurted out to me that they had been "taken." Margaret laughed bitterly, perhaps in self-deprecation, stunned, disillusioned, now rambling her way out of a slowly ending trance about some kind of deep-level hoax. And somehow Baba had known about it and taken pleasure in the sheer game of it; they had expected Baba to reveal a great mystery, his wedding plans with Tatu. I laughed back pitifully with them agreeing that they weren't even near the ballpark. They did not fully see the irony as I could see it. Yet still being cautious with them, I intimated my plans to move on with Surya Das for a tour.

Later that night I took the chance to say a cautious final goodbye to a number of people I was close to. India was visibly heartbroken, this dear girl. She noted in the deep remorse of my tone that I knew something that I could not yet share. I seemed more a fugitive on the run than the robust disciple she had known, stating little more to her than I was being pressed to go "beyond form." Cautiously I warned her not to put her heart in the hands of Baba, the Baba that she understood him to be. I wanted her merely to accept the possibility of one day no longer having to be dependent upon Baba. It frightened her. She could not imagine how she would get along in the world without him.

India wept as I affectionately grabbed her shoulder and left, heading out of the compound toward the ramshackle commercial stalls and jerry-built stands. I wanted to drown my intoxicating despair, back to haunt me yet again, in the public pandemonium, the Coke stalls and floating circus atmosphere, because that was beginning to be the hard answer about my two wasted years. I had been duped in a floating carnival. And now I could examine my due reward—dogs, beggars, mud, fruit-vendors, fleas, photographers and every manner of hawker and hustler and con artist, all mere fleas when compared to the really big con artist in the giant coliseum. My due was a broken heart, a nearly wrecked soul, a penniless pocket, and a grossly undernourished physical body. Yet I had been spared my life. I wasn't sure that the others would all get away so lightly. And I knew that I had to warn them the most powerful way I could at the most receptive time for them.

As I vacantly sipped a Coke I looked out to the glowing lights of the festival. Searchlights lit up the giant central building as it burned up into the night sky like a giant monolith of Satan. A huge Walt Disney-playland clock, 10- to 15-feet in diameter, stood directly above Baba's apartment on a raised tower, its luminescent dial, numerals, and hands glowing in bright multi-colored plastic. Figures walked on the rooftop high up, encircling the donut shape. Desolation, I would tell myself, the scene resembling a Boschian inferno.

Soon Phil's wife Prema, the black hip girl who had gone to Oberlin, sidled up to me like Tina Turner ready to lay down a Motown heavy, swaying just slightly. I primed the pump. "Well, was it impressive?"

"Honey, it ain't impressive, it's depressive."

"You said it. The whole thing was a horror show." I then got to hear her growing doubts, noting her grievances and agreeing. This was the night that Jeanne, a girl who had come in our cab, disappeared and nobody knew where she was.

Later I hastened warily back to the men's dorm room, dodging the nocturnal shufflings of the enemy in red. My spirit was bursting with urgency to leave. I was getting an SOS of a very real and present danger and sensed that it would only be held back so long.

At 5:00 the next morning, as pandemonium started up, I quietly nodded at Surya Das. Now was the time to unobtrusively head out the side gate of the donut-shaped monolith. I carefully resisted my urge to run once beyond the gate, my bags close to my body. Neither of us could endure the place a moment longer. Painstakingly I determined to evade the searching black eyes of Baba, almost thrilled at the challenge of keeping his knowledge of my whereabouts in the dark. In an hour, we were on the early morning train back to Bangalore.

I decided to join Surya Das in the men's dorm at the Regent Guest House. One of our group who had stayed in Bangalore queried me. I remained absolutely silent.

And so I remained till the three ex-friends of Tatu arrived the next day in a cab.

Little did I realize that what was going to happen would pale anything that had ever happened to me in my life.

# Chapter 26

# *Entering the Kingdom of God*

*I*n a private guest room at the Regent Guest House in Bangalore, about seven of us in the room faced the reckoning.

All it took was a look into each other's eyes for us to know that the spell, the enchantment under Baba, was gone forever. It could never be resuscitated. Who was he really? What was the answer? Where do we shunt our wrecked lives from here, at least for those of us who had wholeheartedly invested mind, body, and soul into Baba? There was yet one other viewpoint.

In the usual role of a leader, I began to share with them why Surya Das and I had left Baba, Surya Das often picking up where I left off. They had each had their own inklings about an unwholesome sensuality beneath Baba's holy veneer.

Yet how did this revelation about Baba fit into the cosmology of Vedanta? How about all those millions of pieces to the puzzle: man becoming God, the system of reincarnation, the God-realized guru? My heart, mind, soul, and body shook from the sepsis of this lie. For it was a lie. From the original Genesis lie, across the centuries to Babylon, it filtered down from civilization to civilization.

Its kernel is that man is God, Divine in his essence. According to the Bible, this seductive thought was the cause of the Fall of Man, the reason for his present alienation from God. It is not through pursuing the great lie that man is restored back into fellowship with God. Quite the opposite. Satan told Eve, "You shall be as God."

As Proverbs said, it was as sweet as honey in the first taste but underneath it was as bitter as wormwood. This was the mystery religion of Babylon, the "spiritual harlot" whom God opposed from the foundations of the world and who opposed the true God from time's beginning. This subtle mystical body had shimmered across Egypt's mystery cults, to the Vedantist Brahmins, the Neo-Platonic and Eleusinian cults of Greece, to the Druids, the Sufis, Mayans, and Cabalist Jews, crisscrossing a hundred cultures throughout time, with this enchanting dervish. But this mystery dance was not allowed in the Bible. The scribes of Judah had to wash their hands of it and across the centuries Israel was again and again purged of this deception. What the Bible taught was that the human race had a profound attraction to the great lie, the spiritual equivalent to cocaine. Every taste created a greater propensity for addiction.

Those of us sitting in a circle were now maimed victims of this ancient war. Yet we never would have known it had we just sat back in the West as armchair philosophers, passive mystics, sipping intriguing concepts like fine wine but never entering the heat of the battle. But back home, the sunshine astrologers and weekend meditators were in exactly this predicament. They put their toes into the water just enough to be titillated but they never took the leap. They would therefore never believe those of us who had gone much further down the road. We would be scoffed at as aborted pioneers who somehow didn't have it. Yet they possessed that magical infallibility of intuition to know. The Bible called this blind pride.

A story I had once read by Thomas Mann, "Mario and the Magician," paralleled our situation. It was about a magician of such amazing power that he could totally captivate every will in an audience. Those who escaped could only do it by an utter and thorough gut-level revulsion that held on to nothing of the prior influence. Then fled the magician with a singular act of will, never turning back. I reminded the others, "Remember, if we can't give our lives to him now, then we cannot speak kindly of Baba from a distance or we will float back into his realm like straying asteroids into a black hole."

They asked me who I thought Baba was. Quavering, I recited something I had read on the hill overlooking Puttaparthi, Matthew 24:24: " 'And there shall come Antichrists, false Christs, and false prophets and they shall work great signs and wonders, so as to deceive... deceive... if it were possible, even God's very elect.' It's been in the Bible all along. Baba is an Antichrist who works miracles."

The verse completely caught them off-guard as it did me.

"Then who is the real Christ?" the predominantly Jewish remnant asked.

"Christ." My answer had come so fast and the room became so still that I wondered whether it was entirely my own. "So simple, so incredibly simple," I amended.

It was not so much that I was guiding the course of inquiry, as I was beginning to walk by faith into a greater light as confession removed the scales from my eyes. We had been deceived. We were wrong. If you will, we had sinned. Now, for the first time in my life, I was beginning to see things in an entirely new light, putting me into the center of a miracle that nothing could stop except maybe my own choice to turn away from the light.

It was dawning upon me in full power. I was not God. I was not even a god. I was a bleary-eyed creature lost in the spiritual night. "This is all the Bible has ever said we are. Creatures made by God. Little mortal men, vulnerable little flesh and blood people, made from the common elements and God-breathed with a soul." I was feeling a brokenness that had me on the verge of tears.

I told the rapt listeners about something that happened to me in London the day before I flew to India several years ago.

I was walking down Brompton Road alone, past Harrods. I was approaching my neighborhood of childhood days in Knightsbridge. As then, I was still alone, still seeking. I was stretched by a recent personal anguish and feeling the full weight of my decision to go to India. It had been costly in more ways than one. One of those costs was my lamentation over having to leave a girl I was very close to. My soul was vulnerable.

A most complex, almost nostalgic, forlornness was upon me. Down Brompton Road I went, turning right at Cottage Place, where stood my old childhood home, a four-story affair owned by some earl. I was heading for that very same sanctuary where I used to blind people on Sunday mornings with a giant mirror from my roof, Holy Trinity Brompton Church (I never went to church).

That afternoon I entered the old sanctuary alone, this rear English chapel. In the main chapel an organ rehearsal quietly filled the air with the gentle power of J.S. Bach. I entered the empty side chapel. Alone at the altar, I lay prostrate and started praying to God beseechingly never to let me go, never to forget me, or allow me to be ensnared, to bless me with His love, to have pity on me, to take the reins of my life and guarantee me in this search for the ultimate truth, that I attain the real answer no matter what.

Then I saw those immortal words of Christ carved into the marble altar, "Greater Love Hath No Man Than

He Who Would Give His Life For His Friend." As I left the side chapel I fell against the wall, sobbing. Then I felt a still small voice of assurance reaching down within me, saying, "You are about to go through a dark night of the soul, a great storm, and it will appear to you as though you will even perish. But My hand is on you, and I will provide you a way out. You will be saved in the end, and know the truth." A seal was made. But the truth to be found in India was not its mysticism, yoga, or Eastern philsophy. Rather, it took this grand cycle to bring me full circle to Christ as the only God-man to ever walk the earth.

The salvation of Christ dwarfed Baba's counterfeit tugboat through the ocean of *samsara*, this dark demon god of South India. What a gaudy, papier-mâché imitation.

In front of the others in the room, I was on trembling knees tearfully praying for myself and any who would bow their heads with me as I knelt off to one side of the room. It almost felt like the closing of that ribbon of time back to that moment in the small English chapel. The dark night of the soul had come to an end. I felt like I had passed by the veil of death.

To God and those witnessing my act, I faced the wall and utterly denounced Baba. I admitted the depth of my wrongdoing and sin. Then I confessed that Christ alone is the way, the truth, and the life. And that His name is the only name under heaven and earth given among men by which we may be saved. I confessed Jesus Christ as Lord and Savior, and asked Him to enter my heart, to take over the reins of my life, forever, forever, and forever without end. Amen.

Joy flooded my soul instantly. The terrible insecurities melted away as a million-pound weight that I had carried on my back disappeared. I had hope, real hope, bone-marrow deep, for the first time ever in my life. Truly a miracle had just happened inside me. There

was another feeling that accompanied the taking away
of this great inner weight: Somewhere on the other end
of a long time connection there had been a scream as the
tentacles of some spiritual enemy, those deep inroads of
the empire of Satan on my soul, were torn away and cast
off by God Himself. As though in some dark chamber the
Baba spirit wailed in rage. This was a supreme defec-
tion.

Some people tell me that when they were saved nothing dramatic happened. But when I was transported
from the realm of Satan to the heavenlies of the co-
eternal Christ, it really was as lightning in its soul-
shaking power and immediacy. In an instant I went
from Tal Brooke, dead in his sins, to Tal Brooke, forever
redeemed and crossing that gulf of separation from God
that all creatures in this fallen world experience, to
communion and full acceptance with God.

I would be transported from one kingdom to another,
from one eternal destiny to another, not by my own
merit but by an act of unfathomable grace. It would
happen in less than a second. At one time, the most
obvious answer in the world, and at the other, perhaps
the most difficult gateway to enter. For no other path
requires you to face up to the fact that you are a sinner.
For no other path defines sin as the very words of Christ
do, and herein is a difference as wide as the universe
itself. You and God agree about your blackened condition, your wretched and pitiable unredeemed state.
That as you feel God's holy eye upon you, you are a speck,
most powerless, most small. No merit system of action
can redeem you. Yet, He loves you. And this is when I
began to slowly weep.

When I returned to the chair, I was a different creature, of whom the Scripture says, "Behold, all things are
made new." I could share with them two things that I
had just been "told." The unretractable assurance to

those faithful in Christ, "For I am convinced that neither death, nor life, nor angels, principalities, nor things present, nor things to come, nor powers, nor depth, nor any other created thing, shall be able to separate us from the love of God, which is in Jesus Christ our Lord" (Romans 8:38,39). The other factor pressed into my heart was that I now had a mission, to write another book instead of the pro-Baba book I had been writing. Ringing in my mind was a promise, "I shall bring all things unto thy remembrance."

Several hundred things sealed in the storehouse of my mind about Baba emerged in an unending stream of release. Clear memories where he fell short of deity. When I went on to share some of those discernments about Baba that came railroading out, they all agreed. Mark went on to write his own list, including the observation of the appalling state of so many devotees who follow Baba, their lack of peace, and everything but love and joy. I was amazed to find that he included the fact that Indra Devi had given Baba a private donation of several hundred thousand rupees. The others now agreed that they had never been able to look at the New Testament and interpose Baba in the place of Christ.

What our pursuit then pointed to was an examination of those on the earth who really have managed to lead lives closest to true grace, perfection, love, joy, hope, and contentment. Lives that speak of a goodness that only comes from God. Foremost in my mind were the Carrolls, for they had lived by a standard I had never really seen apart from those living under the lordship of Christ, faithful servants, humbly carrying the lamp of love and service, with qualities of character that no psychoanalytic couch could create in a million years of therapy. These were God-touched lives that came from a form of deep cleansing that no devil could counterfeit, that only God could do.

One of the decoys used by the deceiver was that nominal Christians represented "real" Christians. And the Devil could say, "Look at their fruits, and you can see what sort of Savior they have." But the tragic fact would remain that the lives of these people were only further proof that they had never been saved in the first place, they had never known Christ as Lord and Savior. When Emperor Constantine nationalized the Christian faith, in one fell swoop, the doorway had been thrust open and a haze of confusion resulted when the flock was greatly adulterated, and it really became hard for the outsider to tell the sheep from the goats, the wheat from the chaff.

It was no accident that Christ warned of a large crowd of "goats" to span across the centuries, all in His name whom He had never approved of or gathered. Even great church names, among television stars, self-proclaimed prophets, and founders of cults. Indeed, the goats would include those who had even called Christ "Lord," and worked miracles in His name.

> Many will say to Me on that day, "Lord, Lord, did we not prophesy in Your name, and in Your name cast out demons, and in Your name perform many miracles?"
> And then I will declare to them, "I never knew you; depart from me you who practice lawlessness" (Matthew 7:22).

The criteria for being a Christian would neither be found in man's reason alone nor the declarations of an ecclesiastical body, the church. It could be found solely in the Bible, and Scripture stated clearly that it was a direct person-to-person encounter with the Living Lord through His agency, the Holy Spirit, given as a seal of salvation, and a life that reflected this change.

The Church Universal, the true Church, could be divided by nothing. It was a living kingdom spanning the centuries composed of true Christians. It was, "One body of which there is one Spirit, just as all of you experienced one calling, one hope. There is one Lord, one faith, one baptism, one God, one Father of us all who is the one over all..." (Ephesians 4:4).

This surely exempted "Western Culture" from being that band of true believers. That there had once been an ethics with a Christian base, with at least that world-view reigning for a time, and a state church (never the living church), yes. People mistook that for Christianity. But modern enlightenment philosophy had abolished and replaced almost all that remained of the Christian faith 300 years ago as the motive force behind the West. The philosophy of science became the god of the West, never Christianity. That there had been true Christians, yes, but these were individuals. In this hotel room, God managed to break through this caricature of Christianity that had plagued me and shackled me down my entire life. I had inherited the seeds of doubt from my atheistic father. My peer groups of friends growing up disposed of it mockingly in the most creative ways. Now I had encountered the living God. It was the most sober and holy moment imaginable.

Suddenly I knew what it was to really meet Christ who "stands at the door and knocks" upon the very the door of our souls. I encountered the One who has miraculously changed lives like mine across the centuries.

But there was another problem in reaching those before me, the majority were Jewish. Indeed the majority of all the foreign Baba devotees who had been under me were Jewish, at least three-quarters of them. Many were the scattered sons of Israel who had wandered the nations since Titus wreaked destruction on Israel and its temple. Again, scattered as in the days of Babylon, when they had been found unfaithful to the Living God and sent captive to foreign nations. Then as now their ears had become dull to the voice of their true God. Now they cherished an ethnic identity, seasoned with Yiddish humor, bitterness, cynicism with perhaps a touch of tolerant sensuality to give life a flavor. Their noblest cause had become humanitarianism, but what of pleasing their God, that foremost precedent of their most godly ancestors before Christ? I knew they had deep inbred caricatures that almost inoculated them against Christ. Nevertheless, some were encountering Christ through a new doorway—a New Age ecumenicalism. That was their first look at the New Testament. And I was seeing the damaging effects of some of this now.

# Chapter 27

# *Escaping the Land of Shadows*

*M*argaret, one of the "three friends" of Tatu, claimed Christ as Lord and Savior very shortly after I did. Her conversion appeared long-range and radical, as she and I became very close very quickly. Barbara and Mark, also Jewish, would concede to the purity of Christ and to the demonic nature of Baba. Surya Das would quietly bear through all of this, anxious to go on his spiritual pilgrimage across India. He worried me.

Another girl present whom I did not trust was kept in the dark about what we were doing. I had her marked for duplicity. Mark and Barbara, by my urging, packed their bags for North India and left within days. What this other girl would find in their trail would be heaps of torn Baba photos and memorabilia. To gain greater intimacy with Baba, she played the role of informer. She knew that neither Margaret or I would have a thing to do with her.

For days after that life-changing moment in the hotel room, Margaret and I talked intensely for hours at a time. We went over how deeply we had been deceived and the wider implications of our shift in cosmology and belief.

The main mood for all of us who had left Baba was one of cloaked silence should we be in the presence of those still following Baba who were now moving back to the Whitefield-Bangalore area. A quiet discernment in this spiritual warfare told me not to reveal to them what had happened to us. Though it was immediately evident that the difference between us and the regular Baba contingent was as night and day.

At one point Margaret and I were afraid that we had blundered. We decided to go on a sort of private celebration at the Blue Fox, a modern, plush, thoroughly westernized restaurant just completed. For the first time in 19 months, I would eat nonvegetarian food.

We could, thank God, lead normal lives again. Margaret and I knew that when Christ ate with the publicans and fed the fish to the thousands, he too ate meat, saying, "It is not what goes into your mouth that defiles you, it is what issues from your heart" (Mark 7:15). Both of us had been amazed to discover, when examining Strong's concordance, that rather than supporting vegetarianism, the Bible opposed it as a "doctrine of demons" to emerge in the later times along with enforced prohibition against marriage (see First Timothy 4:3). I had been starving for a steak for two years. My conscience was clear, but I knew by appearances that if we were caught eating meat it would be evidence of our "falling away" and used as the excuse for why we left Baba. But I also knew that from now on I would never be a part of that group again, that I would live as a Christian without Baba.

Just as a large sizzling chateaubriand arrived, Margaret and I looked at the door and our hearts fell. Some of our Baba group, Ram Dass' old New York friends Steve and Leslie, were ushered to a distant table. It was like seeing a sniper. Margaret turned when she saw my eyes light up and I cautioned her to sit still. Our eyes met as if to say, "Oh, well, there goes a good meal but let's eat it anyway." They had been eager friends. I would cooly go over to their table to greet them. They seemed hurt that we had been secretive. I gave them a few hints. They too within a month would leave Baba and be in Nainital North India joining Ram Dass, Neem Korrolli Baba, Surya Das, Mark and Barbara as well as many others. We would learn that Barbara had been hit by hepatitis on the train to Delhi. Mark would commend me for my wisdom in urging them to leave. But many of our group in Nainital would not learn from the Baba deception.

As Margaret and I left the Blue Fox heading arm-in-arm toward Brigade Road yet another unpleasant jolt hit us as we passed Wendel sitting on a railing talking with some of the Baba crowd. We smiled at him and said a quick guarded hello as we walked on. His greeting carried a musing wonder, perhaps even some jealousy. Yet I did not want him to use this (it felt like my first date in two years) as ammunition against us, for I could guess what he was imagining.

It so happened that Margaret, a vibrant full-blooded Jewess, was the prettiest of all the girls as well as imaginative, intelligent, and witty. From the day she arrived, what stuck out was that she was the queen of the girls, beaming with personality. Months back, when we started to meet, we used to joke at the ice-cream stand across from Brindavan. I would ride by on my bike, Margaret would then come over blushing with laughter—she just realized that her divine mission under Baba was to be the "Miss Fab of Long Island." She would be the enlightened housewife walking the beauty queen runway along with other Long Island beauties on television. She would tell them how Baba had done it all, then ride off on a flower-decked float smiling at the viewers while telling them about cosmic consciousness, pranayama, and the asanas. Then Margaret would break into fits of giggles in front of me. This was the same girl who came over to me another time from the girls' table to tell me that they finally figured out who I was in a former lifetime: King Arthur. The joke was that I already had found that out. That was in the old days. Now I was just Tal Brooke the mortal creature created by a transcendent God.

After Margaret and I rounded the corner out of Wendel's view, we felt a certain morbid parallel between our present adventure and a book I insisted that she read entitled *Rosemary's Baby*. The book was a chilling diabolical thriller about a simple demure girl in a hornet's nest of demonic power—people surrounding her, seducing her, and siphoning the life out of her so that she would be the eventual vehicle to carry the devil's baby. Hilda, that sweet old gal, reminded us of the old woman next door, and it went on from there. We wanted sanctuary badly. I also prayed about finances.

When we collected our mail I discovered, by God's timing, yet another $100 check wired to me. This time from Lennie, a Vasser graduate working in Washington and the sister of my best friend Miles Copeland (who today is the famed rock manager of the Police, Sting, the Bangles, and 20 other rock groups). Lennie had just sold the remnant of my stereo system not stolen from her house. It was fully unexpected and the timing was incredible. Margaret wanted to stay on at the Regent Guest House in Bangalore a few more days before moving to the Carrolls' to join me there once Surya Das left for his journey. I felt the utter need to be incognito and gain my strength before battle.

## Sanctuary

Surya Das and I stood on the Carrolls' porch the evening of July 13. Something happened when my eyes met theirs. Something that indicated the astounding power of that event 2000 years ago when Christ walked the earth, but which did not end there. Before I could even tell the Carrolls what had happened to me they knew. Winona Carroll's eyes became teary right there at the door. We were "one in Christ," and they knew it before I could open my mouth. Our sudden joy would be difficult to describe. Here was the love put into my heart by an act of grace that I could not drum up in a million years, reaching out to them in gratitude in a personal bond of fellowship that I had never quite known before. This was a miracle as great as raising the dead.

Of course I was weak, broken, and wretched, carrying many of the scars of two years of hell's discipleship. But if they had seen a bottomless void in my heart before the Ananthapur festival, now they saw a growing torrent of hope in my eyes. A hope filled with faith and joy. I might not be able to articulate the dynamics of this to a hardened skeptic, but he would be faced with that irritating reply given to the Pharisees by the simple congenitally blind man now healed by Christ: "All I can tell you is that wherefore I was once blind, now I see" (John 9:25). A modern miracle of salvation, the greatest of all miracles.

I knew then, as I knew when I finally left them during a deeply emotional embrace, that these guardians of the gospel, these salt-of-the-earth saints, had been considerable agents in my salvation. To them, they were only faithfully serving their Lord, the duty expected of them. To me, this was a cause for eternal gratitude. I knew that in the height of heaven, I would one day look at their radiant faces and wash their feet with my tears. For had they not poured out their lives as a living sacrifice to God, my destiny might eternally be divorced from the face of God. I might be consigned to the most horrible damnation. Instead, they were my spiritual parents as well as brother and sister in the Lord, fellow members of the fold.

Along with my new freedom, I was also a servant and had my own duties ahead. There was an incredible responsibility in being a Christian. Not a pie-in-the-sky easy-believism that the enemy likes to present to dilute the true gospel, but the walk under Christ where we too are used of God, and accountable in the salvation of others—in spreading the Word, living the life, and pouring oneself out to others. My problem was that I had a far from saintly character. I was a natural rebel from the beginning; I had been a problem child, a natural trouble maker. I had it in me to do all sorts of horrors.

A saint by the name of C.S. Lewis would put it very succinctly when I would read his *Mere Christianity*.

> The ... weight ... of my neighbor's glory should be laid daily on my back, a load so heavy that only humility can carry it, and the backs of proud will be broken. It is a serious thing to live in a society of possible heavenly creatures, to remember that the dullest and most uninteresting person you can talk to may one day be a creature which, if you saw it now, you would be strongly tempted to worship, or else a horror and corruption such as you now meet, if at all, only in a nightmare. All day long we are in some degree helping each other to one or other of these destinations. It is in the light of these overwhelming possibilities, it is with awe and circumspection proper to them that we should conduct all our dealings with one another, all friendships, all loves, all play, all politics. There are no ordinary people. You have never talked to a mere mortal. Nations, cultures, arts, civilizations—these are mortal, and their lives are to ours as the life of a gnat. But it is immortals whom we joke with, work with, marry, snub, and exploit—immortal horrors or everlasting splendors.

Clearly Lewis was talking about the resurrection to everlasting judgment, far from the face of God where men would be eternally consigned. Or the bliss of heaven itself, in the very fellowship of highest deity.

The straight and narrow way was costly. The Lord said, "If the world hates you, you know that it has hated Me before it hated you. If you were of the world, the world would love its own; but because you are not of the world, but I chose you out of the world, therefore the world hates you" (John 15:18). What this meant was spiritual opposition and warfare for any Christian who was not neutralized into a diluted belief or a cowardice to say and speak even when his life was on the line. The world was turned upside down at one time when so many believers were martyred for their faith. But they had the blessed hope to look forward to: "Do not be afraid of those who kill the body, but cannot kill the soul. Rather be afraid of the one who can destroy both soul and body in hell" (Matthew 10:28). But when God's clock ran out for human history, the shifting tide would be devastating. God had even stated that this was the reason that He withheld judgment upon the earth, so that more men would turn to Him in the final hour. In my week or two with the Carrolls, they gave me Bibles, concordances, Bible dictionaries, and the best books they had on various subjects.

My clear untutored encounter with the Book of Revelation gave me a perpsective I needed and now knew from my own experience. That the war between good and evil would escalate. Then it would really be the devil's world for a while, the "beast" would get a brief reign, but woe to those who had aligned with him, rejecting God in the process. For surely if God did not hate evil, how could He be good? The New Testament was strewn with passages about the latter days. Days where the world would finally be in waiting for the Antichrist. A not-too-attractive world of ultra-sensual kicks, where men of learning will have cleverly fooled people into laughing off the Truth before they have even given it an honest thought. Paul wrote to Timothy and said:

> But you must realize that in the last days the times will be full of danger. Men will become utterly self-centered, greedy for money, full of big words. They will be proud and contemptuous, without any regard for what their parents taught them. They will be utterly lacking in gratitude, purity, and normal human affection. They will be men of unscrupulous speech and have no control of themselves. They will be passionate and unprincipled, treacherous, self-willed and conceited, loving all the time what gives them pleasure instead of loving God. They will maintain a facade of "religion," but their conduct will deny its validity (Second Timothy 3:1-5).

Paul in the first chapter of Romans would offer an insight into the nature of human rebellion against God:

> They knew all the time that there is a God, yet they refused to acknowledge him as such, or thank him for what he is or does. Thus they became fatuous in their argumentations, and plunged their silly minds still further into the dark. Behind a facade of "wisdom" they became just fools, who would exchange the glory of the immortal God for an imitation....They gave up God; and therefore God gave them up—to be the playthings of their own foul desires in dishonoring their own bodies (Romans 1:21-24).

These and similar hard words were the unpopular side of Christianity, but I was not about to deny them now. I knew they were true. I had always known it in my conscience. Now I need not fear them, I loved them. I loved the truth and hated evil. I loved love and hated those same things God did in the Bible. This was a little new for me. That's because I was beginning to see what evil was doing in the world. It was mangling people's souls in the hands of the adversary, this fallen spirit who used to watch over entire galaxies, whose IQ was probably over a half a million. He didn't need any think-tanks. He was one, a super think-tank, having himself once been described as king of the domain of subtlety. This was the "Lord of the Air" Paul spoke of in his letter to the Ephesians, the one who made war on God's people throughout the centuries. Yet my hatred for him, due to the scars on my own soul, far outweighed any fear I had of him. I was happy to stand against him in Christ.

Almost immediately I was at the very crossroads of spiritual warfare. Apparently I was a rather hot item. I was "marked for total disposal," since I was not the type to stay silent about my knowledge. But now I felt as Paul being lowered in a straw basket down a long drop from the high wall of Damascus. Certainly I had crept away from the massive college in Anathapur that way—secretively. God's people had to be resourceful too. When I left Bangalore, my cloak of secrecy as to my where-abouts would be almost total. God, doubtless, was protecting me, but it was not for me to put Him to the test.

As I would learn the essentials of Christian doctrine from the Carrolls during the day, at night I would face Baba, in my dreams, constantly. He would argue, persuade, hold out great possibilities for me, then, when I didn't succumb, I would be threatened with annihilation. Using the name of Christ, I would blow him out of my presence like a bomb. Every night these dreams went on, even while I was traveling across India. In one dream, Baba was on stage imitating the so-called Saint Sophia miracle. Baba would detect my presence in the auditorium, and there would be a showdown. In another dream, as Baba argued with me, his face began to peel off and swim with maggots.

But there was always victory in the air. One Sunday I went to the Bangalore Mission Church, meeting two missionary friends of the Carrolls, Joe and Edith Mullins who were old friends of John Stott. They looked into my eyes and smiled with a long, satisfied joy. "So you are Tal Brooke. The former Baba zealot. Do you know that the Carrolls and our entire congregation have, over the last six months, been praying for you specifically—that the Lord would deliver you out of the hands of Baba, and reveal to you some hidden aspect of Baba's evil. We and other prayer groups prayed that you might then write another book on him, this time exposing him." I shook hands with these two dear souls, and walked on. I began to get an inkling of the power of prayer, how it had exposed Baba, how it had helped release me.

But should I now be flippant about my salvation, and assume that I could never be deceived? God forbid. And the Carrolls well knew the danger. "Therefore let him who thinks he stands take heed lest he fall" (First Corinthians 10:12). Just as Christ had warned even his apostles, I too would be warned of the leaven of false doctrine. Paul had written to Timothy, his disciple of long acquaintance, to "guard the gospel," even with his life. The Bible was filled with repeated warnings of holding fast to the true faith and avoiding all false teachings. Paul stresses this by saying, "For I determined to know nothing among you except Jesus Christ and Him crucified" (First Corinthians 2:2).

I had seen so many perversions of the truth all my life, that if I came out of this acid test with anything, it was a fearful, loving, and reverential jealousy for the purity of the unblemished Word of God, where I might contend for the true faith.

The apostle John was not "fair-minded" or lax about false teachers. He knew enough to despise them. So did the Holy Spirit who said, "The man who is so 'advanced' that he is not content with what Christ taught, has in fact no God.... If any teacher comes to you who is disloyal to what Christ taught, don't have him inside your house. Don't even wish him 'God-speed,' unless you want to share in the evil that he is doing" (Second John 9–11).

The Carrolls could not stress this enough, even with fear and trembling. They had seen too many people snipped away at the bud by following some self-appointed prophet or teacher who introduced deviations of the truth. To guarantee against this the Scripture is that perfect standard, inerrant and infallible, "delivered once for all the saints." The true Christians stood on an immovable rock, if, like Timothy, we followed His simple commands, abiding in His Word.

"Was it not true that Christendom was in a mess now?" I would ask the Carrolls. Yes, it was, it was swarming with problems of all sorts. But then again the Bible had warned us of this. The adversary, predictably, had attacked from within. He had tried to undermine the Word of God at the turn of the century through a massive academic endeavor.

And then there would be cults galore canvassing neighborhoods with their own tracts and publications: Mormons, Jehovah's Witnesses, Christian Scientists, and a hundred other cults, deviating from the true faith, all founded by individual men or women whose own records were in question. Each cult, systematically, would turn a screw into some fundamental keystone of the faith in an attempt to undermine one or another backbone or key principle of biblical teaching.

On the afternoon of July 20, the Carrolls and I had a final embrace, tears welling up in our eyes. I was a son and a brother now going out into the wilderness again, but forever with the guiding light of God. I was saved, but my life, they knew, was only just beginning. The breadth and depth of the Faith was wider than the universe, and now there was the burden that my life be fruitful and deserving of the Lord, that I die to myself daily, and enter the kind of faithful stewardship that the Carrolls had.

The last time I would see Margaret in India was the night of July 20, when we hugged goodbye on Mahatma Gandhi Road. She insisted coming all the way to town just to say goodbye. I ordered the rickshaw-driver to take care of her as he drove her 12 miles to Whitefield where she would spend her last days with the Carrolls. Meanwhile, I headed to the train terminus to take an all-night train to Pondicherry near the tip of South India where I was to meet Surya Das en route before leaving India. It was near Madras where the grand trunk train to Delhi connected.

On the train to Pondicherry, I felt like Frodo on a mission through Mordor. I wrote to almost no one, being ambiguous even to my parents about why I was leaving India. As the train clickety-clacked, I slowly processed this whole experience in the vast subcontinent of India. Perhaps it could have been no other way for me to come around to the truth. This is what it took for me.

At Pondicherry I was with Surya Das for ten days, getting sea and sun, witnessing to the ashram residents about Christ's salvation; the well-known writer, Sat Prem, turned a cold shoulder, and Diana, a bare-skulled woman renunciant, attendant of the "Mother," just smiled. By God's providence, I got a private darshan with the 96-year-old "Mother," that most occult creature overlooking the domain who resembled a pterodactyl. Again I felt like an assassin. Something drove me to send this woman a spiritual warning of coming judgment. I knew she was demonized. As my eyes fused into her dark orbs, I looked right down them as I said the

Lord's Prayer mentally. Her thick neck bending forward like a giant mesh of cables, eyes fully imbecilic from the side. Yet head-on they were laser-like. As I stared at her in the confidence of the Holy Spirit, having known the other fire, she looked shaken, as if something broke. Her classic tactic had been to penetrate and invade other people through the eyes. With me, she got an inner picture of the fires of judgment. I was told by Diana that this was one of her longest known eye-to-eye darshans. Would this "shakti" of Aurobindo's immortalize her body as she claimed? Hardly, for within three years her obituary would appear in *Time* magazine.

Once I reached Madras, by August 3, I discovered another $100 wired to me, this time for a car I had left with a friend to sell. It had come with a strange kind of timeliness. As I stood on a street corner on Mount Road reading *Newsweek* about some 13-year-old avatar boy-wonder known as Maharajji, and thinking that indeed this is an age of Antichrists, I vomited. By nightfall I had a temperature of 104 degrees. I remembered a dream I had had a few nights before about contracting yellow jaundice. In the dream my urine turned the color of Coca-Cola. Then sure enough that very thing happened. And for three days I lay in a dark, seedy Madras YMCA dorm room, vomiting anything I ate or drank, knowing full well that my liver was disintegrating. This was something that killed some Westerners.

When my temperature subsided, Surya Das and I went hospital hunting before I told him to go on to north India. Madras Central would be a nightmare of rusty needles, crammed rooms of hundreds of thin brown bodies like toothpicks. The red tape to get in would be incredible. It was a scene out of Franz Kafka. I exploded at the bureaucrat who told me it would be three weeks before I got in. Yet I was relieved, for it probably would have killed me. Suddenly, I had to go by Faith with my back already against the wall.

I walked out, got into a cab, and headed for a small, clean, private Catholic mission hospital. Saint Isabell's was beautiful, and for two weeks I ate fish and vegetables, three good meals a day, in a clean private room off a cool veranda. I read the Bible while I felt a quiet strengthening of soul, spirit, and body. This illness, indeed, was more of a natural purging of two debilitating years in India, a peasant's diet, bad water, and heat, and, as I would discover once in London, a colon swimming with large parasitic roundworms which would continue to sap my strength for another six months, but not enough to stop my rapid recuperation from jaundice. In the meantime, I had received a clear command from the Lord to utterly scrap the pro-Baba book about to be released in Calcutta. I sent the press a wire to stop publication. My soul jumped for joy. I felt a much deeper certainty about God's plan for the book that you are now reading.

After two weeks of hospitalization, feeling much stronger, I left the hospital, and almost immediately boarded a Grand Trunk Express to Delhi on August 25. The excitement of the drama burned in the pit of my stomach. Even the wear and tear of the two-day train ride through one cauldron of heat to another would not ripple my purposive joy. For if obstacles came, it would only be to be overcome. I had God in my life, every inch of the way, and how different it was from the other forms of cosmic guidance. When the train finally pulled into the Delhi station I felt a long inner sigh of relief. I had managed to cross all of India without incident. My constant image was Paul being lowered from Damascus in a basket to escape detection.

I took another chance. I took a rikshaw into the diplomatic enclave in New Delhi only blocks from the American embassy to the place I first stayed at, the youth center called the Kendra, built to look like a model European youth hostel. My heart was set on staying there till I flew out of India. I knew I could recover. But my heart sank as I walked in the lobby. The entire complex had been rented by the Peace Corps for a training program that would last three weeks. All wandering Westerners had been turned away. I almost wept I was so tired and disappointed. Then I quietly lowered my head and started praying, talking to God like a needy son. I approached the American director and proposed room and board in exchange for training Americans about living in India in the worst climes, surviving, and handling Eastern philosophy. He admitted that India had the highest attrition rate in the Peace Corps and that they could rarely hang on to people for the full term. I could see him think. Then he looked up.

A miracle! I got a private executive room and all the food I wanted. By the end of two weeks, I had a dedicated group of guys who hung on my every word, big strapping guys as I had once been—ex-football stars from Nebraska and baseball players from Auburn. And when I finally told them the end of my story, and told them the gospel, some of them turned to Christ. By the time they saw me writing all the Westerners at Puttaparthi, they were pulling for me. This was to be my final bombshell, but it would not be dropped in the mail until I was boarding the plane at the airport. I knew Baba's web too well. A premature note could sabotage my attempt to leave.

If things had gone with miraculous smoothness so far, there was another titanic wall to climb before I escaped the land to write my book. You see, since I had been a resident for two years, they had to wire Mysore State to get a police release on my standing, for I had to be cleared. What the enemy might do, I had long ago anticipated, was trump up a civil offense charge against me that would be enough to incarcerate me in a Delhi prison for years.

Here is how it worked. Let us remember that in a state of panic my Calcutta publisher had already written Kasturi about my shocking change of heart, ordering him to scrap the book. It would create a quiet panic in Puttaparthi. Possibly a cable from Delhi to one of Baba's henchmen, the Superintendent of Police, Bangalore, would be felt across the web immediately, thus driving the machinery of Baba into motion, half of the influential citizens of the state, industrialists, and professionals, on up to Dharma Vira, the Governor of Mysore State, all on the grapevine of high priority channels to Baba's throne. The bureaucratic spinning-wheel would roll, false accusations would be drummed up, the more influential the source the better. A resounding "Permission to leave India not granted. Detain suspect for legal action" would leap across the Mysore Teletype to central headquarters in Delhi by early afternoon. Thus Baba might trap me yet, should God not intervene.

First, I had to be financially cleared before I could even apply for an exit visa. In the first week of September, I took a rickshaw across Delhi to a huge office building. If I did not have every receipt for each traveler's check cashed at a bank, then they could legally begin an investigation while detaining me in Delhi indefinitely. I had no receipts at all but the ones just recently cashed in Delhi and Madras.

In a large office, I looked the inspector right in the eye. My receipts had been lost somewhere along the line, possibly on a train. "So you don't have any of them, eh?"

This went on for a while. I remained cool. I suggested to him that after riding in so many trains it was a miracle that I had my passport safe, much less any receipts. He paused, smiled, opened my passport and stamped it with a seal of approval from his office. We cordially shook hands and I calmly walked out.

In order to even apply for an exit visa I needed a plane ticket. That, I would find out after one or two visits to the large office complex near the Delhi Parliament. But by perfect timing my family had picked up a charter ticket within a few days of returning to London from their trip to America. It was the only charter plane of several to leave India within the month, I had the last seat available, the rates were due to go up, and the flight would leave within three days of the ticket's arrival. But if I did not get the exit visa, I would forfeit the entire flight, because that was a charter-flight rule. I could not legally even apply for an exit visa except within 48 hours of the plane's departure. So it was a one-shot affair.

I arrived at the police headquarters in the government enclave. The room was filled with weary foreigners, tormented and bored mystics, all prisoners of red tape, all in the clutches of bureaucratic power-games.

I heard an official say to someone, "But, sir, your passport has expired, it is no good." There was a yell of consummate irritation from some wasted, shaved, skulled renunciant.

I sat down at the inspector's desk the fourth day in a row, finally with a ticket within 48 hours of the plane's departure with all my papers in order, wondering what they would find wrong next. Now all they needed to do was send that fateful Teletype to the police inspector in Mysore.

"But sir, we cannot do anything until Monday."

"Just a second. By then my plane will have left. It is not my fault that there is a government holiday on now. I did what you told me to do. I came here with a ticket within 48 hours of the plane's departure. It is a charter and cannot be transferred. Now . . . you carry the ball."

In a larger office I argued, leaning forward on the desk and watching the official through clouds of acrid smoke. "Listen to me, I came here on a diplomatic passport. Do you think I came here to do anything other than come on my intended mission of inquiry? (I showed him my hardbound Calcutta Baba book.) No, I am a Christian, praise God, I am a Christian."

"Oh, then you are not a follower of our spiritual yoga and gurus then?"

"No, not any more." I responded with grave finality. If I had to sell out on Christ to get out of India, then I would wait for eternity in this office rather than earn an expedient exit visa.

"Well, it seems only you Westerners desire to follow our gurus. Few of our people have genuine interest in these matters any more."

Finally I heard, "Okay, sir. I will wire them in any case. They may have someone there. You come back this afternoon, and if they have replied it will be okay. And if not, I will stamp your passport in any case."

I returned to learn that the Mysore Teletype had not answered. I looked into his eyes and handed him my open passport. Reluctantly, he took out his stamp, looked at it, and pressed the stamp upon the open page. I pressed back the surge of relief within me, extending my hands coolly for the gentleman's handshake.

But it was not all over yet. Mysore might still cable in urgency.

The final night at the Kendra, I masked this incredible drama going on from the Peace Corps group to whom I was giving a seminar (that was another miracle). Later that night, I pondered some alarming Scriptures.

Evil entered the universe eons and eons back in time through the very highest cosmic creature (an archangel), a Spirit Being so vast and powerful that a normal human being would easily mistake it for *a* god if not *the* God in its prior state. His name was "Light Bearer" (Lucifer), now Satan. In Isaiah 14, God explains the act of consciousness that caused this cosmic holocaust and the transformation of this vast cosmic Spirit into Satan.

(It had helped in the construction of the galaxies in some way.)

> How art thou fallen from heaven,
> O Lucifer, son of the morning!
> how art thou cut down to the ground,
> which didst weaken the nations.
> For thou hast said in thine heart,
> I will ascend into heaven, I will
> exalt my throne above the stars
> of God: I will sit also upon the
> mount of congregation, in the sides
> of the North.
> I will ascend above the heights of
> the clouds: *I will be like the*
> *Most High.*
> Yet thou shalt be brought down to
> hell, to the sides of the pit.
> (Isaiah 14:12-15)

Evil, in its ultimate essence and origin was the thought, *"I shall be as God."* And it caused the terrible fall of mankind and the whole world when this same being that fell in the cosmos of the past promised Eve that she would be "like God" (Genesis 3). It was the very first lie, and the most ancient lie. It is the central foundation of the New Age Movement.

As long as I live, I shall never forget that initial sense of intoxicating and delicious pride when I first realized that I had the capacity to be an *advaitin* nondualist mystic. In the company of Vivekananda I could look down my nose on those benighted mortals trapped in the dullards' delusion of *dvaita* (dualism—those who still separated themselves from God seeing a distinction). It was only the spiritual geniuses, we were told, who could grasp nondualism and span the gulf between

Self and God conquering the ultimate riddle. The Bible called this ecstatic insight the ultimate lie. Now I was freed from this terrible delusion.

At 6:00 in the morning I stood with a nervous crowd in the airport waiting room. A previous charter plane the day before had been canceled. But our plane was waiting outside. Those from the other plane would have to wait for another plane. By 7:00, we started to board. I got to the gate. The guard looked at my passport. "Excuse me, sir, but your exist visa was for a plane yesterday evening. It is seven hours expired, sir. You will have to get another." I looked him in the eyes. His superior and other officials sat at a desk behind him. I went right to them. Eyes met. "Is it my fault that the plane was delayed? What in heaven's name can I do now with the plane about to leave. Your office in Delhi is closed right now. This plane is my only chance. Now I want to get on." The official gave the guard a slow nod, and with a red stamp, the guard marked my passport, "Delhi airport, Palam, 14 September, 1971." I walked through the gate giving them a courteous wave. Yes, I even feared being hauled out the plane before the door closed.

I held my breath tensely until we were in the air. Soon we passed beyond the land mass of India—that same face of death staring back out of the sand. Then the clear Arabian Sea sparkled up from below, a radiant emerald green. At that point I exalted, letting out the longest sigh of relief you can imagine. I looked out the window hiding the exploding emotion of joy within. No one could guess what I had been through. Some cheerful stewardess handed me an ice cold Coke. I sipped it slowly, singing a quiet hymn to God. I felt all heaven rejoicing with me. Gone from dominion over my soul would be the Lord of the Air, forever. The throne of my true Lord was in highest heaven.

# *Glossary*

*Advaita Vendanta:* non-dualistic Vendanta, perhaps the most influential interpretation of the Hindu scriptures, systematized by Sankara. It is non-dualistic because it asserts that there is only one Reality and because there is no dualism between the atman and Brahman.

*ananda:* bliss.

*ashram:* an abode or residence, commonly of a saint, sadhu, ascetic, or guru who is usually engaged in some form of religious instruction.

*atman:* the Self or soul, the eternal aspect of a living being. In Sankara's system the Self is identified with Brahman, the one Reality, and so there is truly only one Self. Other Hindu theologians differ from Sankara and, in varying ways, postulate a plurality of souls.

*avatar:* Sanskrit word for the descent or incarnation of a god upon earth.

*bhajan:* a song of devotional love, sung to the accompaniment of musical instruments and chanted in temples or public gatherings.

*bhakti:* Sanskrit word for "love" or "devotion," often used for human devotion to God.

*Brahman:* the supreme Reality, conceived of as one and undifferentiated, static and dynamic, yet above all definitions; the ultimate principle underlying the world, ultimate reality.

*darshan:* literally "sight." One speaks of having darshan of a saint, sage, or a deity, which means being in his or her presence and receiving a blessing by the mere fact. It is of crucial importance to the disciples in an ashram that the guru, in darshan, look directly at the devotee, for his glance, no matter how impersonal and disinterested, correctly forms an important psychic and spiritual link to the master, and through him, to the Absolute.

*dharma:* right, morality, duty, truth, religion.

*dhoti:* loincloth worn by a male Hindu.

*dhyana:* reflection, meditation.

*Kalki:* the final avatar of the god Vishnu. The *Kalki Purana* speaks of him as one whose body is blue, who with sword in hand will ride a white horse swift as the wind, to destroy the race of the Kali yuga, to inaugurate true religion again.

*Kali:* consort of Shiva. She is his female counterpart and symbolizes the projected energy of the Divine Being.

*karma:* the sum total of a Hindu's actions in one lifetime, which determines his fate in the next. Release from karma, whether good or bad, is obtained by "knowledge" and abstinence.

*Kundalini:* The Supreme Power, otherwise Kundalini-Shakti, in the human body. Kundalini is aroused by the practice of tantric yoga. Kundalini is also called the "Serpent Power."

*kurta:* a loose-fitting, collarless shirt.

*leela:* literally "play," but in the religious and mystical sense, the divine sport, the movements and activities of the Supreme Being, which are not subject to the laws of nature or man. The god Krishna, divine incarnation, playing as a child, is *the* example of leela.

*lingam:* a phallic symbol of the Hindu god Shiva.

*mandala:* a symbolic diagram, usually surrounded by a circle, representing a pattern of psychic energy. Incantations are made while inscribing the mandala, and spiritual forces are believed to descent or appear.

*mantra:* a verse, word (Om, Srim, Aum, etc.) or incantation, used to assist in meditation, or to acquire supernatural powers. Each deity is represented by its own mantra; it is only by the correct enunciation of the correct mantra that the deity will descend to enter the body of its image, or will respond to a devotee.

*maya:* a key philosophical, mystical, and practical concept that dominates much of Indian thought. Maya is "God's creative energy," energy that may be described for convenience as "the creative illusion of the Brahman." But maya is also cosmic illusion, becoming magic, art, phenomenal existence. Maya is thus not illusion in the sense of unreality but cosmic play, the divine leela or sport.

*moksha:* liberation, release—usually conceived, in Indian religion, as liberation from samsara.

*nirvana:* a word for liberation in Indian religion and in Buddhism in particular. Literally, it means "the going out," as of a flame—the point being that it is the flame of desire or craving which causes rebirth, and therefore the extinction of craving will bring about liberation from samsara.

*Om:* the chief of all mantras, the universal sound (see *mantra*).

*puja:* worship of gods, usually ceremonial worship, either the daily offerings of flowers, water, and incense to images, or more complex rites in a temple or on an anniversary.

*rishi:* a sage. Any wise or holy man (hence Maharishi—great rishi).

*sadhana:* fulfillment. A course of spiritual teaching leading to a realization of life. A method of training the faculties to realize their potential.

*sadhu:* a Hindu ascetic. The sadhu eschews caste, social position, rank, and authority in order, by gradual stages of purification, to withdraw toward the ultimate reality.

*samadhi:* concentration of thought, intense contemplation.

*samsara:* the passing of the soul through a series of earthly lives. This chain, which invokes so much suffering, is the result of karma, the accumulated debts arising from ignorance, sin, and bad acts and actions.

*sanyasan:* one who has retired from active life to devote himself to spiritual concerns. This possibility is controlled in

Hinduism by the doctrine of four stages of life—that of being a student, that of the householder (i.e., family man), that of one who withdraws from the householder's duties, and finally that of the homeless wanderer or religious mendicant.

*Shakti:* the eternal and Supreme Power, variously described as manifest energy, the substance of everything, the all-pervading. Today, Shakti has been connected to, is identical with, the power of the gods Shiva, Vishnu, or Brahma, the great Hindu triad. From the most ancient scriptural time Shakti, under a variety of names, is intimately linked to Shiva, the Lord of Sleep. Shiva is helpless without the fecundating divine energy, Shakti.

*siddhi:* literally "perfection," siddhi is an occult power gained through the mastery of the higher stages of yoga. The siddha, the person who has the power of siddhi, possesses magical powers according to classical yoga. The yogi is not only able to control his bodily functions (even the non-voluntary ones, like pulse, digestion, and breath), but also can read minds, engage in astral travel, walk on water, bilocate, predict the future, make objects move without touching them, and so on. These immense powers are not used by the more responsible class of yogis, who state that siddhis are distractions, not aids, in the upward ascent of the self to the Self.

*Shiva* (or *Siva*): One of the two great gods of devotional Hinduism (see *Vishnu*). Shiva is often portrayed as rather terrible, and symbolizes the destructive as well as the creative powers of God. As well as being an object of devotion, Shiva is associated with austerity and contemplation.

*swami:* a member of a Hindu religious order and general title for a holy man.

*tapas:* the austerity of an ascetic holy man.

*Upanishads:* (see *Veda*)

*Veda:* literally "knowledge," i.e., sacred knowledge: a word used for the early scriptures of Hinduism, consisting in the

first instance of collections of hymns, the Vedas, to which
were added accounts of the rituals, etc., to which in turn
were added expositions of the inner meaning of religious
acts, the Upanishads.

*Vendanta:* the systematic exposition of the Veda.

*Vishnu:* one of the two great gods of devotional Hinduism (see
*Shiva*). Though an unimportant figure in Vedic religion,
Vishnu acquired, with Shiva, a dominant position in the
period following that of the early Upanishads. Associated
with Vishnu is the conception of "avatara," Vishnu appearing on earth in various animal and human forms, the most
famous being Krishna.

*yajna:* the Vedic ritual of sacrifice. Vedic religion was mainly
one of sacrifices, carefully observed down to the most minute gesture and intonation of phrase. The purpose of the
sacrifices was in part the increase of cattle and food and a
prosperous life for the people, as well as propitiation of the
gods.

# When the World Will Be As One

## —THE NEXT PHASE—
### Beyond the New Age Movement
## by Tal Brooke

In recent years the New Age movement has been touted by many as the spiritual rebirth of modern man. But this popular movement is just one phase of a broad agenda which is only now coming fully into view. The pieces have been shifting into place for a quantum leap more radical than the one that replaced the Dark Ages with the Age of Reason. A momentous global event is upon us—the birth of a New World Order.

# *Other Good Harvest House Reading*

## THE ARCHON CONSPIRACY
by *Dave Hunt*

In a story with unusual relevance for our time, bestselling author Dave Hunt describes a confrontation between supernatural powers and humanity that could someday be as real as today's headlines. Hunt dramatizes the reality of spiritual warfare in this fast-paced novel filled with intrigue and suspense.

## GODS OF THE NEW AGE
by *Caryl Matrisciana*

In a fascinating look at Hinduism and its well-disguised western counterpart, the New Age movement, Caryl Matrisciana prepares us to be spiritually discerning in the days ahead.

## OUT ON A BROKEN LIMB
by *F. LaGard Smith*

F. LaGard Smith explores the biblical meaning of life and afterlife in this answer to actress Shirley MacLaine's autobiography *Out on a Limb*.

## DEATH OF A GURU
by *Rabi Maharaj* with *Dave Hunt*

Descended from a long line of Brahmin priests and trained as a yogi, Rabindranath Maharaj becomes a great Hindu leader. His autobiography, written by bestselling author Dave Hunt, traces his difficult search for meaning, his increasing disillusionment, and his struggle to choose between Hinduism and Christ.